MINORITIES AND THE STATE
IN THE ARAB WORLD

Minorities and the State in the Arab World

EDITED BY

Ofra Bengio and Gabriel Ben-Dor

LYNNE
RIENNER
PUBLISHERS

BOULDER
LONDON

Published in the United States of America in 1999 by
Lynne Rienner Publishers, Inc.
1800 30th Street, Boulder, Colorado 80301

and in the United Kingdom by
Lynne Rienner Publishers, Inc.
3 Henrietta Street, Covent Garden, London WC2E 8LU

Library of Congress Cataloging-in-Publication Data
Minorities and the state in the Arab world / edited by Ofra Bengio and
    Gabriel Ben-Dor.
        p.   cm.
    Includes bibliographical references (p.   ) and index.
    ISBN 1-55587-647-1 (alk. paper)
    1. Minorities—Arab countries.   2. Religious minorities—Arab
countries.   3. Arab countries—Ethnic relations.   4. Religion and
state—Arab countries.   I. Bengio, Ofra.   II. Ben-Dor, Gabriel.
DS36.9.A1M56   1999
305.5'6'09174927—dc21

                                                                98-37994
                                                                CIP

British Cataloguing in Publication Data
A Cataloguing in Publication record for this book
is available from the British Library.

Printed and bound in the United States of America

The paper used in this publication meets the requirements
of the American National Standard for Permanence of
Paper for Printed Library Materials Z39.48-1984.

5   4   3   2   1

Contents

Preface

One of the most bedeviling problems of modern Arab political life has been the place of minorities—national, ethnic, and religious—within the polity and society. The mere mention of the subject has long been taboo in many Arab states, because it clashed with the twin prevailing visions of the territorial state and pan-Arabism over the past half-century. Further adding to the difficulty has been the more recent entry into the Arab political discourse of notions of democratization, pluralism, and civil society, all of which have implications for state-minority relations and pose challenges to entrenched, authoritarian Arab regimes.

The concept of minorities is, of course, a fluid, conditional one. This collection treats minorities not necessarily in numerical terms but in terms of their political standing within the state, that is, their lack of political power. Thus, it addresses the Shi'is in Iraq and Bahrain and the Palestinians in Jordan, all of whom form the numerical majority of the population but do not hold the reins of power or equitably share in it. Also included are those minorities that are active politically and pose a challenge to the integrity of the state, for example, the Kurds of Iraq and the southern Sudanese; those whose political standing has changed over time, such as the Maronites in Lebanon and the Alawis in Syria; the Copts of Egypt, whose problem is perhaps less with the state and more with the society; and the anomaly of the Berbers in Algeria.

It is our pleasant duty to thank here those who enabled this project to come to fruition. First on the list are the contributors themselves, who stoically and patiently bore the brunt of our demands. The previous and current heads of the Moshe Dayan Center, Asher Susser and Martin Kramer, provided indispensable intellectual, financial, and moral support for the project from its inception. Lydia Gareh and Roslyn Loon stitched the manuscript together in their usual exemplary fashion. Amira Margalith, Ilana Greenberg, and Elena Lesnick were helpful in a variety of other organizational tasks. Liat Kozma rendered invaluable assistance throughout. Jean Hay and Shena Redmond at Lynne Rienner have been encouraging and helpful. We are indebted to all and take responsibility for any errors.

Ofra Bengio
Gabriel Ben-Dor

1

Minorities in the Middle East: Theory and Practice

Gabriel Ben-Dor

The study of any given minority inevitably involves analyzing the structure of an entire society: either a minority is defined as such in relationship to a majority or the society as a whole consists of a collection of minorities. Minorities are as varied as there are cleavages in any given society, for example, men and women, old and young, more and less educated, employed and unemployed, and so on. However, the most relevant axis separating minorities from others in modern society is the ethnic one, and thus the primary tool for the study of minorities is the history and political sociology of ethnicity. There is a voluminous literature on this issue, divided into several major contending schools and approaches.[1]

Changing Approaches to Ethnicity

Three major approaches to ethnicity are ethnonationalism, ethnoregionalism, and ethnoreligiousness. *Ethnonationalism* deals with the attempts of ethnic groups to find a territorial expression at the level of an entire state, assumed to correspond to the needs and rights of the nation.[2] *Ethnoregionalism* challenges the powers of the nation-state by demanding greater local-regional autonomy for the ethnic groups or even looking toward a form of independence in the more remote future.[3] *Ethnoreligiousness* assumes an overlap of religious consciousness with some other characteristics of ethnicity—common origin, culture, or language—resulting in a form of ethnic activism that may or may not be territorially oriented but is of obvious political importance.[4]

Clearly some of these forms of ethnicity may overlap and reinforce one another. However, one should be aware that the very foundations for the political awareness and activity involved in ethnic relations are not only subject to different interpretations by the various participants in the political process,

1

but they also change over time. In other words, the structuring of ethnicity is a highly complex process, as dynamic as it is subjective.

The critically important question, therefore, is how and why ethnicity becomes a political fact of life.[5] Three major schools of thought provide different answers to that question.

1. *The economic and rational approaches.*[6] These derive from earlier times via Marxist theories, later modified by Emile Durkheim's sociological approach. The basic idea is that the process of economic development creates the larger communities at the expense of the smaller ones, and that the integration of the smaller and more distinctive units into a more extensive and inclusive societal framework is inevitable as the modern capitalist economy becomes a dominant fact of life in national and international society. A new variation on these themes is to be found in the rational choice approach prevalent in recent years.[7]

2. *The modernization approaches.* These assume that the process of modernization, as commonly defined in the 1960s and early 1970s, virtually creates new entities via the expansion of communication, the spread of literacy and education, the introduction of modern technology, and the intrusion of the idea of mass participation into the political process.[8] Early forms of modernization theory assumed that the creation of such new entities would also create new states that could overcome their premodern identities, much as Karl Marx and Durkheim had also assumed.

However, later and more sophisticated forms of modernization theory—what we may call the *modernization-conflictual* approach—pointed to the opposite possibilities, considered even more likely.[9] These scholars argued that the process of modernization generated and exacerbated ethnic conflict by changing the foundations of more traditional society, confusing issues of legitimacy, and introducing new resources into the arena of political competition. The uncertainties of a massive and manifold process of change, according to this way of thinking, provoke an escape into ethnicity as a form of assurance and safety against the risks and danger of modernity. In addition, those elites in danger of losing access to resources in an arena dominated by forms of competition they find unfamiliar and therefore difficult to control or manipulate tend to resurrect ethnic feelings and solidarity in order to turn them into critical political resources.[10]

Thus, political leaders who find it difficult to adapt to an ideological style of party politics may attempt to create tribal and ethnic parties to counter the ideological impact and legitimacy of their rivals. They inevitably cultivate feelings of pride, solidarity, and identity in the ethnic group they are using, even if such feelings have been long dormant.[11] When even broader groups feel deprived by the redistribution of economic and other resources under modernization, they may also resort to ethnic identity as a source of strength.[12]

3. *The primordial, or authentic ethnic, approaches*. These approaches assume that ethnic groups have an authentic existence of their own and are not merely figments of the imagination to be manipulated or used by leaders and politicians.[13] Such manipulation is indeed possible, but only when there is a strong objective basis for the existence of such a group, which might be revived or utilized in the political process.

More recent variations on this theme emphasize the developmental dynamics involved in ethnic politics.[14] Although an objective basis for ethnicity is likely to exist, ethnic groups themselves "are constantly created and recreated anew. In establishing the political boundaries of Asia and Africa, for example, the colonial powers redefined the size and the scope of the ethnic groups. The expanded political boundaries led to the assimilation and differentiation of ethnic groups: as old groups disappeared, new ones emerged while others simply merged and split."[15]

The authentic ethnic approach inevitably has to deal with the relationship of ethnicity to class structure, an intriguing question that goes back to the days of the Marxist school. According to Saul Newman, Donald Horowitz would argue there is something unique about ethnic identity. "Whereas individuals can overcome their social class and whereas social mobility is possible from generation to generation, ethnic ties are ascriptive. If one is born into an ethnic group, so be it; one cannot maneuver out of one's ethnic identity."[16]

A major contention of this approach is that ethnicity is indeed a comparative concept,[17] which is to say that ethnic groups are inevitably defined as much by their relationship to others as by their perception of any objective characteristics. There is considerable controversy over the implications of this thesis, yet little argument exists that the understanding of ethnicity must involve the psychological relationship between groups in a prominent way. As argued before, the study of minorities and ethnicity is by necessity the study of majority-minority and minority-minority relations as well.

Additional Theoretical Concerns

A particularly important feature of the study of ethnicity in the Middle East is the relationship between minorities and the state.[18] Because of the relatively late creation of states in the region and the difficulty of institutionalizing them in the face of manifold domestic challenges, the ethnic fact of life is particularly acute for the modern Middle Eastern state.[19] When the ethnic politics of minorities overlaps with sectarian-religious identities (at times within a given territory within the state), ethnic groups and minorities can become particularly troublesome. This is particularly true in states where the relatively new variation of nationalism leaves little room for the very acknowledgment of the existence of minorities, which are perceived to challenge the might of the state not only by what they do but also by virtue of what they are.[20]

Although the Middle Eastern state has survived in an impressive fashion, in a harsh and inhospitable environment, it is far from secure. The recent emergence of radical Islamic activity, coupled with increasing ethnic consciousness, poses a new and potent threat to the legitimacy and viability of the state.[21] Yet these states have, so far, demonstrated a high degree of determination and skill in containing this potent threat. If anything, the responses to the recent challenges once again point to the institutionalization of the Middle Eastern state as the overwhelmingly influential fact of life in the contemporary political history of the region.[22]

The confrontation between the state and the new ethnic challenges constitutes one of the most interesting areas of study in contemporary Middle East politics. The authors included in this volume have tried to stress the notion of strategies developed and adopted by state authorities toward minorities, and the strategies utilized by minorities toward regimes and toward states. Although it is still too early to attempt a systematic classification of such strategies, the contributions of these authors help lay the foundation for such a theoretical attempt.[23]

In general, there are few Middle Eastern case studies that would constitute an accepted core of knowledge, based on detailed historical material as well as sound social scientific foundations. As argued in the impressive survey by Charles D. Smith, the historical scholarship has serious lacunae:[24] "However valuable as political history, these studies rarely examine the question of national and regional identities as compatible rather than as conflicting. Moreover, none of these works, with the exception of Bassam Tibi's, concerns itself with theories of nationalism or with the related topics of state formation and the historical and social-science literature pertaining to these subjects."[25]

Yet the social scientists are also at fault: "As for the social sciences, those who specialize in these issues appear to refer more frequently to the theoretical literature in journals of their disciplines than when they investigate comparable subjects in articles or books devoted specifically to Middle Eastern themes."[26] In other words, the historians do not use enough social science concepts, and the social scientists do not use enough concrete knowledge gained from Middle East history.

The present volume is intended to help rectify some of these deficiencies in the field. Editors of such volumes realize how difficult that tends to be. Ideally, there is a common theoretical framework that yields case studies that explore a more or less commonly accepted agenda, hence adding up to a coherent body of new knowledge.[27] In practice, it is neither possible nor desirable to coerce historians into writing questionable social science or to force social scientists into writing just as questionable history. Instead, the production of this volume proceeded in stages that included a workshop where papers were given on the various cases by specialists in the history of the countries. This stage was then followed by the circulation of a theoretically oriented paper (by one of the editors, a political scientist who writes on Middle East politics), whose themes and concerns the participants were requested to address when revising their papers.

This procedure is not exactly the kind of theoretically driven agenda social scientists like to emphasize, nor is this the entirely free and individualistic set of historical studies that country experts seem to prefer. The resulting compromise has produced a series of studies centering around a number of theoretical themes:

1. The centrality of the state and the relations between the state and minorities.
2. The plethora of strategies pursued by both sides in response to constraints.
3. The underlying assumption that while manipulation of identities is very much a fact of life, some form of authentic ethnicity also exists, a variation of the third approach to studying ethnicity described earlier.[28] The characteristics of each such *ethnie* and the dynamics of its political fortunes constitute much of the core of this volume.
4. The importance of the overlap (or lack thereof) of the ethnic characteristics of the minority: nationalist traits, religious awareness, common culture.
5. The sensitivity of Middle Eastern political systems to potential territorial challenges, hence the importance of the differentiation between compact versus diffuse minorities.
6. The importance of timing. We know relatively little about the point in the political dynamics of each country at which a minority undergoes a drastic rise in consciousness and the propensity for collective activity.

The authors explore a variety of domestic political and cultural factors that seem to be relevant, and they also pay attention to regional inter-Arab politics, as well as to such broader international developments as global trends and the regional activities of the Great Powers. Here, therefore, is the beginning of a set of insights and observations that may help generate a theory of timing in the rise of political ethnicity.

What now follows is an introductory exploration of some of the volume's key concerns: in the concluding chapter, the two editors will attempt to draw some preliminary conclusions and look a bit into the future. Thus, we will now consider the politics of primordialism (as a key notion in the third school of the study of ethnicity), the differentiation between compact and diffuse minorities, and the relationship of ethnicity in the Middle East to Islamic radicalism (as the key contemporary issue in the politics of overlap or reinforcing cleavages). Included will be an analysis of ethnic and religious minority problems in Israel as a limiting case study, illuminating by way of comparison and contrast the features of the Arab cases studied in this volume.[29]

The introduction will conclude with a section that undertakes a preliminary exploration of minority problems in Sudan, so featured because, being the most extreme case of reinforcing ethnic cleavages that have led to a protracted and violent civil war, it also may be useful as a limiting case study, one that helps create checks against hasty generalizations from other cases. These introductory remarks on the Sudan—which have an explicit theoretical purpose—should not prejudice the detailed analysis by the country expert included in Chapter 4.

The Politics of Primordialism

The authentic ethnic approach to the study of ethnic politics—the one generally subscribed to by the authors in this collection—emphasizes both the dynamics of change in ethnic identity and consciousness and the more or less objective variables that define majorities and minorities, which tend to endure over time.[30]

Inevitably, the extent to which being a minority is relevant to politics is also a question of the nature of politics in the given society.[31] Not every potential cleavage in society becomes politicized, but sometimes that transition takes place with dramatic rapidity. One influential way to approach this issue is via the classic formulation of primordialism, which has been in existence since the 1960s and is now enjoying a revival, due to the movement away from both the simple theories of modernization and the complexities involved in economic approaches.

The theoretical approach of primordialism is rich and deep; it well deserves centrality in the study of minorities and ethnicity. The original formulation was proposed by Clifford Geertz in an article published in 1963.[32] Geertz, a prominent political anthropologist, argued the importance of primordial ties, those ties that one is born with. At the time, acting according to this inherited identification was considered less modern than the rational, secular, and ascriptive norms of a developed society.[33] This ethnocentric and simplistic approach has been largely abandoned; primordialism has proven to be extraordinarily vital in all societies, and there is no proof that it is particularly strong in any one part of the world.[34] The universality of primordialism is now generally accepted. It seems to be strongest in Eastern Europe with the sociopolitical vacuum that resulted when old institutions and political communities broke down due to the revolutionary wave of the late 1980s and early 1990s.[35]

Geertz gave various examples of the meaning of primordial ties: links based on blood, kinship, religion, clans, presumed historical affinities, and so on.[36] Even though some of them seem to overlap and many appear only imaginary, this does not mean that they are somehow less real, for ideas in the minds of groups of people are political facts of life and are as strong as any objective factors.[37] Yet primordial identities are difficult to work with because they can change so quickly and can appear in surprising forms.[38] These transformations have occurred in societies undergoing rapid change, creating insecurity and thereby encouraging people to go back into their relatively safe shells at the expense of larger political communities. Primordial ties are simple to understand and appear to be permanent and trustworthy. By contrast, larger political communities are more difficult to live with, for they require some adjustment to seemingly artificial ideas and shared characteristics. The contrast in difficulty is readily comprehensible.[39]

Primordial ties are of different magnitudes. Thus, they may threaten to fragment the state either by trying to force it into bigger political communities or by fracturing it into smaller ones. In either case, they threaten the legitimacy of the existing state structures, and this is the fundamental importance that they have for contemporary politics.[40] In the light of political constraints, movements based on primordial ties rarely create states of their own, and when they do, they cannot be successful because they are practically never "clean" of minorities of their own. So we have no real examples of ethnic states in the Middle East and are not likely to have any in the future either.[41] Interestingly enough, even those ethnic groups referred to in the literature as "compact minorities" do not claim to establish states of their own.[42] On the contrary, they appear the most dedicated loyalists of the existing national states in which they wish to do well and even hold a large share of the power inherent in the machinery of the state.[43]

Compact Minorities in the Middle East

Compact minorities include primarily the 'Alawis and the Druze in Syria and, to a lesser extent, the Druze in Lebanon and even less in Israel. Their compactness lies in the fact that they occupy a well-defined geographical territory that makes up only a small part of the state and constitutes a comfortable majority in this region. Although there have been significant Christian and Jewish minorities in the recent history of the Middle East, they never have managed to capture so large a share of the power of the state as, say, the 'Alawis in Syria today.[44] The past policy of the colonial powers certainly helped shape the situation of the 'Alawis, but the combination of space and demography was clearly a major factor in their fortunes.[45]

In general, colonial governments can make a decisive difference in the allocation of resources among minorities. In the case of Syria, for example, the heavy reliance on minority recruitment to the colonial army became a critical factor after independence, when the army became the most important political force in the state after the collapse of parliamentary structures.[46] In the case of Syria, the domination of the minorities may have to do not only with ethnic questions as such but also with such issues as civil-military relations;[47] then the takeover by the military creates minority domination as a by-product.[48]

So the model of the compact minorities in Syria is only one of several possible models, albeit perhaps the most interesting one because the compact minorities are the easiest to deal with in both theoretical and practical terms. Still, the fate of other compact minorities, such as the Druze in Lebanon, is entirely different: they have not been able to capture the machinery of the state, as the state is weak and such machinery is barely, if at all, in existence.[49] Yet the model of the compact minorities is a most useful conceptual tool for analyzing the problem across the region, and a great deal can be learned from such cases against the broader picture of the Middle East as a whole. First, we must ask in what sense the 'Alawis and the Druze are really minorities. They are both Arabic-speaking and not very different in customs and habits from the other Arabic-speaking groups in the state; they are clearly Arabs in a cultural and sociological, if not political, sense.[50] However, both are minorities in the religious sense, having evolved as offshoots of Islam, eventually to the point where they could no longer be considered Muslim.[51]

Clearly, in the case of the Druze the religion postdated orthodox Islam and involved movement from Egypt to the area of southern Lebanon, and then from parts of Lebanon to Palestine and later Syria.[52] From the eleventh century on, being a religious minority also meant being isolated demographically and geostrategically to some degree; it meant being based in the mountains and staying away both from urban areas as well as villages dominated by a Muslim majority. So the Druze developed a strong sense of tribal or ethnic solidarity, enhanced by skill in the martial arts, within a generally insecure environment in which the central government was neither able nor willing to protect such minorities.[53] Their history has led to a distinct ethnic identity, which has in turn witnessed a great deal of adaptability and fluidity in relating to external political forces, without compromising self-identity in any profound sense of the term.[54] It remains to be seen whether this pattern will continue in a more modern setting, in which the traditional patterns of geographic and social isolation may become irrelevant as well as impractical.

The case of the 'Alawis is simpler than that of the Druze. They were not involved in any large-scale movement from one part of the Middle East to another.[55] Although one well-known tradition holds that they are the descendants of one ancient Cana'anite people who came to speak the Arabic language only in medieval times, clearly, at least since the Middle Ages, they have followed the present pattern of being an Arabic-speaking group following a version of the Isma'ili sect of Shi'i Islam, and they have certainly not left their ancient land.[56]

The 'Alawis are a two-thirds majority in the region where they live in the coastal area of northern Syria and its continuation into Turkey. Although small groups of 'Alawis exist in Jordan as well as in Lebanon, basically this is a Syrian sect. The 'Alawis in Syria constitute some 75 percent of the 'Alawis in the Middle East at large, unlike the Druze who have major centers in both Lebanon and Syria, with a third center slowly evolving in Israel. Like the Druze, they also tend to live in mountain villages and emphasize the secret elements in religion. These two factors, secrecy and relative isolation in mountainous regions, have helped maintain a tribal solidarity and distinctness that many other minority groups in the Middle East have lacked. Historical circumstances in Syria led French colonial power to develop a preferential attitude toward these two minorities, which then institutionalized their role in the military, to the point of their later dominating the state elite under the proverbial army-party "symbiosis."[57] It is striking in this context that the 'Alawis, the dominant party in the alliance, have never exceeded one-eighth of the total population of the country.

It is worth thinking about the compact minorities in a broader regional context. Are they the exception that proves a rule, or are they a rule of sorts, and if so, why do we not see more salient cases elsewhere? One immediate example that comes to mind is that of the Kurds, by far the largest ethnic group within the Middle East that can be classified as a minority. Many of the characteristics of the Kurdish case seem completely to fit the model of compact minorities. They live in a number of countries (Iraq, Iran, Turkey, Syria) in areas where they are an overwhelming majority—in each of these cases millions of inhabitants reside in the given area of Kurdistan. (The exact demographic numbers are not known; sometimes the total number of Kurds is described as exceeding 20 million, sometimes substantially less.) The Kurds, like the Druze and the 'Alawis, also tend to live in rural mountain areas and also excel in the martial arts.

Unlike the Druze and the 'Alawis, however, the Kurds are clearly Muslims and Muslims of the majority tradition—that of Sunni Islam. However, the Kurds do not speak Arabic but an Indo-European language, akin to Farsee, which is written at times in Latin and in other cases in Arabic script. In terms of objective parameters, it appears that the existence of a separate language is considered by many scholars as being of decisive significance in defining a distinct minority. In this sense, the "Arabness" of the Kurds is much more in doubt than that of the Druze or the 'Alawis, because they do not live in exclusively Arab countries but are also found in Iran, Turkey, and parts of the former Soviet Union that cannot be considered Arab. (Classic Arab nationalist theory itself put a premium on language as one of the most important characteristics of being an Arab.) Yet their being Sunni Muslim makes them part of the mainstream of the Middle East, so that they do belong to the majority in some ways.[58]

The Kurds can be considered a compact minority in places such as Iraq, where in fact they have tried assiduously to develop various models of political accommodation, some having to do with integration into the political life in the center, and some having to do with the ambitions for territorial autonomy. But the fact that the Kurds are spread all over the Middle East without a clear majority in any single country has made them different from other compact minorities. For example, their geographic spread has made it difficult for them to resolve their problems in any single country because other countries fear the power of precedent for their own minorities. While some have found it expedient to support Kurdish aspirations for reasons of their own raison d'être, others have opposed the Kurdish objectives for the very same reasons.[59] The fate of the Kurds in Iraq in the 1970s is a striking and tragic demonstration of the challenges of building viable, long-term relationships in a region fraught by abrupt change, often engineered by a handful of individuals.

Yet the Kurds resemble a nation in the theoretical sense perhaps more than any other minority in the Middle East, a fact that makes finding their place in the sun more difficult. One advantage that the 'Alawis and the Druze have enjoyed has been that—at least in recent decades—they have not been suspect of supporting potential nation-state alternatives, whereas the Kurds are suspected of doing precisely that.[60] It is more difficult for them to settle for the more modest objectives of the Druze and the 'Alawis because objectively they seem to deserve more, and they seem to possess much greater potential clout. So they are feared more. In the minds of many in the region, the Kurds are a threat not because of what they do but because of what they are. So herein lies an authentic tragedy of this people, which is the largest and most salient cross-national minority in the Middle East. Another obviously crucial factor in the fate of the Kurds was that they never enjoyed preferential treatment at the hands of the colonial powers.[61]

It is not easy to define the alternative to compact minorities, although such alternatives clearly do exist. For example, there are Orthodox Christians who live in various places in Syria, Lebanon, and Israel, and yet they do not enjoy a majority status in a given region, nor do they have a single center. They tend to be politically ineffective, as they lack all the advantages of other kinds of minorities. Their numbers do not make them really important; their voting rights are not important either, as voting in general does not make a real difference,[62] and they lack the political punch of either a strong regional base or a strong connection with the instruments of power (such as the military).[63] This political weakness does not make them unimportant, for they still can leave their mark on cultural life and in business, as indeed was the case decades ago, and particularly with reference to the birth of Arab nationalism. However, as Bernard Lewis observed in the 1970s (in terms of "the Return of Islam," a popular phrase), the more Arab nationalism became accepted by the masses, the more it came to be associated with Islamic themes, a contradiction that the Christians have never been able to resolve.[64] The more they tried to pose ideological alternatives to Islamic politics (such as secular nationalism or socialism), the more those alternatives either became Islamicized or they failed—a classic case of "no exit."[65]

The case of the Coptic Christians in Egypt is somewhat different. Their numbers are significant, around 10 percent, and there has been an occasional upsurge in the level of their political consciousness and aspirations. They have vacillated between the traditional politics of a minority accepting its marginal role and a very assertive political style. The strength of the assertive style became a problem for the Sadat regime, which itself vacillated between two poles: first taking a conciliatory stance toward Coptic activism, later attempting to clamp down on the politicization of religion, an absurd claim in the circumstances of the Middle East. Given the strong Islamic flavor of mass politics in Egypt today, it is hard to see the Copts succeeding in asserting their collective role in politics as a semiautonomous community, as they lack the territorial attributes of the compact minorities, despite the existence of Coptic villages or neighborhoods.[66]

Theoretical and Comparative Implications and Considerations

In trying to assess the theoretical implications of the preliminary comparative analysis, it appears safe to say that there is a model of compact minorities, and that this model has its peculiarities that make it the most visible one. Then there is the model of the semicompact minorities, such as the Kurds, where the situation has been different, even though much of the same potential has been present. The opposite model of the noncompact or dispersed, *diffuse* minorities such as the Orthodox Christians (or the Jews in former times) is at the other end of the spectrum, and there is the case of the Copts in between, close to the diffuse model but not identical to it, due to larger numbers and partial demographic concentrations. So we have different ends of the theoretical continuum—the compact on the one hand and the diffuse on the other—and in between something like semicompact and semidiffuse. This may be a convenient way to get at classifying them for purposes of analysis and comparison. Other variables have to be taken into account as well, including the definition of the majority, in order to understand better what constitutes a minority. As mentioned before, the definition of the majority is not always constant, and it depends on the self-identity of the political community at a given moment in history.

A number of scholars have observed that ethnic identity is malleable and that it can be manipulated. Stephen H. Longrigg, in analyzing Iraqi politics many years ago, coined the apt phrase "Kurds for ministerial purposes."[67] A person can discover his or her identity as a minority under the pressure of political processes, and someone can deny such an identity for any number of reasons as well. In addition, one can and does belong to a number of ethnic and other "primordial" entities at the same time, hence demonstrating what political sociologists call "cross-cutting cleavages." One can be a member of both the majority and a minority at the same time, or a member of several minorities. The results of such multiple belonging can be of different varieties. The classic theory in the West used to hold that cross-cutting cleavages are basically good for society because they moderate one another and thereby lay the foundations for a more pluralistic society in which several different competitive elements and principles coexist.[68]

This theory has been challenged recently in the West, and certainly there is little evidence to support it in the Middle East. Analysts will hasten to add another variable, usually referred to as the level of institutionalization.[69] This theory argues that the technique of building institutions (parties, unions, clubs, electoral processes, and a variety of formal organizations) makes a critically important difference in a country's political fortunes because only institutionalization enables a stable political system to function in an orderly manner, detached from the vagaries of ascriptive competition for resources. At the time this theoretical approach was born, in the late 1960s, the point was repeatedly made by its high priests that the Middle East was generally characterized by a low level of institutionalization, meaning that there were few political entities that endured due to their own strength rather than by being embedded in ethnic and tribal belongings and loyalties.[70]

This theory is still potent, although less popular today, and it does bear directly on the matter of minorities in the Middle East. First, minority identity matters more in societies where there are few complex and stable institutions, simply because the basis for political life and competition is more limited. This also helps to explain why ethnic questions in such societies tend to be more sensitive and lead to more violence. Second, the assets and resources that the given society has in attempting to tackle majority-minority relations are fewer when political institutions are weak, because there is a lack of integrative mechanisms and even neutral arenas where different ethnic identities and entities can meet on mutually acceptable grounds. This lack in turn leads to suspicion and distrust of the existing institutions, which are considered to have been captured by one or more of the competing ethnic interests, thereby reducing their ability to forge political alliances that include a variety of interests and loyalties.

Third, minorities will feel that they can only protect their own interests by establishing institutions of their own or capturing existing institutions, which again make them suspect in the eyes of the majority.[71] All these factors lead to an extremely volatile political life in which the stabilizing influence of enduring political institutions is lacking, with debilitating results for the country. The only truly strong institution in existence is the state, and it becomes the focus of violent competition as the only institutionalized object worth capturing.

Analyzing some of these theoretical observations in the concrete context of Middle East politics, it appears that because there have been fewer institutions and alternative foci of loyalty in the region, ethnic strife between majorities and minorities has endured longer and with more potential for volatility than elsewhere, and this can and should be understood properly against the background of Islam and politics.[72] This is one of the most fashionable subjects in political analysis today, and the discussion that follows will not attempt to enter this general debate about Islam and politics but will make only some observations relevant to understanding the situation of minorities in the Middle East.

The centrality and overwhelming impact of Islam in Middle East politics are so well established that they need no further proof or documentation. However, the implications of these realities for various walks of life are not always properly understood. For instance, the relationship between Islam and ethnicity is a complex phenomenon, and obviously there are different varieties of this relationship in existence.[73] Yet in general it is safe to argue that Islam is not an ethnic religion, like Judaism. Being Jewish, as some Jewish writers have recently put it, is as much a matter of being a "member of the tribe" as it is a matter of practicing or even believing the tenets of Judaism as a religion. The more the modern variety of Jewish nationalism prevails in Israel and makes itself the overwhelming focus of loyalty among Jews in the world, the stronger this tendency, even though it may not be articulated quite so brutally. Evidently, this tendency also reflects the revolt of Jews against their patterns of living for many centuries, characterized by an extreme preoccupation with religious observance at the expense of political life. The other peoples with which Judaism had contact may have been religious in the past, but over the past five centuries they have become increasingly secular in orientation, whereas Jews remained religious until about the middle of the nineteenth century.

As Yeshayahu Leibowitz has observed, until that time the notion of a secular Jew (let alone a secular Jewish community) was practically a contradiction. It has been one of the outstanding challenges of Jewish history since the

mid-1880s to come to terms with the change in this definition and the resulting identity. One reason this redefinition has been so successful is that Jews
do indeed feel a tribal kind of belonging, which has to a large extent compen-
sated for the lack of religious content in Jewish life in most of Israel and
much of the diaspora.

With Islam, things are much more complicated. Whereas Islam can be
considered a political community that is far superior to any single nation-
state, in practice it has meant following the tenets of the Islamic religion.[74]
Although there have been cases of Muslims being forced to align themselves
with their own political community by civil wars, as in Lebanon or Pakistan,
or more recently in Bosnia, the Islamization of a political community has normally meant a higher degree of religious consciousness.[75] Building a Jewish
political community has been basically the work of secular nationalists, long
opposed by most of the religious establishment, whereas building Islamic political communities in recent times has basically been the work of religious
Muslims, often working against the tenets and practice of secular nationalists.
The identity of politics and religion is still a huge problem for those minorities in the Jewish state that are not part of the Jewish nation, as in the case of
Israeli Arabs, but the nature of the Jewish polity presents an interesting contrast to the putative Islamic state.[76]

Because religion is not the sole basis of the Jewish community—many
secular nationalists consider it a bothersome relic of the past—religion in Israel is often regarded as best left to the various religious establishments, which
work more or less autonomously from the state. If anything, the secular-
nationalists resent this abdication of state functions to particular nonstate actors, and they argue correctly that this represents Ottoman traditions that are
badly outdated at the end of the twentieth century. Basically, however, this
arrangement provides a convenient way out for secular Jewish nationalism,
because it allows both the Jewish religious establishment as well as the other
religious establishments to function more or less to their own satisfaction
while maintaining the Jewish character of the state via political and cultural
domination. In this sense, Israel has no problem with religious minorities,
only with political and cultural ones. The Jewish religious establishment is un-
happy only because it has been confined to certain areas of jurisdiction,
whereby most Jews most of the time are not under its influence.

Hence, the Jewish religious establishment desires more power over the
Jews who are not under its jurisdiction, and has little interest in making non-
Jews obey any Jewish laws or tenets. It feels comfortable with the Ottoman
tradition, and when secular liberal Jews argue against religious coercion, they
invariably mean Jews imposing on other Jews, rather than Jews imposing on
non-Jews. The struggle for the Jewish character of the Israeli state is over, at
least in the sense that it is a Jewish state. Whereas the exact meaning of this
term is unclear, in practice the issue has been settled, and the religious estab-

lishment at large has few illusions that it can make the state any more Jewish than it already is through religious legislation. The Israeli state is Jewish because it is populated mostly by Jews, who are in control of politics and who form the cultural elite that manufactures the symbols of living in the country.[77] Those who fall outside this realm of symbols, as do the Israeli Arabs, will always have great difficulty integrating into this cultural definition of the nation, but it is a Jewish state in this cultural-national sense and not in the religious one.

The situation is substantially different in the rest of the Middle East, however. In Lebanon, for instance, the character of the state is not settled, and the Muslim majority is not allowed to dominate political or cultural life.[78] Hence, the militancy of all groups concerned and their ambition to dominate the political center, or at least a share of it, by minimizing the impact of the other religious groups, often manifests through violence. Even if we grant that Lebanon is an exception, as a virtual "nonstate," the struggle for the future character of other Arab states is very much in progress. This struggle constitutes one of the main themes of the Islamic revival, which is so fashionable a subject in intellectual and political circles dealing with the Middle East today. One main theme of this struggle is the distinction between a state of Muslims and a Muslim state, a distinction that is in many ways the crux of the matter in any state claiming to have a religious character.[79]

Practically all observers agree that Israel is a state of Jews more than it is a Jewish state. As a result, there are few attempts to create a radically different way of running the state. Those models chosen for emulation are more likely to be the more successful industrialized nations of the West rather than from the past glories of Jewish history, real or imagined, or from any theoretical superstructure of Jewish political theory. This orientation creates a common language of normative politics in Israel and is a great equalizer between majority and minority, which strive for more or less the same image of the good state.

The situation is quite different in the case of the Islamic forces now so strong all over the Middle East. As the example of Iran demonstrates, the Islamists would very much like to create a state in their own particular image, one that not only differs from but is explicitly trying to defy the modern Western state. In this effort, they share neither a common language nor a common model with non-Islamic forces; and this idea of the Islamic state has the potential to threaten non-Muslims and cause a rift with them. At different periods in the brief history of the revolutionary Islamic republic of Iran, we have already seen grave threats to the Jews and the Bahais. This kind of threat may arise again and again against *all* non-Islamic minorities because, as the saying goes, this is the nature of the beast.

This struggle for the character of the state is still being waged in other states in the region, and the shape of the future state is still in doubt. We can imagine the threat posed to the Egyptian Copts, for example, if the Islamic forces are successful in capturing power in that country. That Egypt is a state of Muslims has already been determined, because 90 percent of its citizens are Muslims and because the Egyptian political elite—despite all pretensions and ambitions of modernization—has preferred to move in the circles of other Islamic countries. But what the forceful wave of Islamic radicalism in Egypt now demands is precisely to take that step toward becoming an Islamic state. No matter how it is defined, this transition will threaten non-Muslims in Egypt. It will inevitably introduce legislation based on the Islamic heritage, at the expense of the universal elements of the modern nation-state, which are more accommodating as far as minorities are concerned.

Hence, the Islamic revival does not involve a return to the "good old days" of Ottoman rule, with their delegation of authority to the different religious communities in a highly decentralized structure.[80] To the contrary, the present Islamic wave represents a bizarre juxtaposition of the centralized power of the modern national state (the very antithesis of the multinational Ottoman Empire), with the leaders' ambitions derived from the eschatological and nostalgic traditions of the Islamic heritage. Perhaps in the future, when there is a clearer definition of what an Islamic state represents, this juxtaposition might either disappear or be transformed in a way that will be congruent with the existence of non-Islamic minorities. For the time being the lot of minorities during the Islamic onslaught is bound to be one of uncertainty and apprehension. In general, Islam is expected to serve as social and cultural content for nationalism, in some ways substituting for the socialism of earlier times: after all, socialism is as alien to the Middle East as the modern nation-state. No matter how universalistic in nature and multinational in demographic terms, however, Islam has been used as the handmaiden of nationalism and not as an alternative to it.[81]

It is not possible to predict the future directions of the struggle for an Islamic state, let alone its outcome. Possibly the Islamic tide will abate, or else it may settle into a moderate pattern that will not threaten the political fate of the minorities. It is quite likely, however, that the present patterns will endure for some time to come.[82] The crux of the present situation may well be that Islam has not really challenged the dominance of the prevailing states in the Middle East. In other words, Islamists have not managed to present commitment to a broader Islamic framework, such as the proverbial Islamic Umma, as an alternative to existing states, notwithstanding the theoretical possibilities inherent in Islamic frameworks. In practice, the Islamic wave has settled in most cases into an alliance between the nationalism defined by the loyalty to a single state and the broader loyalties such as Arab and Islamic sentiments as the overall framework of faith and values.[83]

Without a doubt, the resulting amalgamation is an uneasy one, full of tensions that are both logical and practical-political. Thus, the Iranian Islamic entity has fought with other Islamic entities in bloody battles and has tried to call on the Islamic loyalties of its own population. Because the enemy was also Islamic (although accused of having become secularized and unfaithful), the Islamic appeal was not sufficient in this particular case. Nationalist themes had to be mobilized, so that nationalism was virtually recycled, not in a pure form but one congruent with the Islamic character of the regime.[84] For example, the attraction of Shi'i Islam, the state religion of Iran, was mobilized against the Sunni character of the Iraqi elite.[85] The Sunni-Shi'i cleavage brings us back to the question of just what defines a minority in the Middle East.

Although there are many sayings to the effect that "the house of Islam is one," in practice this is far from true. The split between Sunnis and Shi'is has been such a central fact of life in the political history of the Middle East that it cannot be ignored. Do the Sunnis constitute a minority in Iran, and if so, does the term *minority* carry the same connotation as in the case of an ethnic-linguistic minority like the Kurds? If the reply is in the affirmative, then we have at least three definitions of minorities in the Middle East: ethnic, religious, and intra-Islamic. When two or more such cleavages coincide, we are likely to find a more serious problem with minorities, but normally in the Middle East this complication does not arise. Thus, the Kurds are an ethnic minority, but they are Muslims, albeit Sunni Muslims, which aggravates definitions in a Shi'i country such as Iran. However, the main theoretical question is how to treat the case of a country such as Iraq.[86]

We do know that in Iraq the ruling Sunnis in fact represent a minority of the population—the Shi'is have a numerical but not a political majority. In terms of political and cultural dominance, the urban Sunni elite has been very much in control since the inception of the modern Iraqi state. Yet we will rarely find a reference in the literature to the case of the Sunnis in Iraq as a minority, which they technically are, especially if we refer only to Arab, that is, non-Kurdish, Sunnis in Iraq. This failure is interesting, as it demonstrates that demography is only one of the elements that shape how we treat groups in society, and that other elements also enter the picture.[87] The Sunnis in Iraq are rarely if ever considered to be in a similar position to the compact minorities in Syria, even though there is some resemblance between them. If in the course of Iraqi history the Shi'is capture power and come to dominate the political center, it is possible that we shall indeed start hearing more references to the Sunnis there as a proper minority.

Elsewhere in the region intra-Islamic minorities definitely exist and are normally treated as such by scholars as well as politicians. The Shi'is in the various states of the Arabian Peninsula are but one example, and there are numerous others. Indeed, with the assertion of Shi'i self-confidence, backed by Iran, the salience of such minorities is likely to grow.[88] Obviously, the Shi'is are being increasingly politicized, and they are not going to be bought off easily by slogans of loyalty to Islam, because their brand of Islam is so different from that of the Sunnis: this difference has many political implications. Precisely because they are found within Islam, the intra-Islamic minorities may well enjoy the highest degree of legitimacy to be politically active as minorities and to differ from the norms of a given country. The implications of this kind of minority activity are not yet fully understood because the process is relatively new.

The Extreme Case of Sudan

Sudan represents an interesting and important case in the ethnic makeup of the Middle East.[89] It is one of the largest countries in the region, along with Saudi Arabia and Algeria, spreading over approximately 2.5 million square kilometers and stretching from the Egyptian border in the north deep into Central Africa. In terms of population, Sudan is split into two widely differing parts, an Arabic-speaking Islamic north, and a linguistically and ethnically different south, partly Christian and partly followers of traditional African religions. (They are hence considered pagan by the Muslims and Christians, though polytheistic is probably a more useful characterization.) Sudan has suffered from a very long and rather intense civil war between north and south almost from its very inception. This civil war seems to end every once in a while in a negotiated agreement, which then breaks down in short order due to the inevitable strains in the complex relationship of the two sections, with the underlying causes of conflict rarely being addressed in the various agreements.

The case of Sudan represents perhaps most clearly the divisive cleavages that underlie the entire Middle East. The main cleavage may be considered the religious one, which divides the Islamic community from the rest. This cleavage firmly puts the north in the family of the Islamic nations and the south in the family of black African nations. Others will argue that the main cleavage is the one that makes the north Arab rather than Islamic. In no other place in the Middle East can we see a major part of a country inhabited heavily by a population that is neither Muslim nor Arab. Moreover, this split is also territorial, which is to say that the non-Islamic, non-Arab population occupies a territory of its own, a territory that is relatively far from the political center of the country and hence difficult to control.

A comparison of this case with others in the region shows its uniqueness. There are significant numbers of Christians in Lebanon, with the Maronites having a substantial territorial concentration in a mountainous area that is difficult to reach. They are Arabs, however, and their acknowledgment of this identity forms a key part of the National Covenant. The Kurds are concentrated in several countries rather than one; no less important, the Kurds are Sunni Muslims, so that their ethnic-linguistic minority status is *not* reinforced by the religious factors that are so important in Islamic countries.[90] This case reflects the uniqueness of Sudan, whose potential instability is also exacerbated at times by the extreme factionalism of the majority Islamic-Arab population.[91] This case also resembles most the classic ethnic cleavages now ravaging such countries as the former Yugoslavia. Elsewhere, I have analyzed the possible benefits of a federal solution to the problems of Sudan, and indeed some such experiments with autonomy have periodically been made.[92] But we need to reserve judgment on this solution, as attempts to implement it have so far usually failed.

The case of Sudan exhibits another characteristic of many societies in the Middle East: extreme factionalism among both the majority and the minority. (Most estimates speak of a two-thirds majority and a one-third minority.) This factionalism has to be understood in order to comprehend the complexities of Sudanese politics. Yet factionalism at times inhibits finding a solution to ethnic conflicts. It makes it more difficult to find consensual support for models of coexistence and of course, in the case of the south, it makes for internal strife and violence as widespread as the conflict between majority and minority. This pattern, while seemingly extreme in Sudan, also exists in Lebanon and makes politics there that much more difficult to comprehend and manage, let alone transform to a higher level of stability. However, we do not have a theoretical explanation as to whether extremely factionalized societies tend to have more serious strains with minorities, or perhaps it is the other way around:[93] fragmented societies with minorities also tend to factionalize internally the majority and each of the minorities.[94]

Concluding Observations

As the analysis reveals, there are evidently many different kinds of minority situations.[95] A country that has no majority but only minorities is Lebanon. A large majority, with a clear minority situation, exists in Egypt. Syria has a minority situation together with a clear majority, although the majority is not in control of the political center. A minority dominates the majority and another very large minority in Iraq. In the Arabian Peninsula a clear majority dominates, but there is also a large foreign presence of alien workers along with strong intra-Islamic minorities. We have the case of Sudan, with a sharp cleavage between an Arab, Muslim north and a non-Muslim, non-Arab south. All over the Middle East the cases fall more or less into one of these patterns.[96] We are not able at the present time to generalize about all these cases. For example, we are not able to state whether one pattern is more amenable to intergroup accommodation than another, or whether one pattern is more likely to lead to violent rivalry. But we are able to state that these patterns are not peculiar to the Middle East as such, as they can be found elsewhere in the world.

It makes sense to assume that a large single majority is able to enjoy more stable rule than smaller majorities, and it makes sense to assume that multiple minorities are more difficult for a majority to handle than a single minority.[97] Diffuse minorities constitute, as a rule, less of a political threat to the majority than do compact minorities that have a territorial base; in fact, this observation is one of the points worth elaborating upon in further research. Land and territory seem to make a big difference in the impact of ethnic groups in the Middle East, and it remains to be seen how broadly this is true. The importance of a territorial base has been recently observed in new entities emerging from the ruins of the former federations of Yugoslavia and the Soviet Union. Other examples are to be found in well-known cases of ethnic strife in Africa and Asia, from Zaire to Cambodia. One common denominator of these cases appears to be the territorial dimension that transforms the putative minority into a concrete ethnic force.

National political patterns have to be considered against the patterns of the status of minorities. We have seen that the Middle East has both compact minorities and their opposite, the diffuse minorities ('Alawis as contrasted with Greek Orthodox Christians, for instance), and it exhibits ethnic as against religious distinctions: by religious, we mean the differentiation between Islam and all others. However, there is one further dimension, the difference between the varieties of Islam that are important enough to make the groups involved also equivalent to majorities and minorities. Here again it is difficult to theorize, so we shall only suggest some lines for future research and analysis. For example, we may consider the hypothesis that in the foreseeable future intra-Islamic minorities are likely to gain further importance because their legitimacy is going to be higher than that of other groups. The lot of the Kurds in Iraq may improve, almost as an analogy to the former colonial situation in other countries, where the colonial powers used to prefer the compact minorities. The international support for Kurdish autonomy in the north in the wake of the 1991 Gulf War may be a belated historical quirk that functionally fills the same role as the older colonial preferences for compact minorities in Syria. Obviously, this support is much less stable than the old colonial one, but its impact for the future may still be decisive.

Many other elements and variables make a difference in the fortunes of the minorities in the Arab world. However, the interplay of the main themes referred to in this preliminary analysis—compact versus diffuse minorities, the nature of the primordial ties, Islamic radicalism, the colonial legacy—set the stage on which the continuing drama of Middle Eastern minorities unfolds. We hope that this background has respected the advice of Charles D. Smith: "Historians of the modern Middle East should be willing to question fashionable theories and to evaluate their relevance rather than assume an automatic congruence of experience based on terminology. Likewise, scholars in the social sciences should discuss their theoretical literature more fully in work on the Middle East."[98]

Notes

1. On the survey of prevailing approaches to the study of minorities and ethnic groups, see Saul Newman, "Does Modernization Breed Ethnic Political Conflict?" *World Politics* 43, no. 2 (April 1991), pp. 451–478; Donald D. Horowitz, *Ethnic Groups in Conflict* (Berkeley: University of California Press, 1985); Joseph Rothschild, *Ethnopolitics: A Conceptual Framework* (New York: Columbia University Press, 1981); Anthony D. Smith, *The Ethnic Revival* (Cambridge: Cambridge University Press, 1981); Edward D. Tiryakian and Ronald Rogowski (eds.), *New Nationalisms of the Developed West: Toward an Explanation* (Boston: Allen and Unwin, 1985). The article by Newman is particularly useful in trying to classify and categorize the various approaches.

2. Variations of this focus have been the subject of the bulk of the literature in Middle Eastern history and politics. For a survey of recent works in this field, see the review article by Charles D. Smith, "Imagined Identities, Imagined Nationalisms: Print Culture and Egyptian Nationalism in Light of Recent Scholarship," *International Journal of Middle East Studies* 29, no. 4 (November 1997), pp. 607–622. This is a review based on the survey of Israel Gershoni and James P. Jankowski, *Redefining the Egyptian Nation, 1930–1945* (Cambridge: Cambridge University Press, 1995). A large number of other works are instructive, and most of these are referred to in the Smith article. In addition, see, for instance, Philip S. Khoury and Joseph Kostiner (eds.), *Tribes and State Formation in the Middle East* (Berkeley: University of California Press, 1990).

3. For an instructive recent example along similar lines, see Nelida Fuccaro, "Ethnicity, State Formation, and Conscription in Postcolonial Iraq: The Case of the Yazidi Kurds of Jabal Sinjar," *International Journal of Middle East Studies* 29, no. 4 (November 1997), pp. 559–580.

4. For a penetrating variation on this theme, see Fouad Ajami, *The Vanished Imam: Musa al-Sadr and the Shia of Lebanon* (Ithaca, N.Y.: Cornell University Press, 1986). Another interesting case in point is Yitzhak Nakash, *The Shi'is of Iraq* (Princeton, N.J.: Princeton University Press, 1994).

5. It seems that the most comprehensive treatment of this issue is to be found in Rothschild, *Ethnopolitics*. An ambitious attempt to explore the relationship between ethnicity and politics in the context of the Middle East is Milton Esman and Itamar Rabinovich (eds.), *Ethnicity, Pluralism and the State in the Middle East* (Ithaca, N.Y.: Cornell University Press, 1987).

6. See the good survey in Newman, "Does Modernization Breed Conflict?" pp. 453–456.

7. As exemplified in Ronald Rogowski, "Causes and Varieties of Nationalism: A Rationalist Account," in Tiryakian and Rogowski, *New Nationalism*.

8. See, for example, the essays in Clifford Geertz (ed.), *Old Societies and New States: The Quest for Modernity in Asia and Africa* (New York: Free Press, 1963).

9. See, for instance, Walker Connor, "The Politics of Ethnonationalism," *Journal of International Affairs* 27, no. 1 (January 1973), pp. 1–21.

10. Extensive examples and items of the relevant literature are to be found in Gabriel Ben-Dor, *The Druzes in Israel: A Political Study* (Jerusalem: Magnes, 1981).

11. Nathan Glazer and Daniel P. Moynihan, *Ethnicity: Theory and Experience* (Cambridge, Mass.: Harvard University Press, 1975); Crawford Young, *The Politics of Cultural Pluralism* (Madison: University of Wisconsin Press, 1976).

12. This is one major theme pursued in Ben-Dor, *The Druzes in Israel*.

13. This is argued in sophisticated detail in the influential *Ethnopolitics* by Roth-schild. However, the earlier and deservedly influential formulation is to be found in Clifford Geertz, "The Integrative Revolution" in Geertz, *Old Societies.*

14. See Horowitz, *Ethnic Groups in Conflict.*

15. Newman, "Does Modernization Breed Conflict?" p. 464, paraphrasing Horowitz.

16. Ibid.

17. Ibid.

18. See the argument and the literature in Gabriel Ben-Dor, *State and Conflict in the Middle East: Emergence of the Postcolonial State* (New York: Praeger, 1983) and Ben-Dor, "Ethnopolitics and the Middle Eastern State," in Esman and Rabinovich, *Ethnicity, Pluralism and the State.*

19. See Bassam Tibi, "Old Tribes and Imposed Nation-States in the Modern Middle East," in Khoury and Kostiner, *Tribes and State Formation.*

20. Many instructive examples are referred to in the useful review by Charles D. Smith, "Imagined Identities, Imagined Nationalisms." This survey also contains a rather extensive bibliography of the literature relevant to this argument. See also the example of Egypt as analyzed by Sa'd al-Din Ibrahim, referred to later in this volume.

21. There is, as is well known, a most extensive literature on this. For one instructive set of insights and examples, see Bruce Maddy-Weitzman and Efraim Inbar (eds.), *Religious Radicalism in the Greater Middle East* (London: Frank Cass, 1997).

22. This point is argued in great detail in Gabriel Ben-Dor, "Stateness and Ideology in Contemporary Middle Eastern Politics," *The Jerusalem Journal of International Relations* 9, no. 3 (September 1987), pp. 10–37.

23. A good example of how such historical knowledge may crystallize into the understanding of state strategies is to be found in the classic by Reinhard Bendix, *Nation-Building and Citizenship: Studies of Our Changing Social Order* (New York: John Wiley and Sons, 1964). For the more general argument see Theda Skocpol and Margaret Somers, "The Uses of Comparative History in Macrosocial Theory," *Comparative Studies in Society and History,* 22 (1980), pp. 174–197.

24. Smith, "Imagined Identities," p. 608.

25. Ibid.

26. Ibid. Smith points to "important exceptions" to this general criticism and includes Ben-Dor's *State and Conflict in the Middle East* among them.

27. For some of the classic dilemmas of using case studies in the study of politics, see Harry Eckstein, "Case Study and Theory in Political Science," in Fred I. Greenstein and Nelson W. Polsby (eds.), *Handbook of Political Science, Strategies of Inquiry,* vol. 7 (Reading, Mass.: Addison Wesley, 1975), pp. 80–104; Arend Lijphart, "Comparative Politics and the Comparative Method," *The American Political Science Review* 65, no. 3 (September 1971), pp. 682–693; and Joseph LaPalombara, "Macrotheories and Microapplications in Comparative Politics: A Widening Chasm," *Comparative Politics* 1, no. 1 (October 1968), pp. 52–78.

28. This concept, referring to a "real ethnic core," derives from the work of Anthony Smith, quoted in Charles D. Smith, "Imagined Identities," p. 609. See the original formulation in Anthony Smith, *The Ethnic Origins of Nations* (Oxford: Oxford University Press, 1986).

29. As it turns out, the contrast between the two also masks surprising similarities, a contrast that calls to mind Raymond Aron's famous remark that the heart of social science lies in the edict: "See the dissimilar in that which appears similar, and seek the similar in that which appears dissimilar."

30. See the many pertinent examples and the literature quoted in Esman and Rabinovich, *Ethnicity, Pluralism and the State*. For a recent, and different, view on some of the same issues, see Ted Robert Gurr, "Peoples Against States: Ethnopolitical Conflict and the Changing World System," *International Studies Quarterly* 38, no. 3 (September 1994), pp. 347–377. Gurr predicts the continuation of massive ethnic conflict in the post–Cold War era in the poorer, weaker, and more heterogeneous states, primarily in Africa. See also Joseph V. Montville (ed.), *Conflict and Peacemaking in Multiethnic Societies* (Lexington, Mass.: Lexington Books, 1987).

31. Indeed, the self-definition of minorities, as that of other social groups engaging in political activity, is subject to dramatic changes with the circumstances, in the Middle East as elsewhere. See Augustus Richard Norton, "The Future of Civil Society in the Middle East," *Middle East Journal* 47, no. 2 (spring 1993), pp. 205–216.

32. Clifford Geertz, "The Integrative Revolution," in Geertz, *Old Societies and New States*. This article has been deservedly influential in all subsequent studies of ethnic politics and minorities, as surveyed in Gabriel Ben-Dor, "Ethnopolitics and the Middle Eastern State," in Esman and Rabinovich, *Ethnicity, Pluralism and the State*. See also Pierre L. van Den Berghe, *The Ethnic Phenomenon* (New York: Elsevier, 1981) and George M. Scott, Jr., "A Resynthesis of the Primordial and Circumstantial Approaches to Ethnic Group Solidarity: Toward an Explanatory Model," *Ethnic and Racial Studies* 13, no. 2 (April 1990), pp. 147–171.

33. There are many alternative conceptions, some of which have been also very influential, for instance Samuel P. Huntington, *Political Order in Changing Societies* (New Haven, Conn.: Yale University Press, 1968).

34. Since the disintegration of the Soviet Union, much publicity has accompanied the pronouncements of Senator Daniel Moynihan, who argues that toward the end of the twentieth century ethnic conflict will be the "defining mode" of conflict in world politics. Some of this is also echoed in Huntington, who speaks of cultural conflict in more or less the same vein. See Samuel P. Huntington, "The Clash of Civilizations," *Foreign Affairs* 72, no. 3 (summer 1993), pp. 22–49; and Huntington, *The Clash of Civilizations and the Remaking of World Order* (New York: Simon and Schuster, 1996). See also Benjamin Barber, *Jihad Versus McWorld* (New York: Random House, 1995) and Thomas Sowell, *Race and Culture: A World View* (New York: Basic Books, 1994).

35. Indeed, the events in Central and Eastern Europe, as well as in many parts of Africa, seem to back up much of what is contained in the theses of Moynihan and Huntington, in both relatively developed and less developed parts of the world.

36. Geertz, "The Integrative Revolution."

37. Gabriel Ben-Dor, "Ethnopolitics and the Middle Eastern State."

38. This is argued in great detail by Norton, who says that such "identities are malleable." Conference on Democratization in the Middle East, McGill University, Montreal, May 1993.

39. Such insecurity is one of the main facts of life in modernizing societies. See Ben-Dor, *The Druzes in Israel*. In turn, insecurity of this kind breeds anxiety and also tends to breed violence, which explains some of the connections between the processes of modernization and ethnic violence.

40. This point is of crucial theoretical importance. See Ben-Dor, "Ethnopolitics and the Middle Eastern State" and Ben-Dor, *State and Conflict*.

41. On ethnic groups and ethnic problems in contemporary Arab states, see Saad Eddin Ibrahim, *Management of Ethnic Issues in the Arab World* (Cairo: Al-Ahram Center for Political and Strategic Studies, 1995). This booklet presents useful data,

ideas, and insights into the nature of problems of ethnicity in the various Arab coun-tries. In general, Ibrahim argues that the correct way to handle these problems is for Arab states to make more progress toward democracy, federalism, and civil society. His bibliography contains useful references to contemporary Arab publications in the field.

42. "Compact minorities" is a term coined by Pierre Rondot and made current by Albert Hourani, as quoted in Itamar Rabinovich, "The Compact Minorities and the Syrian State, 1918-45," *Journal of Contemporary History* 14, no. 4 (October 1979), pp. 693–712.

43. Ibid; Ben-Dor, *The Druzes in Israel.*

44. Albert Hourani, *Minorities in the Arab World* (New York: Oxford University Press, 1947) is the classic exposition in this field. See also Hourani, *Syria and Lebanon: A Political Essay* (New York: Oxford University Press, 1946).

45. For a comparative perspective on such developments, see Bendix, *Nation-Building and Citizenship.*

46. See Rabinovich, "The Compact Minorities."

47. A huge literature exists on military intervention in Middle East politics, and some of it does emphasize the centrality of the minorities in this process. See, for in-stance, Manfred Halpern, *The Politics of Social Change in the Middle East and North Africa* (Princeton, N.J.: Princeton University Press, 1963); Amos Perlmutter, "The Arab Military Elite," *World Politics* 22, no. 2 (January 1970), pp. 269–300; Eliezer Beeri, *Army Officers in Arab Politics and Society* (New York: Praeger, 1969); and Gabriel Ben-Dor, "The Politics of Threat: Military Intervention in the Middle East," *Journal of Political and Military Sociology* 1 (spring 1974), pp. 57–69.

48. This process also raises the interesting theoretical and practical question of what happens to the controlling minority when the attempt is made to reduce the level of military intervention and to free up the political process for greater civilian involve-ment. See Gabriel Ben-Dor, "Civilianization of Military Regimes in the Arab World," *Armed Forces and Society* 1, no. 3 (May 1975), pp. 317–327.

49. This argument is made in detail in Gabriel Ben-Dor, "Stateness and Ideol-ogy," where the literature on Lebanon is surveyed and analyzed.

50. See Hourani, *Minorities in the Arab World*, and *Syria and Lebanon.* I find that quoting such classics, when—as in this case—they are *not* out of date, is one of the most pleasant duties of a scholar specializing in fields where classics do in fact exist.

51. Bernard Lewis, *The Middle East: 2000 Years of History, from the Rise of Christianity to the Present Day* (London: Weidenfeld and Nicholson, 1995).

52. For a detailed survey of the history of the Druze, see Ben-Dor, *The Druzes in Israel* and Ben-Dor, "Intellectuals in the Politics of a Middle Eastern Minority," *Middle Eastern Studies* 12, no. 2 (May 1976), pp. 133–158.

53. See Gabriel Ben-Dor, "The Military in the Politics of Integration and Innova-tion: The Case of the Druze Minority in Israel," *Asian and African Studies* 9, no. 3 (1973), pp. 339–369.

54. This ties in strongly and naturally with the notion of *taqiyya*, the permission to pretend to be what one is not in order to survive. The notion may derive from Shi'i Islamic sources, but it appears to have to do more with the realities of minorities in the region than with theological considerations as such.

55. See Rabinovich, "The Compact Minorities."

56. See Abbas Kelidar, "Religion and the State in Syria," *Asian Affairs* 61 (1974), pp. 16–22.

57. A term coined by Itamar Rabinovich in his book *Syria Under the Ba'th, 1963–1966: The Army-Party Symbiosis in Syria* (New York: Praeger, 1971).

58. Interestingly, the literature on the Kurds is not quite as rich as one would expect, at least in proportion to their numbers and importance, although recently there has been something of a belated revival, due probably to the events of the Gulf War and its aftermath. See, for instance, David McDowall, *A Modern History of the Kurds* (London: I. B. Tauris, 1996) and Abbas Vali, *Kurdish Nationalism: Identity, Sovereignty and the Dialectics of Violence in Kurdistan* (London: I. B. Tauris, 1996). This may have to do with the relative inability of the Kurds to capture even a share of power, or—at least until until the 1991 Gulf War—to institutionalize a minority role in quest of self-government, with international salience. This contrasts sharply with the 'Alawis in Syria, or for that matter, with the Palestinians in the areas under Israeli control. See also the sources quoted in Servet Mutlu, "Ethnic Kurds in Turkey: A Demographic Study," *International Journal of Middle East Studies* 28, no. 4 (November 1996), pp. 517–541.

59. It is not one of the main purposes of this volume to compare how regimes try to develop strategies for dealing with minority problems. (On this see, for instance, Fred W. Riggs, "Ethnonationalism, Industrialism and the Modern State," *Third World Quarterly* 15, no. 4 [December 1994], pp. 583–611.) However, if this were a major objective, the treatment of the Kurds in the various countries clearly constitutes the most natural target of inquiry, when governments not only seem to differ substantially but also to treat the Kurdish question inside and outside their borders very differently.

60. This is a crucial difference between various minorities, particularly in a region of the world where state building has only recently reached a critical threshold, and where nation and state do not easily coexist. See Ben-Dor, *State and Conflict in the Middle East* and "Stateness and Ideology"; Elie Kedourie, *Democracy and Arab Political Culture* (Washington, D.C.: Institute for Near East Policy, 1992); Halpern, *Politics of Social Change.*

61. In other words, the patterns of social and political mobilization of the Kurds differed vastly from those of other compact minorities. See the classic formulation in Karl W. Deutsch, *Nationalism and Social Communication: An Inquiry into the Foundations of Nationality* (Cambridge, Mass.: Harvard University Press, 1953).

62. Free and orderly elections, contrary to some earlier romantic views, make a huge difference in modern political life, and even more for the minorities than for the majority in society. A more democratic Middle East, therefore, might be a more hospitable area for minorities. See Rex Brynen, Bahgat Korany, and Paul Noble (eds.), "Theoretical Perspectives," in *Political Liberalization and Democratization in the Arab World*, vol. 1 (Boulder, Colo.: Lynne Rienner, 1995).

63. And this may make even more difference in the specific context of Middle East politics than elsewhere. See Elie Kedourie, *Politics in the Middle East* (New York: Oxford University Press, 1992).

64. *Commentary* (January 1975), pp. 32–48, elaborated upon in his *The Political Language of Islam* (Chicago: University of Chicago Press, 1988).

65. See also Fouad Ajami, *The Arab Predicament: Arab Political Thought and Practice Since 1967* (Cambridge: Cambridge University Press, 1992). In this book Ajami pursues his famous and controversial argument as to the failure of Arab nationalism to resolve the major dilemmas it has faced.

66. The case of the Copts is also interesting in that Egypt is the most statelike Arab country (as argued in Ben-Dor, "Stateness and Ideology"), with clearly defined boundaries, a strong sense of identity within them, a tradition of allegiance to central

rule, and at the same time, a single majority and a single minority. At the very least, the parameters of the problem are delineated more sharply than in practically any other case.

67. These are examples of what is referred to at times as "synthetic neo-particularism," as surveyed in Ben-Dor, *The Druzes in Israel.*

68. See, for instance, Joseph LaPalombara, *Politics Within Nations* (Englewood Cliffs, N.J.: Prentice Hall, 1974).

69. This notion is identified, above all, with the work of Huntington in his *Political Order in Changing Societies.* However, for the complexities involved, see Gabriel Ben-Dor, "Institutionalization and Political Development: A Conceptual and Theoretical Analysis," *Comparative Studies in Society and History* 17, no. 3 (July 1975), pp. 309–325.

70. See, for instance, Perlmutter, "The Arab Military Elite."

71. The ultimate institution to be captured in such cases may be no less than the state itself, as argued in Ben-Dor, "Ethnopolitics and the Middle Eastern State."

72. See James A. Bill and Robert Springborg, *Politics in the Middle East,* 4th ed. (New York: HarperCollins, 1994).

73. Interestingly enough, the vast literature on Islam in recent years deals with questions of ethnicity and minorities much less than with general ideological and political considerations.

74. See P. J. Vatikiotis, *Islam and the State* (London: Croom and Helm, 1987).

75. See Samir Khalaf, *Lebanon's Predicament* (New York: Columbia University Press, 1987).

76. On the ideas of the Islamic state, see Nazih Ayoubi, *Political Islam: Religion and Politics in the Arab World* (London: Routledge, 1991), pp. 1–35. The bibliography of this book contains most of the relevant sources up to the beginning of the present decade.

77. In a way, all this only demonstrates the huge difference between the idea of the Jewish state, in which religiousness may well be less important than nationalism, and the idea of the Islamic state. In the latter case, the religious component is much weightier, and the nationalist component is often found in another sphere altogether, as in Arabness and the like. See the detailed argument in Ben-Dor, *State and Conflict.*

78. Many analysts consider Lebanon indeed a nonstate. See Ben-Dor, "Stateness and Ideology."

79. This dilemma, at least until the Iranian revolution of 1979, was best demonstrated by the problematical situation in Pakistan, the only state founded explicitly as Islamic.

80. This picture may, however, be an idealized and nostalgic version of reality. See William R. Polk and Richard Chambers (eds.), *Beginnings of Modernization in the Middle East* (Chicago: University of Chicago Press, 1968).

81. This is argued emphatically in Kedourie, *Politics in the Middle East,* chapter 6 (pp. 268–246), and throughout Vatikiotis, *Islam and the State.*

82. Indeed, some pundits, such as Bernard Lewis, are already inclined to argue that the wave is past its peak, due to disillusionment with the Iranian revolution, an inability of the Islamists to articulate a credible and coherent political doctrine, the strength of the incumbents, and many other factors.

83. Indeed, the history since the late 1970s gives further credence to the argument (Ben-Dor, *State and Conflict*) that it is the state, and not Islam, Arabism, socialism, or ethnicity that will continue to dominate Middle East politics in the foreseeable future.

84. In the Iran-Iraq war of the 1980s, the term *occupied land* was used by Iraq not to refer to Palestine but to Khuzistan, a province of Iran.

85. See Martin Kramer, *Shi'ism, Resistance, and Revolution* (Boulder, Colo.: Westview, 1987).

86. The lack of basic definitions and good typologies demonstrates not only the considerable theoretical confusion in the field but also the need to do much "pretheoretical" work, as Harry Eckstein put it in his writings, namely working out the basic concepts and dividing them into workable categories. See Eckstein, "On the Etiology of Internal Wars," in Bruce Mazlish, Arthur D. Kaledin, and David B. Ralston (eds.), *Revolution* (New York: Free Press, 1971), pp. 31–34.

87. In other words, as Israeli anthropologist Emanuel Marx put it in June 1985, ethnicity is also "situational." His remark was made at a conference on ethnicity and politics at the Hebrew University, Jerusalem.

88. See James Piscatori (ed.), *Islamic Fundamentalism and the Gulf Crisis* (Chicago: University of Chicago Press, 1991).

89. The case of Sudan is analyzed in great detail in Chapter 4. However, I am trying to show here the utility of the case method in developing and testing theoretical considerations. After all, the idea of producing a volume of different cases all over the Middle East is not just to show the rich variety in the region but also to try and study the similar and the dissimilar among them. On the utility of the case method for theory building and other purposes there is a large literature associated with the names of Harry Eckstein, Arend Lijphardt, and Alexander L. George. See, for instance, Alexander L. George, "Case Studies and Theory Development: The Method of Structured, Focused Comparison" in Paul Gordon Lauren (ed.), *Diplomacy: New Approaches in History, Theory and Policy* (New York: The Free Press, 1979), pp. 43–68. Extreme, or limiting, case studies like that of Sudan help us with generating hypotheses and ideas, as well as testing other, existing ideas and insights in different situations.

90. See Amin Hassanpour, *Nationalism and Language in Kurdistan, 1918–1985* (San Francisco: Mellen Research University Press, 1992).

91. Because it is such an extreme case, its features constitute a useful check against hasty generalizations, while at the same time allowing us to test in a preliminary way some of the more obvious conclusions arising from comparing other cases. See Alexander L. George and Timothy J. Mckeown, "Case Studies and Theories of Organizational Decision Making," *Advances in Information Processing in Organizations*, vol. 2 (1985), pp. 21–58.

92. Gabriel Ben-Dor, "Federalism in the Arab World," in Daniel Elazar (ed.), *Federalism and Political Integration* (Ramat Gan, Israel: Turtledove, 1979).

93. Compare the fascinating picture of segmentation in John Waterbury, *The Commander of the Faithful: The Moroccan Political Elite, A Study in Segmented Politics* (New York: Columbia University Press, 1970), an extreme case of fragmented political processes and institutions.

94. A fascinating study of one such example is to be found in Nakash, *The Shi'is of Iraq.*

95. For a picture of the deployment of the minorities in the region, see Robert D. Mclaurin (ed.), *The Political Role of Minority Groups in the Middle East* (New York: Praeger, 1979).

96. The case of Jordan, analyzed in Chapter 5 of this volume, does not appear to fall clearly into any of these neat categories, but analysis reveals that it has a single ruling group that is the minority (the East Bankers), and the majority group outside the political establishment (the Palestinians) is often referred to as the minority. For a

comparative picture with other regions in the world, see Larry Diamond and Marc F. Plattner (eds.), *Nationalism, Ethnic Conflict and Democracy* (Baltimore, Md.: Johns Hopkins University Press, 1994).

97. Some theories of military intervention tend to attribute the high incidence of military coups in Iraq and Syria to a large extent to this ethnic factor. See Perlmutter, "The Arab Military Elite."

98. Smith, "Imagined Identities," p. 619.

PART ONE

Arab Africa

2

The Berber Question in Algeria: Nationalism in the Making?

Bruce Maddy-Weitzman

The Berber seems to be content to be drawn gradually into and assimilated by his country's general ethos, to lose his identity in Arab society. Berber nationalism has become an outmoded doctrine, if it ever existed in the first place. The Berber of today may remember the tales of his father's father, of the glory of the Berber tribes; but he will not attempt to emulate his fore-bears. Instead, when asked his identity, he will say he is an Arab or an Algerian or Moroccan. *Imazigher* [sic] is a forgotten word.[1]

The original inhabitants of North Africa between Egypt's Western Desert and the Atlantic Ocean have been known to the outside world since antiquity by the once contemptuous epithet "Berbers" (from the Greek word *barbaroi*, meaning "barbarian"). Their social organization was traditionally tribal; their defining characteristic remains their various spoken dialects of a single language, whose origins remain obscure, but which seems related to the language of ancient Libya, Libico-Berber, an Afro-Asiatic (formerly Hamito-Semitic) language.[2] Berber dialects are often incomprehensible to speakers of other Berber dialects from different regions. Despite the problems involved in the very term *Berber,* it has been gradually adopted by the people who speak variants of the Tamazight language, although many also use the term Amazigh (free man).

Berbers present special problems for any analysis of minorities in the modern Middle East, for they defy neat definitions according to well-established categories. Unlike the Copts or the Christian minorities of the Fertile Crescent, the Berbers were thoroughly Islamized over the course of centuries of Arab conquests. Today, nearly all are Sunnis of the Malikite school, as are their non–Berber Arab compatriots in North Africa. The Kurds' "semidiffuseness" partially resembles the Berbers' territorial concentration in a few main areas. However, the degree of Arabization experienced by the Berbers, while varying from place to place, was greater, on the whole, than comparable processes of Arabization, Persianization, and Turkification experienced by the Kurds. Moreover, the Kurds, while constituting a majority in their mountainous habitats, remained an ethnolinguistic minority amidst their neighbors. In North Africa, the vast majority of the population descends from the original Berber stock. Perhaps half of all North Africans have been so thoroughly Arabized over the centuries that they have lost all semblance of their Berber origins. Neither Libya nor Tunisia, for example, contain Berber communities of any significant size. The remaining substantial Berber communities in Algeria and Morocco are products, in varying degrees, of an Arab-Berber fusion or synthesis, linguistically, politically, and socially, thus further complicating any efforts to pin down the essence of being Berber and forcing one to employ the very term *minority* with great caution, depending on the particular context.

Their modern experience, dating from France's occupation of Algeria in 1830, is an additional defining characteristic. Initially in Algeria and later in Morocco, French colonial policy was directed toward distinguishing Berbers from Arabs, to consolidate French control. Politically, this effort was an utter failure: in Algeria, in particular, Berbers played central roles in the 1954–1962 war for independence, whereas in Morocco, the infamous Berber *dahir* (decree) of 1930, which established a system of customary law tribunals for Berbers separate from other Muslims, served as a rallying cry for Moroccan nationalists of all stripes. Socially, economically, and culturally, however, the impact on Algerian Berbers of both specific French policies and the colonial experience per se were profound. To be sure, this is true for Maghreb societies as a whole, as exemplified by the centrality of the French language in public life and the influence of French culture even today, notwithstanding decades of Arabization policies. The lasting influence of the French experience in North Africa contrasts vividly with both Britain's legacy in Egypt, where the British carried with them nothing comparable to France's *mission civilisatrice* (civilizing mission), and the Fertile Crescent, where French penetration was less far-reaching than in the Maghreb. Writing in 1972, Ernest Gellner declared that "in his heart, the North African knows not merely that God speaks Arabic, but also that modernity speaks French."[3] Nonetheless, questions regarding language and cultural orientation resonate differently for Berbers than Arabs, particularly in Algeria.

Still, another complicating factor for any analysis is the fragmented nature of Berber society: on the microlevel, many tribal fractions lived, until recent decades, a relatively autonomous existence in remote mountainous regions with only minimal reference to their wider surroundings. On the macrolevel, modern Algeria alone has four distinct Berber communities with different geographic "home bases," each speaking a distinct dialect, each having a particular history and socioeconomic configuration. Berbers in Morocco, who constitute more than 40 percent of the population, present a similarly varied picture. What distinguishes Morocco from Algeria in this regard is that regime policies in Morocco have been somewhat more flexible toward contemporary manifestations of Berber culture.[4]

Given these unique features, one may ask whether the Berbers constitute a minority at all. It is clear that they do not meet all of the conventional categories associated with minorities in other states. At the same time, it is probably not useful to go the other extreme, as some Berber activists do, and define Algerians and Moroccans as overwhelmingly Berber, whose identity merely needs to be reawakened. A more nuanced and in-depth understanding of North African societies compels one to pose a different set of questions: How do the historical, socioeconomic, and cultural dimensions of Berber life affect contemporary realities, both among Berbers and between Berbers and the state? In what ways have the processes of modernization and political upheaval promoted the integration of Berbers with their wider surroundings? In what ways have they stimulated or enhanced a particular Berber self-consciousness?

It is the intention of this chapter to address the relationship of these issues to the ongoing existential crisis in Algeria, focusing on a number of critical questions. Can one speak, for the first time, of an emerging proto-nationalist, or even explicitly nationalist, movement among the Berbers, whose appeal extends beyond a small circle of Berber intellectuals based in France and North America? If so, what forces are shaping its emergence, and how are they related to the experience of previous decades? What is the relationship between the movement's cultural and political aspects? What is its agenda, and what are its prospects?

A Brief Profile of Algerian Berbers

Most estimates place the number of people in Algeria speaking Berber, either as a first or second lanaguge, at 25 percent to 30 percent, although a recent study views these figures as inflated, and speaks of perhaps 20 percent at the most.[5] Historically, Berber dialects were almost exclusively oral. More recently, some preliminary practical steps have been undertaken toward standardizing the language with a common script and dialect. Much discussion has accompanied this matter, which is far from merely academic, as it touches on core questions of Berber and modern Algerian identities. Whereas Berber activists favor the adoption of a Latin-based alphabet, both Islamists and many Algerian officials insist on the use of the Arabic script.[6]

Approximately two-thirds of Algeria's Berbers are Kabylians, from the Kabylia mountainous region southeast of Algiers. The second largest group, slightly less than one-third of the Berber population, are Chaouias, from the mountainous Aures area further eastward, south of Constantine. They are separated from Kabylia by a fairly narrow Arabic-speaking zone.[7] The two remaining Algerian Berber groups are the small Mzab (Ibadi Muslim) community in the area around Ghardaia in the south, and the Touareg nomads of the Sahara Desert, cutting across the boundaries of Algeria, Mali, Niger, and Burkina Faso. The latter two are insular communities with little effect on national life. The regime is generally unsympathetic to their needs, especially in the case of the Touaregs.[8] The Chaouias are "compact" and less cosmopolitan than the Kabylians; they emigrated from their home region in fewer numbers and are French-speaking to a lesser extent.[9] Kabylians, in contrast, constitute the heart of the Berber community and are an integral part of Algerian society as a whole, having had the greatest degree of contact with the outside world (Arab Algeria and France) through both emigration and commerce. Thus, the Berber question in Algeria has been, for the most part, synonymous with the Kabylia question. However, one must also take note of increasing manifestations of Berber cultural activism in recent years among the Chaouias as well.

Like the term *Berber, Kabylia,* the "land of the Kabylians," is European in origin (French, in this case), coming into usage in the sixteenth century. Prior to the French conquest, the Kabylians defined themselves mainly through their membership in various tribes; indeed, *qaba'il* is the Arabic word for "tribes."[10] Kabylia is commonly divided into two areas, Greater and Lesser Kabylia, the former being topographically more rugged and thus less accessible to invaders. Kabylia's rough terrain was an ideal refuge for dissidents. Consequently, Berber manners and customs, social mores, communal structures, and the practice of Islam remained more fully intact in Greater Kabylia than elsewhere. The process of cultural and linguistic Arabization, which was stimulated in Algeria by the immigration of the Banu Hilal Arabian tribes during the eleventh century, occurred more slowly and more partially in the Kabylia heartland than elsewhere. Similarly, France was able to impose its rule on Kabylia only in 1857 and after much resistance, twenty-seven years after its troops landed in Algiers.

Despite Kabylia's topographic, climatic, and sociohistoric similarities with parts of Lebanon and Syria, Kabylian Berbers did not develop into a compact minority like the Druze or Alawis. The harshness of temperatures, rocky terrain, dense forests, and poor soil quality of Greater Kabylia stimulated both emigration to more hospitable climes among the Arabs of the plains and coastal areas, and the development of a Kabylian trade network involving the manufacture and sale to the Arabs of commercial crafts, spearheaded by members of the Rahmaniyya religious brotherhood. The Rahmaniyya was the most important religious brotherhood in all of Algeria and provided the leadership and organizational backbone of the failed revolt against French rule in 1871.[11] This duality—strong manifestations of Kabylian particularism and social, economic, and political interactions with surrounding currents—has been an enduring feature of the Kabylia reality up until the present day.

The Impact of Colonial Rule

Notwithstanding, or perhaps even owing to the Kabylians' fierce resistance to French rule, France quickly developed a "Berber policy," based on the Berbers' real and supposed distinctiveness vis-à-vis Algerian Arab Muslims, to consolidate French rule. It was a classic case of France's traditional divide-and-rule strategy throughout the Middle East. The Berbers, so went French thinking, had been Islamized only superficially, and could thus be weaned from their essentially primitive, naturalistic folk religion in preparation for "civilizing" them. To this end, Islamic courts were abolished in Kabylia beginning in 1874, and the application of customary tribal law was encouraged. Islamic courts would be reinstituted alongside the French-inspired judicial system only after the attainment of Algerian independence. Similarly, in Morocco, the French authorities were to remove all Berber regions from the jurisdiction of the sultan and the shari'a (Islamic law).[12] To be sure, Kabylia itself did not witness French-inspired development, and on the eve of World War II was more poverty stricken than ever.[13] Nonetheless, present-day Algerian Arab and Islamist opponents to the Berbers accuse them of having received preferential treatment from the French, thus calling into question the Berbers' nationalist and Islamic credentials.

The impact of French policies on the Kabylians was far reaching, though not entirely as had been intended. The Kabylians' disproportionate participation in the newly established French educational system resulted in French becoming the Kabylians' second language to an even greater extent than among the rest of Algeria's Muslims. Kabylian emigration patterns were also reoriented toward France, beginning at the end of the nineteenth century, and became numerically significant in the years after World War I. Exposure to modern education also directly affected the Kabylians' place within Algerian Muslim society. The Kabylian diaspora in the coastal Algerian cities came to include an important stratum of merchants, capitalist farmers, and white collar professionals such as doctors, lawyers, administrators, and teachers. Decades later, this would be translated into an overrepresentation of Kabylians in the Algerian state apparatus. Indeed, between 1891 and 1950, nearly all of the state-recruited teachers for Algiers were Kabylians.[14]

By the mid-1920s, the number of North African workers in France totaled about 100,000. Of these, the vast majority were Algerians, most of whom, in turn, were Kabylians. Their politicization soon followed: in 1926, the North African Star (Étoile Nord Africaine), the first permanent Maghrebi political organization in France, headed by Messali al-Hajj (who himself was not a Kabylian), was founded with the support of the French Communist Party.[15] By the mid-1930s, it had divested itself of the Communists' internationalist agenda in favor of an explicitly nationalist one. Messali began to attract followers inside Algeria as well, and the seeds for Algeria's war of independence were planted.

An essential component of the nationalists' rejection of French domination was the articulation of a modern Algerian identity, based on territory, Islam, and affiliation with the Arab world. This formula remained the guiding theme of Algerian nationalism throughout the anticolonial movement. Still, it was not entirely bereft of controversy. In the late 1940s, Kabylian intellectuals and activists challenged Messali's domination of the nationalist movement, with some of them rejecting the dominant formula of Arab-Muslim Algeria in favor of Algerian Algeria. Algerian identity, they declared, was intimately linked with the population's employment of Berber dialects and Algerian colloquial Arabic, as opposed to the modern standard Arabic being developed in Egypt and the Fertile Crescent, with which most Algerians were not familiar. Some of the group also rejected an explicit Muslim religious orientation, preferring secular and Marxist criteria as a basis for national identity.[16] Algerian ulema responded by calling for the repression of Kabylia media outlets, saying that the Kabylians would not be real Algerians so long as they continued to speak the "jargon" that "burns our ears."[17] Messali felt threatened enough by the opponents of Arab-Muslim Algeria to condemn their ideas as "Berberism."[18] As it happened, the advocates of Algerian Algeria won little following in Kabylia or elsewhere and played no role in the struggle for Algerian independence. It is noteworthy, nonetheless, as a precursor to developments in the years after attaining independence.

Juxtaposed with the Berber extremists in 1949 was another Kabylian, Hocine Ait Ahmed, who subsequently attained the status of one of the historic chiefs of the revolution. Ait Ahmed had impeccable familial credentials: the house he was born in was a pilgrimage site, owing to his late grandfather, Cheikh Mohand el Hocine, one of the spiritual leaders of the Rahmaniyya and known for his resistance to French rule. His mother's family possessed similar anticolonial credentials. Ait Ahmed's challenge to Messali was on the grounds of the latter's excessive monopolization of power and unwillingness to adopt more militant action against the French, not on the basis of an explicitly Berber or Kabylian agenda. He subsequently wrote that conservatives and legalists used the pretext of accusing more radical elements of the nationalist movement of Berberist tendencies in order to remove them from power.[19] Nonetheless, Ait Ahmed's power base would remain overwhelmingly Kabylian. During the years of struggle against France and the subsequent decades, Ait Ahmed's activities, guided by the notion that Kabylians were the avant-garde of Algerian patriotism, would reflect much of the complexity and ambiguity of the Berbers' place in Algerian society.[20]

From Resistance to Independence

Kabylians played an essential role in the struggle for independence, at both the elite and mass levels. The first spasm of revolt against French rule occurred in Kabylia in 1945. From 1947 onward, a small group of Kabylians, under the leadership of Belkacem Krim, clandestinely organized anti-French activities. Ait Ahmed joined them in 1949. They became the core group of the 1954 revolt, which began in Kabylia and spread throughout Algeria. It would seem that Greater Kabylia's importance as a center for resistance to Algerian rule reinforced the prominent place that Kabylians already had in all strands of the Algerian independence movement.

By late 1956, Kabylians held commanding positions or were disproportionately represented in nearly every political and military grouping involved in the struggle against French rule. It was only following the catastrophic defeat in the battle of Algiers (autumn 1956 to summer 1957) that the Kabylians lost their hegemony over the movement.[21]

To be sure, as William Quandt has stated, a Kabylian leadership group with close ties to the Kabylian population at large never developed during the 1950s, and other sources of intra-elite cleavage, such as personal relations, were more important than Berber-Arab distinctions. This continued to be true during the early days of independence. However, as Quandt himself takes care to point out, there was a Kabylian dimension to the power struggles that engulfed the Algerian elite in the aftermath of independence. What came to be known as the Tizi-Ouzou group, established in July–August 1962 and led by Belkacem Krim, was initially the largest armed group opposing Ahmed Ben Bella's and Houari Boumedienne's efforts to consolidate power in newly independent Algeria (Tizi-Ouzou is the largest town in Greater Kabylia, although neither the group's leaders nor its followers were exclusively Kabylian). That Kabylia was a problematic area for Algeria's new power bosses was demonstrated by the fact that it registered the lowest percentage of voter participation in the September 1962 referendum confirming Algeria's independence and new political system. This pattern repeated itself in the September 1964 legislative elections. Interestingly, the radically different context notwithstanding, it did so again in the 1996 presidential elections.

Hocine Ait Ahmed belonged to the Tizi-Ouzou group in 1962. His opposition to the Ben Bella–Boumedienne group led him to establish a party, the Forces des Fronts Socialistes (FFS), in 1963 and to mobilize his supporters in armed revolt, not, to be sure, in the name of Kabylia or Kabylian rights, but in the name of opposing the emerging hegemony of the Front de Liberation Nationale (FLN). As Charles Micaud puts it, "the revolt had . . . no separatist objective; Kabyle peasants were used by some Kabyle leaders in Algiers as a power base to increase their authority in the central government. There was no attempt at opting out of the political system—but rather at demanding greater participation and integration in the new nation-state."[22] Moreover, the FFS did not speak for all Kabylians: half of the Kabylian deputies in Algeria's national assembly condemned their actions.[23] Nonetheless, at least some of the new ruling hierarchy were convinced that the Kabylians were secessionists, and favored a policy of isolation of the region and then afterward destruction.[24]

Ait Ahmed's efforts were in any case a failure. His arrest, October 1964 death sentence (which was commuted to life imprisonment in April 1965 by Algeria's president Ben Bella), and escape from prison and flight to Switzerland on 1 May 1966 seemed to mark the end of the Berber question in Algerian political life.

Writing in the late 1960s, Quandt suggested that Algerian political life during the next decade would not be seriously colored by Berber-Arab rivalries. Moreover, he hypothesized that the combination of existing government policies promoting economic development in rural Berber regions and the avoidance of overt discrimination against Berbers in political and administrative life was likely to lead to the integration of Berbers into the Algerian nation without major conflicts, and the probable decline, over time, of Berber particularism among the masses. At the same time, he held open the possibility of Berber "ethnic particularism" emerging as a consequence of modernization and the creation of a Berber leadership with links to the masses. This might be given further impetus, he suggested, by governmental policies of rapid Arabization, economic neglect, and discrimination in hiring practices for administrative posts. Overall, however, the regime's apparent sensitivity to the potential for Kabylian discontent—manifested in enhanced development projects for the region and its relatively strong, centralized authority—seemed to preclude any serious Berber problem in the foreseeable future.[25]

The Reassertion of Kabylian Identity

As it happened, the regime's policies of socioeconomic development and vigorous repression of linguistic-cultural expressions of Berber particularity, even including a ban on giving Berber names to children, combined to move Berber-Arab relations along a different course. The authorities' efforts to promote development in Kabylia contributed to a boom of sorts in Tizi-Ouzou, whose population almost doubled between 1966 and 1977 (from just under 27,000 to 45,000), and to a greater degree of economic and social integration within the region. The ironic twist was that the regime's efforts to centralize its authority and promote national integration had the contrary effect of strengthening a collective Amazigh consciousness, stimulating what Anthony Smith calls the processes of historical reappropriation and vernacularization of political and cultural symbolism.[26] But this would have been attenuated had the government been more attuned to Kabylian sensibilities in the cultural sphere. Ahmed Ben Bella's declaration upon returning from exile in 1962 to assume the presidency of newly independent Algeria that *"nous sommes des Arabes"* ("we are Arabs") had been adopted without serious debate as the regime's guiding ideological formula. Its implementation, through a more strident policy of Arabization, posed both cultural and material threats to the Kabylians, particularly owing to their disproportionate status in public administration and the educational system.

Thus, by the early 1970s, there were a number of manifestations of Berber (i.e., Kabylian) disquietude with the state of affairs.[27] New Kabylian popular songs reiterated and expanded on existing collective sentiments. In 1974, when Arab singers replaced Berber singers at the annual Cherry Festival in Laiba-Nait-Iraten, they received a hostile reception from a Kabylian audience that turned into a riot (perhaps premeditated), which had to be suppressed by troops and police. In 1977, at the final game of the national football championship pitting a team from Kabylia against one from an Algiers suburb before a mostly Kabylian crowd, the Algerian national anthem was drowned out by the shouting of Kabylian nationalist slogans such as *"A Bas les Arabes"* ("Down with the Arabs"), *"Imazighen, Imazighen,"* and *"Vive la Kabyle"* ("Long live Kabylia"). The scene was repeated at the end of the game during President Houari Boumedienne's presentation of the cup to the victorious Kabylian squad.[28]

These outbursts were linked, at least ideologically, to an amorphous Berber Cultural Movement (MCB), made up largely of Kabylian students supported by Berber intellectuals in France, whose agenda was both Berber/Kabylian and national: opposition to compulsory Arabization, insistence on official recognition of the Berber language and culture, including its teaching in the educational system, and a demand for Western-style political liberalization and democratization. As explained by one author sympathetic to the Berber agenda, the repressive nature of the Boumedienne regime necessitated confining their demands to the cultural sphere and avoiding, at that stage, overt political challenges to the regime's authority. Doing so also "had the added advantage of being attractive to Berbers across the political, ideological and social class spectrum." At bottom, however, the Berberists saw democratization as the only way to guarantee their cultural and ethnic rights within the Algerian state.[29]

Ait Ahmed, for his part, was fully in accord with the emphasis on democratization and human rights, and made them central planks of the FFS's published platform in 1979. Demands for the recognition and promotion of the Berber language were also included in the platform, an indication that Ait Ahmed was cognizant of the changes that Kabylia had undergone and determined to remain firmly ensconced in his core constituency.[30]

Apart from the hostile incidents directed against the Algerian regime, the politicization of Kabylian Berbers gathered steam away from the public eye.

But in March 1980, it burst forth in open confrontation with the authorities in what came to be known as le Printemps Berber (the Berber Spring), an evocation of the cultural flowering in Prague in 1968 before the Soviet crackdown. Mezhoud argues that it was "by far the most important, perhaps most revolutionary event" in the history of independent Algeria up to that time. As such, it inaugurated "a new era of opposition to the Algerian regime," and thus prepared the ground for the October 1988 riots and ensuing events that have shaken the Algerian state to its core.[31] One may take issue with his categorical linkage between the two episodes, but the Berber Spring was nevertheless a seminal development in the history of Kabylian-state relations.

The immediate background to the disturbances was an official commission's decision in December 1979 to Arabize entirely primary education and the social sciences and humanities in the universities, increase the process of Arabization in the secondary schools, and place greater emphasis on religious education in primary schools.[32] Implementation remained another matter. Nonetheless, the Berber/Arab-Islamic cultural and linguistic battle lines were being drawn more sharply. Concurrently, the demise of the "last tolerated symbol of Berber culture," a Kabylian Berber-language radio program, was rumored to be imminent.[33] The spark came with the authorities' banning of a scheduled 10 March 1980 lecture by Mouloud Mammeri, a well-known Berber writer and anthropologist, on Berber poetry, at Tizi-Ouzou University. The students went on strike and demonstrated in protest against cultural repression of the Berbers. Sympathy protests were organized in Algiers and other areas, as well as strikes in Tizi Ouzou. In the early hours of April 20, the police began cracking down against both students and workers in Tizi-Ouzou. Between thirty and fifty persons were killed and hundreds wounded in five days of clashes between activists and the police.

The regime spoke of colonialist plots and agitation by the exiled Ait Ahmed, who denied any responsibility.[34] At the same time, it sought to mollify the Kabylians: those arrested during the unrest were released, and promises were made to address the Berber cultural agenda, including increased Berber-language courses, the creation of university chairs in Berber studies, and the allowance of popular culture programs.[35] In general, their implementation was short-lived, and the regime restored its authority with seemingly little difficulty.

On the surface, then, the Berber Spring appeared to have been merely a spasm. But appearances were deceiving. A number of factors combined to politicize growing numbers of Kabylians during the 1980s: the legacy of Kabylian self-assertion embodied in the Berber Spring resonated with increasing vigor; the regime failed to draw the proper conclusions from the 1980 events and remained inattentive toward Kabylian grievances; and Algerian society as a whole became increasingly polarized along a number of fault lines (e.g., rich/poor, regime/opposition, and religious/secular). One especially important factor for Berber activists was the increasing Islamization of Algerian society, in which the regime sought to relegitimize its rule by competing with newly assertive Islamist trends for the possession of Islamic virtues.[36] "Islam in Algeria," wrote one scholar, "[had] been nationalized exactly like the land and the industry."[37] The growing current of Berber particularism and self-consciousness, and the emphasis by Berber activists on the priority of democratization of Algerian life, was clearly a response, in part, to the increased Islamization of Algerian society. In turn, this response left them open to charges that they were "enemies of Islam."

Manifestations of a developing civil society among Kabylians, apart from, or even in opposition to the regime, included the establishment of the Committees of the Children of Martyrs, the Berber Cultural Association, and the Algerian League for the Defence of Human Rights.[38] Consequently, the Kabylian activists were well placed to take advantage of the sudden opening up of Algerian political life in 1989, in the aftermath of the October 1988 riots. Ironically, the upheaval in Algeria's main urban centers did not extend to Kabylia, as Berber activists reportedly chose to avoid provoking the regime's contingency plan for a brutal crackdown in the event of disturbances.[39]

The Berbers and the Implosion of Algeria

A leading expert on Kabylia had written at the time of the Berber Spring that there was "not the slightest basis for separatism in Kabylia," and that what was at issue was "the participation of the Kabyles in Algerian cultural, economic and political life at the national level. . . . The essential objectives of the Berberist movement can be seen to be entirely assimilationist in nature."[40] This remained true a decade later, if by "assimilationist" one avoids the connotation of losing one's individual and collective identity in the larger whole, and limits the term to encompass political and cultural pluralism within a unified entity. But the struggle for Algeria's soul inaugurated by the democratic explosion in the wake of the October 1988 intifada, followed by the implosion of both state and society beginning in mid-1991, placed the Berber/Kabylian question in a very different context. To what extent did the old maxims still apply?

Two parties have articulated the Berber/Kabylian agenda during the past six years and competed for the support of the Kabylian populace. The leading party was the FFS, led by the aging but still formidable Ait Ahmed, who returned from exile in December 1989. Ait Ahmed's continued appeal was based on what one Berber activist called "his pristine record of honesty and historical prestige."[41] The second group, the Rassemblement pour la Culture et la Démocratie (RCD), was headed by Dr. Sa'id Sa'di, one of the leading Berber activists as far back as 1980. It lacked the broad social base of the

FFS, constituting a much narrower strand of intellectuals, artists, white collar professionals, and activists. Whereas the FFS continued to promote a national agenda from its Kabylian base, the RCD's agenda, by contrast, was more explicitly modernist-secular Berber. To the RCD, Ait Ahmed was sadly out of touch with Algerian contemporary life.[42]

Despite, or perhaps even owing to, their competition, the Kabylian/Berber cause was significantly advanced. On one level, the activities of the two groupings denoted an effective division of labor. Concurrently, expressions of Berber identity and culture between 1989–1991—festivals, colloquiums, journals and newspapers, and university activities—proliferated in the newly liberalized atmosphere of Algerian public life.[43]

The two Kabylia-based parties took diametrically opposed positions regarding the countrywide 1990 municipal and provincial elections. The FFS boycotted the process, calling it a farce, because the elections were to be conducted according to the ruling FLN's interests. In Ait Ahmed's view, the proper method of exercising popular sovereignty at this juncture was to dissolve parliament and elect a new constituent assembly that would define the power of all institutions.[44] Democracy, in Ait Ahmed's view, had not yet been properly ingrained into Algerian life. Without fundamental changes such as the ending of the virtual slavery of women, massive investments in education, and the guaranteeing of free trade, Algeria's democratic experiment, he feared, could prove to be a false dawn.[45] In a show of strength, up to 200,000 persons marched in Algiers on 31 May in support of the FFS's boycott, condemning the violence against women and bars serving alcohol, which was perpetrated by the Front Islamique du Salut's (FIS) shock troops, and demanding the abrogation of the 1985 family law. Ait Ahmed's diagnosis was trenchant, but his preoccupation with the regime's manipulation of events caused him to underestimate the strength of the FIS, which he called "completely artificial."[46] The boycott of the municipal elections was partially observed but constituted a tactical error, for it left the field open to the RCD, which opposed the boycott and, more importantly, the FIS. The possibility of the FFS becoming a true third force on the Algerian political scene was thus weakened.

The real story of the elections was the sweeping victory of the FIS candidates, who won approximately 55 percent of the just under eight million valid votes cast (61 percent of the more than thirteen million eligible), giving them 853 of 1539 municipalities and 32 of 48 provinces. Candidates of the formerly hegemonic Front de Liberation Nationale (FLN) finished a distant second. The RCD's candidates received 5.65 percent of the votes in municipal elections and 2.08 percent of the provincial election votes. The RCD's support was, as expected, concentrated in Kabylia, where they won a majority in 87 municipalities and one provincial assembly, that of Tizi-Ouzou.[47] Sa'di was quick to call the FFS boycott a mistake. His opposition to the FLN, which still dominated parliament, was no less vehement than Ait Ahmed's.

But his concern with the FIS's success led him to again differ with Ait Ahmed on the proper course to pursue during the subsequent months. Postponing the upcoming parliamentary elections, even if it meant maintaining the current FLN-dominant Parliament, and establishing a government of "national transition" was, in Sa'di's view, the only way to forestall the FIS from attaining power. Ait Ahmed, however, favored a continuation of the electoral process in which he was now prepared to participate (having recognized the error of his ways in boycotting the municipal balloting).

The confrontation between the emboldened Islamists and the hard-pressed Benjedid regime steadily escalated during the remainder of 1990 and throughout 1991, and tore further at the already tattered fabric of Algerian society. The Algerian constitution, issued in 1989, had declared Arabic to be the sole official language of the state. In a move clearly designed to counter the FIS's appeal by demonstrating fidelity to Arab-Islamic values, the FLN-dominated Parliament passed a measure in late 1990 insisting that official institutions be fully Arabized by July 1992, and all institutions of higher learning by 1997. For good measure, it forbade the importation of computers, typewriters, and any other office supplies that did not have Arabic-language capabilities, and threatened the closing of businesses that employed French in advertising or labeling of merchandise.

The regime's accelerated measures of Arabization occasioned a large-scale protest demonstration in Algiers organized by the FFS. Nonetheless, the regime's promotion of Arabization further reinforced the outsider status of the Kabylians of both the FFS, with its more national agenda, and the RCD, with its more explicit Berberophone emphasis. Appearing at great risk was their common vision of modern Algerian culture: the Kabylian synthesis of village customs and rituals, many undoubtedly pre-Islamic in origin, an attenuated Islam, Tamazight (the Kabylian version is known as Taqbaylit), and French-centered modernity, epitomized by the French language spoken by much of the intelligentsia and middle and upper classes.[48]

Throughout 1991, Ait Ahmed refused to take sides between the FIS and the authorities. Thus, he sharply condemned the regime's postponement of the June 1991 parliamentary elections, the crackdown on the FIS leadership, and reported large-scale human rights violations against detained Islamist activists. At the same time, he insisted that the FIS should not be allowed to maintain a monopoly on public life. "Nous refusons," he told an interviewer, "le faux choix entre la république intégriste et l'état policier. Nous voulons casser ce dilemme en redonnant la parole à la population." ("We refuse the false choice between the fundamentalist republic and the police state. We want to rescind this dilemma and restore the voice of the population.")[49] He viewed with favor the appointment in the summer of 1991 of a government of technocrats, headed by Ahmad Sid Ghozali, for it took power out of the hands of the FLN's old guard and included at least one overt FFS supporter: the new economy minister, Professor Hocine Benissad, one of Algeria's better-known economists, who would have been an FFS candidate for Parliament.[50]

Sa'di, however, supported the crackdown on the FIS and postponement of the June elections. The FIS, he told an interviewer, should be dissolved, for it "uses democracy to organize civil disobedience . . . [and] believes that violence is a strategy to take power."[51]

The two Kabylia-based parties also differed, at least in nuance, regarding the role of religion in public life. Unlike Sa'di, Ait Ahmed refrained from explicitly advocating the formal separation of religion and state. Instead, he evoked a religion that promoted "de culte et de méditation, de tolérance et de fraternité" ("veneration and meditation, tolerance and brotherhood").[52]

Ait Ahmed's vision of a pluralist, tolerant democratic Algeria was swiftly overtaken by events. Nationwide parliamentary elections, finally held in late December 1991, produced an overwhelming triumph for the FIS, which won 188 out of the 231 seats decided in the first round of elections, with a total popular vote of 3.2 million out of 6.9 million valid ballots.[53] One hundred ninety-nine seats remained to be contested in runoff elections in mid-January. With the FIS only 28 seats short of an absolute majority after the first round, its domination of the new Parliament was assured. FLN candidates garnered 1.6 million votes, but only 15 seats. The FFS received 510,000 votes. However, owing to their overwhelming concentration in Greater and Lesser Kabylia districts, it won 25 seats, making it the second largest grouping in Parliament, with the prospect for a few additional gains in Algiers in the second round. The RCD fared poorly, garnering only 160,000 votes (2.9 percent) and winning no seats. Sa'id Sa'di was himself defeated in Tizi-Ouzou by an FFS candidate.

The crucial question for Algeria at this juncture was whether the FIS would be allowed to gain control of parliament through the completion of the electoral process.[54] True to form, the two Kabylian parties differed on the next step. Sa'di was openly in league with those sections of the Algerian political, military, economic, and cultural elites who favored a nullification of the process, which, if carried forward, would "bury" Algeria and condemn it to chaos. Ait Ahmed, however, declared that the cancellation of the second round of elections would make Algeria look like a banana republic and insisted that one couldn't destroy a democracy in order to save it.[55] On 2 January, an FFS-sponsored demonstration, attended by over 300,000 persons, called for the strengthening of democratic institutions, including the presidency and the Constitutional Council, which would oversee the numerous challenges to results in specific elections districts. Only thus could the threats posed by both the hard-liners in the regime and the Islamists be rebuffed.

Yet as has so often been the case in modern Algerian history, events took a different course than that advocated by Ait Ahmed. The military's deposition of President Benjedid on 10 January, the nullification of the electoral process, and the banning of the FIS inaugurated a new, more violent epoch in Algerian politics, one whose outcome, six years later, continued to be undetermined. What is certain is that the no-holds-barred struggle between armed Islamist movements and the security forces has apparently cost more than 60,000 lives, broken Algerian society asunder, and left the populace terrorized.

Throughout the civil war, the FFS doggedly stuck to its established principles. The only alternative to the regime's "scorched earth logic," declared Ait Ahmed (who had returned to dividing his time between Switzerland and France), was a "dialogue for historic reconciliation." Direct dialogue with the Algerian Army, the only possible guarantor of a democratic solution, was absolutely essential. FFS demands from the regime included lifting the state of emergency, the release of political prisoners, the abrogation of special courts and laws, and guaranteeing freedom of political activity. Following a transitional process to be monitored by a national parliamentary committee, it favored parliamentary elections under a system of proportional representation, underpinned by a democratic constitution.[56] The most recent manifestation of the FFS's all-Algerian posture was its participation in a January 1995 conference of eight opposition parties, including FIS representatives, in Rome, which concluded by recommending the restoration of the rule of law and the democratic process in Algeria and the re-legalization of FIS in return for the cessation of violence.

As Algerian society as a whole became more polarized, the Berber aspects of the crisis were brought into sharper relief as well. Kabylian Berber artists were physically attacked during the years of civil war by the Islamists, not as Berbers as such, but as symbols of a decadent, evil culture that they promised to eradicate. The fact that some of the artists were militantly opposed to the Islamists made them even more inviting targets. However, ascribing a Kabylian dimension to these attacks is unavoidable. Two prominent examples were the murder of Tahar Djaout, a Kabylian writer and polemicist, and the kidnapping and ultimate release of the singer Lounes Matoub. The latter incident brought 100,000 Kabylians into the street in Tizi-Ouzou demanding his safety. Following his release, Matoub gave an interview in which he characterized Ait Ahmed's participation in the Rome conference as tantamount to supporting terrorist operations in Kabylia against the Berbers.[57]

Notwithstanding the criticism of Ait Ahmed, a process of convergence between the FFS and RCD, under the rubric of the MCB was also underway. Their common interests were highlighted anew by President Liamine Zeroual's attempts to initiate a dialogue with the Islamists during 1993 and 1994, which the Kabylians feared would result in a deal at their expense. The dialogue, said Sa'id Sa'di, "was merely a relentless pursuit of the same old policy. If it is to enable the [political] clans to survive by plunder, we know where that will lead us." What was needed, he insisted, was for the government to step down and "free the state from the clans," and comprehensive resistance by all forces in Algerian society opposed to both the government and the fundamentalists. Strikes, boycotts of schools, and armed self-defense were all means to be employed.[58]

In Kabylia, his call increasingly fell on receptive ears. Kabylian villages organized their own self-defense militias against the Islamists. Three widely observed general strikes during the fall of 1994 were conducted in Kabylia in support of the longstanding Berber demand for official recognition of Tamazight and Berber culture, the last in protest against President Zeroual's failure to refer to Berber grievances in a nationwide television address.

Most impressive was the extended school strike throughout Kabylia, begun in the fall of 1994, on behalf of Tamazight. Berberism as a political and cultural agenda could be ignored no longer. Testimony to that came in the Rome declaration in January 1995, in which Ait Ahmed participated, and whose other provisions the RCD opposed: "The components of the Algerian character are Islam, Arabism, *Tamazight* [my emphasis] and the two cultures and languages contributing to the development of that character. They should have their place and should be strengthened in the institutions, without any exclusion or marginalization."[59] Three months later, the legitimacy of Tamazight was publicly acknowledged by the ruling authorities as well. Following weeks of negotiations to end the school strike in Kabylia between President Zeroual's representatives and a broad spectrum of Berber groups, the government announced that it would create a "body with executive powers, attached to the presidency, [and] charged with the rehabilitation of Tamazight [culture] . . . one of the foundations of the national identity, and the introduction of the Tamazight language in the systems of education and communication."[60]

The declaration was a milestone in the Berbers' long struggle for recognition. It came only a few days after massive demonstrations in Kabylia had commemorated the fifteenth anniversary of the Berber Spring, a show of force that cut across the Kabylian political spectrum. Nonetheless, satisfaction with the declaration was not universal. Sa'di's wing of the MCB (MCB—Coordination Nationale) supported the statement and its accompanying call for an end to the school boycott. Yet the FFS wing of the MCB (MCB—Commission Nationale) and the autonomous Union of Education and Training Workers withdrew from the talks before they were concluded. Ironically, it was the FFS that was now the more militant proponent of Berber rights, declaring that the government had not gone far enough in giving official recognition to the national character of Tamazight. The opposing stands of the RCD and the FFS derived from their contrary orientations vis-à-vis the regime: the RCD continued to maintain a common cause with the authorities in the struggle against the Islamists, whereas the FFS remained part of the political opposition to the regime. As is so often the case, culture and politics were intimately intertwined.

Subsequently, however, the regime's newfound openness regarding the Berber agenda proved to be limited at best. Efforts by Zeroual to institutionalize and legitimize his rule through presidential, parliamentary, and municipal elections, and through constitutional reform, were met with increasing opposition in Kabylia. In November 1995, while the FFS boycotted the presidential election, Sa'di ran as a candidate, winning 9.3 percent (1,115,796) of the vote. However, in 1996, the RCD refused Zeroual's entreaties to join the regime and renewed its strident opposition to what it called a "presidential dictatorship." Although the new draft constitution recognized that Amazighité (Berber identity) was part of Algeria's common heritage, along with Islam and Arabism, it failed to recognize Tamazight as Algeria's official second language. Moreover, it insisted on not using the three components of national identity for party propaganda or for politicking. The constitutional amendments were overwhelmingly approved in November 1996; however Kabylian opposition was palpable: the voter turnout in Tizi-Ouzou was only 25 percent, 63 percent of which voted against the amendments.[61] Algerian political life was clearly perceived in Kabylia as falling far short of the desired genuine pluralist order.

Conclusion

Given the FLN regime's utter failure during a quarter-century of rule to forge a modern Algerian political community on an exclusively Arab-Islamic, socialist basis, the fact that "Berberism in Algeria remains on the defensive" in the face of regime policies and demographic shifts,[62] and the special place Kabylia and Kabylians have held in Algerian history and society, it is hardly surprising that Kabylian Berbers have acquired many of the attributes of a modern *ethnie:* a "named unit of population with common ancestry myths and historical memories, elements of shared culture, some link with a historic territory and some measure of solidarity, at least among [its] elites."[63] Algeria's current crisis, now existential in nature, has sharpened matters further. To be sure, one finds Berber-speakers and Kabylians, all across the Algerian political spectrum, from the so-called hard-line eradicators in the Algerian security forces to the Groupe Islamique Armé, the most vicious and uncompromising of the Islamist armed groups. Nonetheless, the Amazigh appear to fit the definition of a "national minority" *ethnie* coexisting uneasily with state authorities, with groups and parties that articulate its needs.

To be sure, one might argue that the promotion of Berberism is, at best, a matter of proto-politics. After all, the demand for *political* autonomy, a feature common to the programs of many national minorities, has been almost completely absent up to now from the Kabylian agenda. Given Kabylia's paucity of resources, the intertwining of Kabylians within the larger fabric of Algerian

society, and the FFS's consistent articulation of a national agenda in which
Berber grievances could be properly addressed, the proposed ideal formula of
one leading Berber scholar, "*un projet autonomiste dans un cadre fédéraliste*"
("autonomy within a federal framework"),[64] let alone separatist demands,
would be difficult to sustain, at least under current conditions. Thus, Algeria is
not a case in which the dynamics of majority-minority relations pose a threat,
in and of itself, to the state's territorial integrity. Rather, the Berberist agenda
operates within the existing state framework, while seeking to institute a liberal, democratic, multicultural order in which their own cultural identity can be
developed unhindered. If the Kabylians are practicing a secular form of
taqiyya,[65] then it is of the subconscious variety. At the same time, one must
take into account the existential crisis of the Algerian state and the fluidity of
its circumstances. One possibility is the de facto breakup of the state into various regions controlled by different authorities—the military, the Islamists, local groups, or various combinations thereof. One can envisage in this scenario
a set of common interests between Kabylians and officials in the security services seeking to combat the Islamists and maintain their dwindling power
wherever possible. There is already considerable evidence of Berber militias
enjoying the regime's support. A sweeping triumph by the Islamists might
have much the same effect. In the meantime, the continued escalation of violence and overall political stalemate promises to further politicize the Kabylian
community and sharpen its collective self-consciousness. Writing in 1987, a
leading scholar of the Berber language and culture was pessimistic about the
prospects for Berber culture to develop unhindered, in light of what he called
"Arab-Islamism's totalitarian tendency . . . [and its] inability to tolerate the existence of the Other."[66] However warranted his pessimism (and the proposition
itself is at least debatable), it is clear that at this point, any serious efforts to
pull Algeria back from the abyss, achieve a modicum of civil peace, and begin
the herculean task of reconstructing Algerian society will have to take the
Kabylian/Berber agenda into account. The Berber "genie" cannot be simply
stuffed back into the bottle, a fact that seems to have been acknowledged, however grudgingly, by important components of both the regime and the opposition (even including some more moderate Islamists).

A final note: the Algerian Berber revival is paralleled, in a less politicized
fashion, to be sure, in Morocco, and has stimulated activities among the
Berber diaspora in Europe and North America.[67] Pan-Berberism, in the sense
of political unity at the expense of the current state framework, is unimagin-
able. But the political dimension of the Amazigh revival is now manifest in
Algeria, and latent in Morocco. Its contours are still evolving, and its course
will depend on developments too numerous to predict. To be sure, the Algerian Berbers' strategic goal of a liberal, democratic, and multicultural order appears to be, for now, beyond the horizon. In any case, whatever direction
events in Algeria take, the degree to which the Berbers exploit the partial

opening provided by the regime to further crystallize their collective identity and promote their agenda will no doubt play an important part in determining the future relationship between the Amazigh and the Algerian state.

Notes

1. William E. Hazen, "Minorities in Assimilation: The Berbers of North Africa," in R. D. McLaurin (ed.), *Political Role of Minority Groups in the Middle East* (New York: Praeger, 1979), p. 152.

2. For a discussion on the roots of the Berber language, see L. Galand, "Berbers: Language," *Encyclopedia of Islam*, new edition (hereinafter: *EI 2*), vol. 1 (Leiden, Netherlands: E. J. Brill, 1960), pp. 1180–1185, and Ernest N. McCarus, "Berber: Linguistic 'Substratum' of North African Arabic," *The Washington Report on Middle East Affairs* (January–February 1995), p. 31.

3. Ernest Gellner, "Introduction," in Ernest Gellner and Charles Micaud (eds.), *Arabs and Berbers: From Tribe to Nation in North Africa* (Lexington, Mass.: Lexington Books, 1972), p. 19.

4. But Moroccan tolerance clearly has its limits as well. A number of Berber activists were imprisoned on 1 May 1995 for publicly calling for the recognition of Tamazight as an official language and for its teaching in schools. They were released in July as part of a large-scale royal amnesty.

5. Michael Brett and Elizabeth Fentress, *The Berbers* (Oxford: Blackwell, 1996), p. 3.

6. Salem Chaker, "Constantes et Mutations dans l'Affirmation Identitaire Berbère," in S. Chaker (ed.), *Berbères, Une Identité en Construction,* Revue de l'Occident Musulman et de la Méditerranée, no. 44 (Aix-en-Province: Centre Nationale de la Recherche Scientifique [CNRS], 1987), pp. 28–29. The Touareg Saharan nomads use a script called Tifinagh, which stems from an ancient Libyan script that had thirty-seven geometrical signs written from right to left (McCarus, "Berber: Linguistic Substratum"). The first Amazigh texts written with the Latin alphabet date back to 1889. Before that, the Arabic alphabet was used by those trying to write Tamazight. The father of modern Tamazight, Mouloud Mammeri, developed a writing system during the 1970s based on both the Latin and Tifinagh alphabets. (Amara Lak, "On Tamazight and Its Writing," *The Amazigh Voice* 4, no. 1 [March 1975], pp. 7–8).

7. G. Yver-[Ch. Pellat], "Berbers: Distribution at Present," *EI 2,* vol. 1, p. 1177.

8. The larger Touareg communities in Mali and Niger face severe repression from the regimes there. The Algerian authorities have shown little sympathy for their cause.

9. William Quandt, "The Berbers in the Algerian Political Elite," in Gellner and Micaud, *Arabs and Berbers,* pp. 285–286.

10. Jeane Favret, "Traditionalism Through Ultra-Modernism," in Gellner and Micaud, *Arabs and Berbers,* p. 321.

11. Hugh Roberts, "The Economics of Berberism: The Material Basis of the Kabyle Question in Contemporary Algeria," *Government and Opposition* 18, no. 2 (spring 1983), pp. 219–220; Jamil M. Abun-Nasr, *A History of the Maghrib in the Islamic Period* (Cambridge: Cambridge University Press, 1987), pp. 266–268.

12. Abdallah Laroui, *The History of the Maghrib: An Interpretive Essay* (Princeton, N.J.: Princeton University Press, 1977), pp. 342–343; Charles-Robert Ageron, *Modern Algeria: A History from 1830 to the Present* (London: Hurst, 1991), pp. 72–73.

13. Albert Camus wrote a series of eleven reports, "Poverty in Kabylia," in 1939 for the newspaper *Alger-Republicain,* depicting the extreme destitution of the region. Thanks to Rabah Seffal for providing me with this information.

14. Roberts, "The Economics of Berberism," pp. 221–223; Quandt, "The Berbers in the Algerian Political Elite," pp. 288–289; Favret, "Traditionalism," p. 323.

15. John Ruedy, *Modern Algeria: The Origins and Development of a Nation* (Bloomington: Indiana University Press, 1992), pp. 136–137.

16. Ibid., p. 154.

17. Hocine Ait-Ahmed, *Mémoire d'un Combattant. L'Esprit d'Indépendance* (Paris: Sylvie Messenger, 1983), p. 51, quoted in Amar Ouerdane, "La 'Crise Berberiste' De 1949, Un Conflit a Plusieurs Faces," in Chaker, *Berbères, Une Identité En Construction,* p. 41.

18. Roberts, "The Economics of Berberism," p. 227.

19. Pierre Monbeig, "Une Opposition Politique dans l'Impasse, Le FFS de Hocine Ait-Ahmed," in Pierre Robert Baduel (ed.), *L'Algérie Incertaine* (Aix-en-Province: Institute de Recherches et d'Etudes sur le Monde Arabe et Musulman [IRE-MAM], Revue du Monde Musulman et de la Mediterranée [REMMM], 1994), pp. 126–127.

20. Ibid., p. 131.

21. Hugh Roberts, "The Unforeseen Development of the Kabyle Question in Contemporary Algeria," *Government and Opposition* 17, no. 3 (summer 1982), p. 328.

22. Charles Micaud, "Conclusion," in Gellner and Micaud, *Arabs and Berbers,* p. 436.

23. Favret, "Traditionalism," pp. 307–324.

24. Tassadit Yacine, "Du 'Bastion' au 'Reduit' Kabyle," in Reporters Sans Frontiers, *Le Drame Algérien: Un Peuple en Otage* (Paris: Éditions la Découverte, 1994), p. 128.

25. Quandt, "The Berbers in the Algerian Political Elite," p. 303.

26. Roberts, "The Economics of Berberism," pp. 223–227; Anthony D. Smith, *Nations and Nationalism in a Global Era* (Cambridge: Polity Press, 1995), pp. 65–67.

27. For the roots and evolution of Berber cultural reaction, see Brett and Fentress, *The Berbers,* pp. 278–282.

28. Ibid., pp. 229–230.

29. Ibid., p. 228; Salem Mezhoud, "Glasnost the Algerian Way: The Role of Berber Nationalists in Political Reform," in George Joffe (ed.), *North Africa: Nation, State and Region* (London: Routledge, 1993), p. 153.

30. Monbeig, "Une Opposition Politique," pp. 132–133.

31. Mezhoud, "Glasnost the Algerian Way," p. 143.

32. Colin Legum (ed.), *African Contemporary Record* (hereinafter: *ACR*), vol. 13, 1980–1981 (New York: Holmes and Meier, 1981), p. 7.

33. Mezhoud, "Glasnost the Algerian Way," p. 150.

34. Legum, *ACR,* vol. 13, 1980–1981, p. 8.

35. Mezhoud, "Glasnost the Algerian Way," p. 144; Colin Legum (ed.), *ACR,* vol. 14, 1981–1982 (New York: Holmes and Meier, 1983), pp. 5–6.

36. Bruce Maddy-Weitzman, "The Islamic Challenge in North Africa," in Maddy-Weitzman and Efraim Inbar (eds.), *Religious Radicalism in the Greater Middle East* (London: Frank Cass, 1997), pp. 171–188.

37. Mohamed Arkoun, "Algeria," in Shireen Hunter (ed.), *The Politics of Islamic Revivalism: Diversity and Unity* (Bloomington: Indiana University Press, 1987), pp. 173–174.

38. Definitions of "civil society" are numerous and not always complementary. The Hegelian definition, as used by Bernard Lewis, "denotes those interests, associations, organizations, loyalties and authorities between the family and the state." In the Middle East context, Lewis extends and redefines the notion of family to include additional "involuntary automatic loyalties by birth ethnic group, tribe, clan, and—in a downward spiral—religion, sect, faction, region and locality." (Bernard Lewis, "Why Turkey Is the Only Muslim Democracy," *Middle East Quarterly* 1, no. 1 [March 1994], pp. 46–47.) As used generally by Western scholars, "civil society" evokes "secularism, citizenship, civism, civility, [and/or] civil liberties." (Eva Bellin, "Civil Society: Effective Tool of Analysis for Middle East Politics?" *Political Science and Politics* 27, no. 3 [September 1994], p. 510). Clearly, in the case of the Berbers, the developing manifestations of a civil society drew on, and were complemented by, more involuntary loyalties.

39. Mezhoud, "Glasnost the Algerian Way," pp. 159–161.

40. Hugh Roberts, "Towards an Understanding of the Kabyle Question in Contemporary Algeria," *The Maghreb Review* 5, nos. 5–6 (September–December 1980), p. 120.

41. Private communiqué, 1995.

42. A journalist sympathetic to the RCD, which, he said, "represents a break with the past and openness toward a new future," subsequently characterized Ait Ahmed as a man "with no political future; he is 70 years old and a constant loser, who misread history." Interview with Ahmad Fettani, *al-Watan al-'Arabi*, 20 November 1992, Joint Publication Research Service, Near East and South Asia, 1 February 1993.

43. Salem Chaker, "Quelques Evidences sur la Question Berbere," *Confluences Méditérannée: Comprendre l'Algérie*, no. 11 (summer 1994), p. 108.

44. Radio Algiers, 3 April—Foreign Broadcast Information Service, The Middle East and North Africa, Daily Report (hereinafter: DR), 4 April 1990. Ait Ahmed was blamed by opponents for wanting to create "Algerian Kurdistan" (Yacine, in Reporters Sans Frontiers, *Le Drame Algérien*, p. 128).

45. Patrick Bishop in the *Daily Telegraph*, reprinted in the *Jerusalem Post*, 14 March 1990.

46. Francis Ghiles, in the *Financial Times*, 11 June 1990; Algerian Press Service, 31 May—DR, 1 June 1990.

47. Radio Algiers, 14 June—DR, 15 June 1990, and Algeria Press Service, 21 June—DR, 22 June 1990.

48. For a sensitive and revealing description of an American-trained engineer's rediscovery and elaboration of Berber village culture, see Rabah Seffal, "Remember Me?" *The World and I*, September 1992, pp. 612–623.

49. *Le Figaro*, 7 June 1991, quoted in Monbeig, "Une Opposition Politique," p. 134.

50. *Financial Times*, 19 June 1991.

51. Paris, Inter-Radio Network, 5 June—DR, 6 June 1991.

52. Monbeig, "Une Opposition Politique," p. 134.

53. It is interesting to note that FIS candidates received 1.2 million votes *less* than in the 1990 municipal elections. The turnout for the two elections was approximately the same. But over 900,000 ballots, nearly 12 percent of the total, were invalidated. Whether these votes would have strengthened or weakened the FIS cannot be known. Similarly, the FLN suffered a drop of approximately 630,000 votes. Fawzi Rouzeik, "Algérie 1990–1993: La Démocratie Confisquée?" in Baduel, *L'Algérie Incertaine*, p. 44.

54. It appears that the elections were marked by widespread irregularities, some of which may be attributed to bureaucratic chaos but also to manipulation by FIS-controlled municipalities. Francis Ghiles, "Algeria Again at the Crossroads," *Middle East International,* no. 417 (24 January 1992), pp. 3–4.

55. *Financial Times* 2, 6 January 1992; *Libération,* 1 January 1992.

56. Ait Ahmed's interview in *al-Sharq al-Awsat* (London, Jidda, and Riyadh, daily), 9 February—DR, 11 February 1993.

57. *El Pais,* 10–16 May 1995.

58. *Le Figaro,* 30 March 1994; *Middle East Quarterly* 1, no. 2 (June 1994), pp. 92–94.

59. *Al-Sharq al-Awsat,* 14 January—DR, 18 January 1995.

60. "Amazighté—Communiqué De La Présidence," issued by the Embassy of Algeria, Washington, D.C., 23 April 1995.

61. Meir Litvak, "Algeria," *Middle East Contemporary Survey (MECS),* vol. 19 (1995), pp. 220–221; and vol. 20 (1996), pp. 225–234.

62. Brett and Fentress, *The Berbers,* pp. 275–277.

63. Smith, *Nations and Nationalism,* p. 59.

64. Chaker, "Quelques Évidences sur la Question Berbère?" p. 110.

65. *Taqiyya* is a Shi'ite doctrine of extreme quietism, stipulating that one may not only submit to illegitimate power, one may also conform and pretend to believe if necessary for survival. Bernard Lewis, "The Shi'a in Islamic History," in Martin Kramer (ed.), *Shi'ism, Resistance, and Revolution* (Boulder, Colo.: Westview, 1987), p. 23.

66. Chaker, "Constantes et Mutations dans l'Affirmations Identitaire Berbere," p. 31.

67. Joel Donnet, "Renaissance Berbère au Maroc," *Le Monde Diplomatique,* January 1995, p. 18.

3

Egypt's Coptic Pandora's Box

Ami Ayalon

A shadowy curtain has long veiled the Coptic issue in Egypt, a curtain woven of intense sensitivity, perpetual denial, and a profound reluctance to discuss what is behind it. Not quite a unique Egyptian phenomenon, such sensitivity and denial seem to have stemmed from a perplexing cultural predicament prompted by the changes of modernity. It has been marked by an irritating uncertainty about communal identity, about the role of religion in society, and about relations with the rest of the world, in particular the West. The status of the Copts, a religious minority in an otherwise homogeneous society, and their relations with the state and with the Muslim majority, has been problematic for more than a century. The issue has been so intricately entangled with other national dilemmas, and its implications have often been so confusing, as to elicit a general aversion to touching it. One typical symptom of this situation has been the mist engulfing the question of Coptic demography: How many Copts are there really in Egypt and what is their share of the population? Church sources have claimed that no less than 18 percent of all Egyptians are Christian. The government has chosen to speak of "around 6 percent" (5.7 percent, according to the 1986 census), with certain official publications quoting still lower figures. A noted Egyptian scholar in the mid-1990s adopted the loose and rather standard assessment of 7 percent to 10 percent (to wit, between 4.2 million and 6 million Copts at the time), a figure he still offered with a word of caution.[1] Such discrepancies have reflected the general puzzle of the Coptic issue and the discomfort of being specific about it.

Long kept quiet, the issue became particularly sensitive in the last quarter of the twentieth century. The change occurred as a side effect of a more momentous development, that is, the rise of Islamic militancy, the product of cultural disorientation and material hardship from which the faith seemed to offer an escape. In the process, Egypt's Christians were targeted by their agitated Muslim compatriots and fell prey to their rage. Copts, it should be

noted, suffered from the very same national tribulations as Muslims and responded to them concurrently. By the time they became victims of their
neighbors' violence, they had already been contending with a serious sociopolitical and cultural crisis of their own. Their problem, further aggravated
by this deepening friction, continued for a while to be largely overlooked by
the government and public alike, as both were preoccupied with what seemed
to be more pressing troubles. The Coptic issue was suddenly brought out into
the open in early summer 1994, when an academic conference on minority
rights in the Middle East convened and probed the state of the Copts, among
other topics. A heated public controversy on the matter erupted, which shed
new light on hitherto shady corners of the Muslim-Christian arena and, more
important, on some of Egypt's intricate cultural dilemmas.

Monarchy and Revolution:
From Integration to Marginalization

The historical status of the Copts as *dhimmis,* a protected minority in the Islamic state, implied certain distinct political and economic handicaps. That
system, however, also had the advantage of clarity in defining the Copts' place
in the state and society. The dissolution of the old Ottoman order in Egypt in
the late nineteenth century therefore evoked questions of communal identity
among the Christians—as it did among their Muslim neighbors—that were
further compounded by the bewildering encounter with Europe, its missionar-
ies, thinkers, and occupiers. The problem was at first mostly cultural-ideologi-
cal rather than material: the changes the country experienced did not cause a
particular economic crisis for its Christians, and in some ways they even
opened up new opportunities that improved their lot. Yet the problems of identity were irritating enough. Haunting both Muslims and Copts, they eventually
spawned political difficulties as well. By the turn of the century interfactional
tension was brewing in Egypt, and it would turn violent on the eve of World
War I. Then, for a brief historical moment during the interwar period, there
was an interval of peaceful coexistence and even cooperation, as Muslims and
Christians joined hands in the grand battles for independence and nation building—a period later to be remembered with nostalgia (relying, as all nostalgia
does, on a somewhat selective memory). The facade of solidarity began to
crack in the mid-1930s against a backdrop of a severe socioeconomic and cultural crisis that brought confessional tensions back to the surface. Soon the
1952 revolution would banish the Copts to a corner of the national arena with
no role to play. Such bewildering vicissitudes within a few short decades im-
mensely exacerbated the crisis of communal orientation for the Copts.[2]

The solutions Egyptian Christians found for their identity problems under the monarchy were of the familiar kind under such circumstances. They

included defiant assertiveness; an attempt at redefining the frame of communal reference for all of Egyptian society so as to place themselves comfortably within its confines; and, when these two approaches failed, emigration. Talk about a distinct Coptic identity began around 1900, accompanied by a call for cultural and linguistic revival and measures to reform the church. Among these measures were the opening of a clerical seminary in Cairo and the establishment of a Sunday school network for young Copts, religious projects that developed into a social support system and would later assume a political role. Christians discussed the needs of the "Coptic nation," and some of them called for the formation of a political party to defend Christian rights. Such ideas were abandoned during the interwar phase of Muslim-Christian collaboration. But in the late 1940s, as confessional tension resurfaced, Coptic activists founded an organization in Cairo entitled Jama'at al-Umma al-Qibtiyya (Coptic Nation Society), which became a political party in 1952 in response to the vocal rising of Islamic sentiments of the time.[3]

More illuminating was the Copts' effort to reformulate the country's communal guidelines and eliminate or minimize the role of religion in Egypt, as it was emerging from its Ottoman past. The most obvious option for a new community was one based on territorial nationalism—"Egyptianness"—as distinct from a pan-Islamic or regional identity of any kind. Egyptian nationalism was born on the eve of World War I and became popular in the country during the struggle against foreign domination; Christian leaders were among its chief advocates and ideologues, as it was both consonant with the Coptic historical legacy and politically beneficial. Other Copts adopted a "Mediterraneanist" orientation for similar reasons.[4] The appeal of these two options—defiant assertiveness and integration—alternated with the changing political circumstances, and the Christian community wavered between them without landing firmly on solid ground.

The July Revolution and the quest for pan-Arabism, which it substituted for Egyptian territorialism, disconcerted the Copts still further. On the morrow of the Free Officers' coup, they found themselves in cultural straits more serious than ever before. Pan- Arabism, its Islamic undertones undeniable despite its professedly secular call, was highly problematic for the Christians as a frame of reference. What made the transition to a military regime even more of a crisis for them was its adverse effect on their economic and political standing. The confiscation of extensive Coptic property and the nationalization of Christian-controlled businesses deprived the Coptic elite of its public influence, as did the abolition of political parties, the main avenue of political participation.[5] Under the new rules, the channels for social and political mobility were the military and state-controlled civil bureaucracy. Copts, however, were traditionally scarce among army officers (there was none among the Free Officers and in the Revolutionary Command Council), and thus could have little access to top civilian posts except through the president's goodwill. The

new government discriminated against them in recruiting people to state and
public-sector positions, and the Copts could hardly protest. Age-old feelings
of deprivation, once brushed aside by the shared zeal of patriotic cooperation,
now reappeared along with an acute sense of communal isolation. Under the
regime's firm grip, divested of economic options and effective means of political self-expression, Copts for the first time in their history turned to a third
type of solution for their problem: emigrating from their ancestral land in
large numbers, mostly to the United States, Canada, and Australia.[6]

The July Revolution, with its vision of national pride and individual re-
demption and with its charismatic leader, Gamal Abd al-Nasser, at first appeared to offer a total remedy for the country's ills. It would later prove a dis-
appointment, prompting a crisis perhaps graver than the one it initially set out
to alleviate. For the Copts, ill-treated by the officers' regime from the outset,
frustration came much earlier. When Nasser's leadership was still being
hailed by the majority of Egyptians as holding great promise, the Christian
minority was at a low ebb materially and spiritually. It was marginalized in
the state and society, away from the limelight of exciting national and international action, its grievances overlooked. A "Coptic problem" was an unknown
notion except, it seemed, to the Copts themselves. Egyptian society was too
preoccupied with dramatic or dramatized events to pay much heed to the increasing plight of its small and ancient minority.

The 1970s: Roots of a Violent Clash

On 6 November 1972 a Coptic church was set on fire in Khanka, north of
Cairo. A protest demonstration by Coptic religious leaders developed into a
Muslim-Christian skirmish, and a parliamentary commission of inquiry was
established to investigate Coptic complaints.[7] This was an isolated incident—
some five peaceful years would separate it from the next wave of violence—
and a minor one compared to what was in store for the two communities. But
it was an augury for the future, as well as a symptom of tension already bub-
bling below the surface. Under President Anwar al-Sadat the social and political situation of Egypt's Christians took another turn for the worse. This was a
period in which the attention of most Egyptians turned away from the grand
foreign battles of the recent past to more burdensome domestic issues. Growing disillusionment with the state and erosion of the hope for a better future
produced a renewed attachment to faith and the phenomenon of religious radicalism. Sadat, more orthodox than his predecessor, at first did little to check
the development of the latter; until close to the end of his presidency he even
encouraged it in certain sectors for political expediency.

The new religious forces that were taking shape, including militant
groups, did not concern themselves initially with the non-Islamic minorities.

Their main adversary was the state, their primary objective a revision of society's values. Copts represented a secondary if not altogether marginal consideration: their role in state institutions should be modified, the radicals believed, but that would be settled anyway once the country was governed by the shari'a.[8] Still, the intercommunal atmosphere continued to heat up, in part the indirect result of Muslim radicalization with Sadat's blessing, but in another part, as we shall now see, the outcome of the Copts' own attitude.

Sadat's accession to the presidency coincided with a portentous change in the Egyptian church: the election of Shenuda III as Coptic pope and spiritual head in the autumn of 1971. Shenuda, forty-seven years old upon assuming his post, was a charismatic, dynamic, and uncompromising leader with sharp political instincts, in marked contrast to his recent predecessors.[9] No sooner had he taken office than he brought the church's standing within the community to unprecedented centrality. Starting his tenure at a time of severe crisis for the Copts, Shenuda inspired a line of assertiveness, encouraging his disciples to voice their complaints and demands aloud and to seek improvement of their situation through passive struggle and otherwise. The concurrence of rising Islamic activism and a bold Christian leadership effected a far-reaching change in the Coptic problem: from oppressed marginalization to open and sometimes violent conflict between Copts and Muslims.

One of the most bitter complaints Christians now aired vocally (and an obvious priority for Shenuda) concerned discrimination in building houses of prayer. The law relating to the construction of churches was based on the Ottoman *hatt-i humayun* (noble rescript) of 1856, which guaranteed equality between Muslims and non-Muslims in the empire but also required government licensing to erect a church. A 1934 Egyptian government decree further specified ten restricting conditions for the construction of churches, including a minimum distance between churches and between a church and the nearest mosque, as well as the absence of objection on the part of Muslim neighbors.[10] Getting a license to build a new church became an increasingly tedious matter, with the government never too enthusiastic to grant it. Such restrictions, harsh enough when the decree was issued in the 1930s, became quite unbearable later on. Demographic developments, particularly the growing concentration of Copts in the cities due to internal migration, as well as rising religiosity among them, rendered the need for more places of worship urgent, while the parallel rise in Islamic sentiments made the government less prone to accede to Christian requests. Improvised solutions, namely, the illegal building of churches (often under the guise of "philanthropic societies"), were liable to be taken as provocations by Muslim neighbors, and they sometimes reacted violently. Such was the case in Khanka, where the church attacked in 1972 had been unlawfully erected. For the Copts this was a source of much anguish, especially given the rapid expansion of mosques, which required no license to construct.

Nor were Christian complaints about the absence of religious freedom limited to the building of churches. Copts were alarmed by the mounting pressure from Islamic religious circles to impose Islamic law on all Egyptians. One such Islamic initiative, publicly considered in the mid-1970s, was the "apostasy law" (*qanun al-ridda*) that sought to apply the shari'a-prescribed death penalty to apostates, including Christians who had converted to Islam temporarily (a common practice among Copts, for certain practical reasons). Another demand, put forth toward the end of the decade, was for the shari'a to be proclaimed "the main source of legislation" in Egypt. The government dropped the apostasy law following a Coptic uproar, but then succumbed to Muslim pressures and adopted the latter demand, changing the constitution accordingly in May 1980.[11] Such readiness by the state to introduce discriminatory religious measures—whether yielding to radical Islamic pressures or due to its own pro-Islamic prejudice—was highly worrisome to the Copts. "That a single Muslim should embrace Christianity is an unbearable scandal and an assault on the public order," Mirit Butrus-Ghali, a leading Copt thinker, charged bitterly, "while it is permissible, acceptable and desirable for hundreds of Copts to convert to Islam. [The state] makes things easy for [such converts to Islam], providing them with benefits and gifts, and joyful celebrations and parades are organized for them in the streets," he noted.[12]

Religious intolerance was one area in which the Copts felt oppressed. There were other grievances: in education, from the imposition of Islamic-oriented textbooks on Christian children to discrimination in the allocation of funds for higher education; in free expression and publication, with Christians exposed to unchecked Muslim propaganda attacks while being themselves subject to more rigorous censorship; and in political representation, where it was fairly easy for Copts to prove their deprivation in parliamentary, ministerial, governorship, and top public-sector positions.[13] There was little novelty in these complaints as such. But their open and vocal expression by Copts in the 1970s under their stalwart leader was new. Airing such claims in times of rising Islamic activism, however, was a recipe for mutual suspicion, tension, and eventually violence.

By the late 1970s, the Muslim-Christian conflict was no longer latent. It had evolved into an overt encounter, one that would persist with intensifying waves of violence into the 1980s and 1990s. Agitated by the rising tide of ill-boding Islamism, the Copts under Shenuda defended their cause vehemently. A Coptic convention gathered in Alexandria in January 1977—the first in sixty-six years—and presented a series of explicit Christian demands that from then on were voiced repeatedly, loud and clear, at times accompanied by strikes and fast days.[14] Beyond verbal protests, Coptic students were reportedly organizing in groups on university campuses to counter similar activities by their Muslim counterparts.[15] Such open assertion of sectarian claims and organized action by Christians were anathema to Muslim leaders and provoked their rage, thus stepping up the momentum of rising tension. Rumors, mostly anti-Christian, were another ingredient of this hazardous recipe. Reports originating in the street or mosque, circulated in pamphlets, and echoed in the marketplace and on university campuses, accused Christians of engaging in clandestine organizational activities, amassing weapons, building illegal churches, and plotting to "return" the country to Christian control. The Copts angrily denied these accusations, openly criticized the government for acquiescing in them, and demanded its protection.

But the state was not quite in a position to offer effective protection to its non-Muslim minority, given its own strained relations with the radicals. Moreover, the firm stance Christians now displayed in lieu of their past docility often upset the regime, which viewed it as undermining its own efforts to stabilize the domestic scene. On several occasions Sadat expressed his irritation with Coptic conduct. In May 1980 he reminded them that he was "a Muslim head of a Muslim state," accused them of political intrigue, and even repeated the "Coptic state" conspiracy rumors.[16] Sadat's offensive also exposed another dimension of the unfolding Christian problem: the personal antagonism between two charismatic figures, the president and the Coptic pope. With the former ever groping for popular legitimacy and the latter daringly raising delicate issues, confrontation between them was all but unavoidable, with a fatal effect on the intercommunal arena.

Other important factors were at work in the evolving conflict. Coptic demands were voiced not only inside Egypt but also, more freely and vociferously, by Copt immigrants abroad. Their communities in North America, Australia, and France published periodicals and pamphlets, organized street demonstrations in times of violent outbursts in Egypt, and mobilized public opinion in their countries to exert pressure on the Egyptian government. Such activities served to incite their brethren back home, arousing further doubts among Muslims about the Copts' patriotism, and upsetting and even embarrassing the government.[17] At home, too, there was another complicating factor. Much of the open Muslim-Christian confrontation took place in Upper Egypt, where there were large concentrations of both Copts and radical Islamists (according to one count, 78 percent of all attacks on Copts between 1971 and 1993 occurred in towns in Upper Egypt—in the provinces of Bani Suwayf, Minya, Fayum, Asyut, Suhaj, Qina, and Aswan).[18] In these places far from the capital, where police control was less potent than at the center, the social tradition of blood vengeance (*tha'r*) was very much alive and common among Muslims and Christians alike. This powerful custom had a perpetuating effect on the confessional conflict there, regardless of the religious motives that had initially sparked it.[19] Finally, the conflict in Egypt evolved against the backdrop of rising Islamic sentiments in neighboring countries and growing pressure on non-Muslim minorities—in postrevolutionary Iran and elsewhere—which encouraged Egypt's fundamentalists and increased the Copts' anxiety.

Under these troublesome circumstances a dynamic of mutual animosity and violence developed. Local incidents, like the one in Khanka, occurred again in the autumn of 1977 in Fayum and Asyut, continued on a more violent scale in Asyut and Minya in early 1978, and rapidly gathered momentum thereafter. By the end of the decade such incidents had become a common feature in Upper Egypt, spreading to the capital and the Delta. Violence peaked in an unprecedented bloody explosion in the poverty-stricken Cairo suburb of al-Zawiya al-Hamra in June 1981, resulting in scores of casualties and hundreds of arrests. The sociopolitical order in Egypt, an Egyptian observer sadly noted, "reverted back hundreds of years" as the country was witness to a "Lebanese scene."[20] Known as "the *fitna* of al-Zawiya al-Hamra," the event was the grievous highlight of the stormy prelude to the assassination of Sadat four months later.

Violent Peaks: Targeting the "Enemies of God"

President Husni Mubarak inherited a Coptic dossier as tangled as ever. For a while the Muslim-Christian front was quiet: the 1981 blast in suburban Cairo, Sadat's brutal death, and the ensuing tough clampdown on Islamists had a paralyzing effect that lasted for several years. Also contributing to the calm was that during much of this period Pope Shenuda was kept in confinement in a remote monastery, to which he had been banished by Sadat in September 1981. Still, all the factors of intercommunal strain remained, waiting to resurface. The material and ideological woes besetting both communities persisted, and mutual mistrust perpetuated itself in a vicious circle. The Copts remained intensely nervous about Islamic militancy and critical of the authorities for their impotent handling of the problem. Radical Muslims, for their part, adhered to deep suspicion of the Copts, of their demands and rumored plots, and continued to view them as a legitimate target in the battle against society's ills. The Islamists were now equipped with a *fatwa,* a religious ruling issued sometime around Sadat's death by their authoritative blind shaikh 'Umar 'Abd al-Rahman, which stated:

> Christians belong to three categories: those who kill Muslims, those who support the church with money and arms in order to harm Muslims, and those who do not cause any harm to Muslims. An eye for an eye must be exacted from Christians in the first category, while Christians in the second category must be deprived of their wealth. But no harm should come to Christians in the third category.[21]

Early in 1987 the intercommunal arena flared up again. As so often before, it was a rumor that ignited the encounter, this time about Copts secretly spraying women's veils with a chemical that caused cross-shaped markings to appear on them after a while. Wide-scale riots broke out across Upper Egypt, following the sadly familiar pattern of rumor-assault-counterassault-arrests.[22] Once sparked, the fire persisted with periodic outbursts in the southern towns and villages. One typical instance was the incident of March 1990 in Abu Qurqas, an agricultural town in the Minya province. Rumors about an illicit love affair between a Coptic boy and a Muslim girl incited tension and rage. Islamists circulated a leaflet entitled "Wipe Out the Disgrace, Oh Muslims!" charging "Nazarenes" and "Crusaders" of seducing Muslim girls with drugs and money to act in pornographic films. A fiery Friday sermon in the local mosque sent hundreds of Muslim youths armed with sticks and firebombs to the streets to attack Coptic property, and by the end of the day two churches, a hospital, and other buildings had been badly damaged. The police apprehended about 100 of the assailants but failed to quell the tension, and for the next two weeks more Christian property in nearby villages was devastated. Then, at the order of the president, leaders of the two communities moved to contain the crisis, and cabinet ministers were sent to address a "national reconciliation meeting" in Abu Qurqas. In a closing scene, Muslim and Christian leaders marched through the shabby town hand in hand, chanting "Long Live the Crescent with the Cross (*yahya al-hilal ma'a al-salib*)!"[23] A murky curtain closed on the gloomy show, scarcely masking the hatred and fear that continued to seethe behind it.

The short years of tranquility preceding this gory wave became an episodic interim. Once more violence spread to the Cairo vicinity, inflaming its gloomy neighborhoods that were overcrowded with southern rural immigrants, both Muslims and Copts. There, radical Islamists succeeded in establishing temporary semiautonomous strongholds, reportedly imposing a poll tax on their Christian neighbors, "the enemies of Allah." Intercommunal clashes broke out in 1990, 1991, and 1992 in the suburbs of 'Ayn Shams and Imbaba, commencing as ordinary disputes between neighbors and evolving into riots with casualties and extensive damage.[24] These events demonstrated the high explosiveness of the situation in close proximity to the authorities in the capital. But the hub of the conflict remained in the south, where, one observer noted, it was easier to buy a gun than a chocolate bar. The Islamists' animosity to the Copts no longer derived from presidential inducement: the devil had long since come out of the bottle. A decade after Sadat's death, confessional tension had returned to its 1981 peak. The frequency and cruelty of riotous encounters had long surpassed it.

A further upturn in the scale of violence occurred in mid-1992. Muslim militants upgraded their struggle to a more vicious stage, one far more costly for the state. They now aimed at such vulnerable targets as tourism and foreign business and launched frontal attacks on security forces, causing enormous damage.[25] Christians were not a prime target in this sweeping offensive, but they were easy prey and were hit hard. No fewer than twenty-two Copts

died, and many others were wounded in thirty-seven attacks aimed directly at
Copts in 1992 alone, according to one count. Similarly intensive attacks on
Christians during the following two years resulted in scores of casualties.[26]
Reports from Upper Egypt, especially from Minya, Asyut, and Qina, depicted
incessant Muslim-Christian clashes and excessively fierce assaults by the former on the latter. Public and governmental attention was focused on the ominous Islamist challenge to the regime's stability and survival, the dangerous
malady that seemed to dwarf the intercommunal sore.

For the Copts this was a troublesome period in other ways as well. In the
early 1990s, discord broke out between the Coptic Church and lay community
spokespersons, as well as within the church itself. It revolved mostly around
Shenuda's style of leadership: there was mounting criticism of his overin-
volvement in politics, his tyrannical conducting of community affairs, and his
ill-disposed treatment of senior church functionaries. Such censure was
voiced both in Egypt and in the Coptic diaspora, preoccupying the community alongside its other pressing struggle. Although Shenuda's leadership
seems to have been still acknowledged by the great majority of Copts, the
community, now under heavy Muslim siege, was less than unified.[27]

How did Mubarak's government, engrossed in combating an Islamist
peril of more than one stripe, view the Coptic problem? Curiously, the regime
shared certain important objectives with the Copts. For both of them Islamic
militancy was a threat. Both were interested in a basically secular orientation
for the state, and neither wished to see accelerated implementation of the
shari'a. Mubarak's interests in these issues, however, were dictated by considerations other than concern for the Copts and their grievances. For him the intercommunal strife was an irritating by-product of the bigger challenge his
regime was facing. That bigger problem acutely exacerbated the delicate
Christian issue and disrupted the long-term efforts to settle it. But that was
only one, and certainly not the most hazardous, aspect of the Islamist challenge. Once it had been contained, Mubarak assessed, the Coptic problem
would revert to its old, basically harmless state.

Mubarak therefore applied a low-key approach to the problem, employ-
ing palliatives to pacify that front as best he could. Having learned Sadat's
bitter lesson, he was cautious not to play the lethal game of evoking anti-
Christian sentiments among Muslims. Instead, his officials preached
Muslim-Christian friendship and made it a point to minimize the matter
whenever asked to comment on it. Sectarian sedition was "not an issue in
Egypt," they claimed, but rather an exaggeration of simple sociocultural differences by the opposition and the hostile foreign media.[28] The government
retained the measured quota of Coptic ministerial representation according
to their officially stated share in the population—two portfolios (with brief
intervals of one) throughout Mubarak's tenure, as against a single Christian

minister during most of Sadat's time.[29] Such measures, the president hoped, would help defuse the tension on this front.

A Glimpse into the Box

In spring 1994 the Cairo Ibn Khaldun Center for Development Studies announced its intention to hold a conference in May of that year, to discuss the rights of Middle Eastern minorities, including the Copts.[30] The announcement stirred a public storm in the country. That the delicate question of minorities in the region should be openly debated, and that Egypt's Christians should be considered under that rubric, was abhorrent to publicists, politicians, and religious leaders. Far more candid than would be conceivable in any other Arab country, and highly passionate, the debate yielded hundreds of polemic articles—many still marked by the old equivoque, others bolder and more frank—along with several serious studies on the subject. They opened a unique window into the complex sensitivities associated with the Copts. More instructive, the debate shed much light on broader social and cultural issues. It reflected something of a predicament, illustrated by the tension between the reluctance to regard the question of minorities in the region as a problem and the call to confront it boldly, between the desire to revert somehow, without an encounter, to the old communal equilibrium and the sense that only an honest exposure of all relevant aspects would lead to that desired end. More broadly, it mirrored the battle over Egypt's cultural soul in recent decades, between the traditionally oriented trend and the secular-rationalist one.

Critical reactions to the conference idea appeared from the second week of April on, at first in a relatively mild tenor. But on 22 April, the veteran writer Muhammad Hasanayn Haykal published an article in *al-Ahram* entitled "Egypt's Copts Are No Minority but Part and Parcel of Egypt's Human and Cultural Fabric," in which he bitingly assailed the conference concept and its organizers. His attack prompted a spate of reports, essays, and interviews in the Egyptian and Arab press during the following weeks, most of which echoed Haykal's arguments and advocated his stance, with only a handful of objections to them. Members of the Ibn Khaldun Center, led by their robust chairman, the sociologist Sa'd al-Din Ibrahim, handled the heavy fire valiantly and clung to their decision to hold the conference and address the Coptic question. As the heat intensified and shifted from criticism to threats, they were forced to make two alterations in their plan: they transferred the conference from antagonistic Egypt to Cyprus; and they dropped from its title the notion of "minorities" (*aqalliyyat*)—a term often taken to imply elements extraneous to society's main body—replacing it with "religious communities, sects, and ethnic groups" (*al-milal wal-nihal wal-a'raq*). The conference took place in Limasol on 12–14 May 1994 and concluded with what the Ibn Khaldun Center described as a solid success. The Copts were discussed both in open sessions and in a special closed session. Encouraged by the achievement, the center convened a follow-up symposium in Cairo in November, where the problem and its ramifications were further considered.

Haykal's article, whose themes inspired much of what was written later, epitomized the basic concept of the conservative trend concerning the Coptic issue: harmful to the national interest if explicitly debated, it is best denied or depicted as a nonissue. Coming from a celebrated rationalist thinker, such reasoning was particularly effective. Haykal's essay presented two basic arguments: (1) The Copts are not an ethnic, sectarian, or religious [*sic*] minority like other such groups in the region; rather, they are an integral part of the country's multicolored fabric, a multitude that had always lent Egypt its vigor; and (2) treating the Copts as a minority is thus false and dangerous, for it may serve the interests of Egypt's enemies; moreover, such a wicked idea must be a product of alien conspirators seeking to weaken the country from within.

Disregarding Haykal's skillful rhetorical techniques (he repeatedly digressed to side issues, some with dubious relevance, so as to create a broader context for his reasoning),[31] his argumentation could be taken as an authentic expression of deep-rooted Egyptian concerns. It articulated the old aversion to viewing the Copts as anything but an integral part of the Egyptian body, perhaps even its most ancient part. Referring to them as a minority, let alone an oppressed one, contradicted that common view and jeopardized the community's self-image as a cohesive body. Anyone raising the issue in such terms must therefore be the enemy or its pawn.

These points were reiterated and elaborated with many variations in the following weeks. The Copts, it was argued, were "Egyptians in the full sense," historically, culturally, and legally. If they had special problems, as some writers were prepared to acknowledge, these problems emanated from circumstances that were not particular to Christians but troubled other Egyptians as well in one way or another. Such was their victimization by militant Islamists: many innocent Muslims shared that fate with them. Presenting the Copts as a minority was inconsonant with their being loyal Egyptians, evoked the damaging notion of Christian separatism, and was insulting to the Copts themselves. Such talk meant a return to the old imperialistic thinking that had once sought to divide and rule; it was necessarily a plot by such foes as the U.S. Central Intelligence Agency and the Israeli Mossad, as well as by Copt emigrants abroad who were rendering their brethren in Egypt a ruinous disservice. The whole project, then, was a threat to national unity. "Saying that the Copts in Egypt are an ethnic or cultural minority who are separated from the rest of the community is an affront to all Egyptians," Tariq al-Bishri, an eminent thinker, told an interviewer. "I cannot imagine anybody accepting the notion that Egypt's Copts are a minority."[32] Haykal's rebuke for the Ibn Khaldun Center was likewise vigorously echoed, with the accusation that its activities were politically and not scientifically motivated. There was even a demand for police action against the center and its chairman. Of the scores of writers who joined the fray (no fewer than 300 in Egypt and abroad, according to Sa'd al-Din Ibrahim),[33] the great majority expressed such critical views.[34] At base they were conveying a major genuine concern, which none of them expressed more clearly and succinctly than Haykal: "Should our economy become ill, we will remedy it. Should we stray in our political course, we will find the right path. Should our thinking get confused, we will one day rectify that as well. But should the national cohesion of this country be cracked—God forbid!—that would be beyond our capacity to repair."[35]

As against this, the voices of those defending the conference idea were few and, given the general uproar, quite feeble. They wrote fewer than 10 percent of all the pieces published on the subject.[36] Most of them were members of the Ibn Khaldun Center, who, finding access to the popular media difficult, pronounced their position in the center's courageous but small-circulation monthly newsletter *Civil Society*. Rejecting Haykal's attack as "intellectual terrorism" and the assaults on the conference and the center as "full of inaccuracies, insults, and despicable offenses," they reiterated their principal concept: the problem of the Copts as a religious minority does exist and should be discussed earnestly, for only a sincere effort to face it would benefit national unity.[37] "Ignoring the problem does not deny its existence, or decrease its malignancy," argued Amina al-Na'ash (Naqqash). "The first step to circumvent it is to shed light on it and expose it, whilst engaging in a responsible dialogue in order to prevent the miseries that could result if we turn a blind eye."[38] The public offensive soon led the conference defenders to focus on the need for an open discussion rather than on the grievances of the Christians. The conference itself did consider the difficulties facing the Copts in the areas of education, freedom of religion, freedom of expression, and political representation, for all of which it offered recommendations. Yet its most important statement, everybody felt, was the fact that it took place at all and dared to open the delicate Egyptian Christian file in public.[39]

From a Coptic perspective, the public debate of early summer 1994 revealed a disheartening reality. The unusual scope of the discussion and its intensely emotional tone attested that, far from being a nonissue, the problem was very much a fact of life in Egypt. It was widely conceived as a disturbing fact of life—however, one that should remain untouched, undiscussed, concealed. Their troubles, Copts were told resoundingly, represented a Pandora's box for Egypt. They contained a potential menace to the sociopolitical order that could weaken the nation's defenses against its enemies. Opening it would therefore be irresponsible and unpatriotic. Nor would it be in the Christians' own interest, for it would most likely invite more Islamist violence against them. Equally frustrating for the Copts, many of their members shared the fright and preferred not to touch the box. Christian spokespersons invited to attend the conference refused,[40] and some even joined its critics.[41] Pope Shenuda himself found it expedient to distance himself and his followers from the fire. "We are not a minority in Egypt," he hastened to state as soon as the question hit the headlines. "If the Copts have certain problems or demands, these matters should be resolved in a spirit of amity in the same homeland without resorting to such terms as 'minority' and 'majority.'"[42] As for the government, it remained conspicuously silent: the mainstream of expressed opinion and Coptic complicity was comfortably consistent with its own strategy on the matter.

Why was the mainstream of the Egyptian political community so sensitive about the status of non-Muslims in their society? The question relates to broader dilemmas involved in Egypt's quest for a proper role under the sun following two centuries of complex relations with the world. Clearly, the Copts differed from the rest of Egyptian society. Otherwise, there would have been no special institutions to run their affairs, no special legislation concerning their religious rites, no special quota for their political representation. Equally clear, their main distinction was their religious faith. It was primarily their standing as a religious minority in a predominantly Sunni Muslim society—an undeniable fact, at least in the technical sense—that most participants in the public debate sought to conceal or dismiss.

But treating the Copts as a religious minority would define the Muslim majority as a religious community as well. And underscoring religion as the primary determinant of Egypt's collective identity would diminish the weight of its other parts, including the legacy of ancient Egypt and the Arab heritage binding it with its neighbors. Moreover, granting religion such a leading status would signify reverting to premodern values—those associated with the Ottoman and pre-Ottoman past—while minimizing later developments that underlay Egypt's claim to modernity. It is thus easy to see why such an option was objectionable to many in the liberal educated class who participated in the public debate. For this class, thinking of the Copts in such terms was a matter of a past that should be left behind. If, they felt, the status of Christians was still ridden by problems as the Ibn Khaldun Center people insisted, these should be viewed in their true limited proportions, reduced to insignificance or, better still, overlooked altogether in the service of more important interests.

This tension between past values and those considered desirable for the present and future was further highlighted by the state's open conflict with the Islamists. Preaching religious tradition to the exclusion of all else, the Islamists sought to harass the Christians as such. And because they were so adamant on targeting the Copts, those aiming to check the radicals rejected the notion of "religious minority" as part of the anti-Islamist struggle. In this, the educated class was joined by the government, which tacitly concurred with the vocal rejection of opening the Coptic file. Deeming the Islamists' call dangerous, the regime viewed the militants' anti-Christian offensive as part of their drive to undermine its own legitimacy. Thus, while secular-minded intellectuals and the government had their respective outlooks and considerations for obscuring the issue, both considered such a tactic an essential tool in the battle against militant Islam. Only a small group among the educated class, vocally represented by members of the Ibn Khaldun Center, thought otherwise and favored a different approach.

The views of other groups—the great mass of Egyptian society, which did not take part in the public debate—have not been examined in this discussion. Exploring them would require a different approach and different research tools. Clearly, the popular response to the Islamist message was far from consensual rejection. On the contrary, in its less aggressive version the message seemed to appeal to large sections of society. It would thus perhaps make sense to assume, tentatively and broadly, that the silent mass of Egypt's Muslim population not examined here held views on the Christian minority that were somewhere between those of the political and educated elite and those of the Islamists.

The Box Left Open

Once unsealed, the Coptic trouble box remained open in the country's public domain. The plight of Christians and their relations with their neighbors now won widespread attention. But, as both the government and Coptic leaders had once feared and now came to learn, more attention meant more tribulation. For the militant Islamists, attacking Christians who were now in the limelight could buy them well-desired visibility. In Upper Egypt, Copts remained a soft target, and the radicals managed to strike at them periodically even after having been destabilized by the regime's counteroffensive in the mid-1990s, thus scoring useful propaganda gains. In one such typical attack in February 1996, Muslim gunmen opened indiscriminate fire on passers-by in the village of 'Izbat al-Aqbat, Asyut province, killing eight. In a more brutal one a year later, a band of armed militants broke into a church in Abu Qurqas and massacred twelve young men and women during a religious meeting. Another thirteen Copts were slaughtered in one day in Qina province four weeks later, rendering the toll in Christian lives within one month the highest in recent memory.[43] Accounts of these last incidents indicated that the victims were attacked for their refusal to pay *jizya,* or poll tax—a tribute levied from non-Muslim minorities in Islamic states of the past, which the radicals now sought to impose on Christians as a kind of "protection fee."[44] With the Coptic problem still the focus of public attention, this idea had an explosive potential and the militants were not the only ones to exploit it. Heads of the Muslim Brotherhood—the big religious movement likewise under the regime's clampdown—stated in April 1997 that in Muslim Egypt Copts should pay *jizya* and be excluded from the army because their loyalty could not be trusted.[45] The Brotherhood later backed down from the statement, but not before it had generated a public uproar that kept the Christian problem burning.[46]

Nor were the Islamists the only ones whose activity was effected by the publicity of the problem. The Christian voice was also heard louder now, especially that of the diaspora Copts. Their community in North America became vociferously active in raising the issue of Coptic civil rights in Egypt as a consideration in Egypt-U.S. relations. In summer 1997 they were accused by a popular Egyptian weekly of working to sabotage U.S. aid to Egypt, a charge that added fuel to the fire of Muslim-Christian polarization.[47] "Never have those relations been more frayed than at present," a seasoned observer of Egypt assessed in early 1998, some four years after the issue became a matter of public debate.[48]

In this agitated atmosphere, the government's policy of minimizing the problem and veiling it became more difficult. It was increasingly harder to appease the Christians without antagonizing the Islamists. Still, the government continued to adhere to this strategy as the best option under the circumstances. This was seen during the parliamentary elections of fall 1995, when the ruling National Democratic Party's list of candidates included no Copts, not even in constituencies with a Christian majority. From among the Copts themselves—soberly pessimistic after the recent redemarcation of their boundaries—no more than seventy-seven joined the race through other parties or independently, a mere 1.97 percent of a total of 3,890 candidates. When none of them was elected, Mubarak, acting upon his constitutional prerogative, appointed six Copts to the Assembly, none of them a prominent figure.[49] Such measures to marginalize the Christians were coupled with traditional vocal expressions, well orchestrated and often televised, of national unity following violent Islamist attacks on them. With the government locked in a tough battle against its militant adversaries, this was hardly an appropriate time for measures effectively improving the lot of the Copts.

The government recourse to the old shadowy veil for covering the brutal action on the Muslim-Christian stage could not hide it from the actors themselves. The Copts, who will always remember Sadat for encouraging Islamic radicalism and thus turning them into victims of their neighbors' fury, will conceivably remember Mubarak's era as one in which too little was done to reverse that trend.[50] For much of the last decade of the twentieth century, Copts continued to feel isolated within their own society and witness their problem denied. Developments on the ground seemed to indicate that the situation was likely to persist to the end of the century and possibly beyond.

Notes

1. For a discussion of these data, see Sa'd al-Din Ibrahim, *Al-Milal wal-nihal wal-a'raq; humum al-aqalliyyat fi al-watan al-'Arabi* (Cairo: Ibn Khaldun Center, 1994), pp. 382–384; J. D. Pennington, "The Copts in Modern Egypt," *Middle Eastern Studies* 18, no. 2 (April 1982), pp. 158–159. In some of his other publications Ibrahim most often quotes the figure of approximately 5 million Copts. See also Youssef Ibrahim in the *New York Times*, 15 March 1993 (speaking of 17 percent, i.e., about 10 million), and Jumhuriyyat Misr al-'Arabiyya, wizarat al-difa', *Al-Aqalliyyat fi al-mintaqa al-'Arabiyya wa-ta'thiruha 'ala al-amn al-qawmi al-'Arabi* (Cairo, [199?]), p. 152, where the total number of Copts in Egypt, Sudan, and Syria [*sic*] together is given as 4.1 million.

2. For historical studies of these developments, see B. L. Carter, *The Copts in Egyptian Politics, 1918–1952* (Cairo: American University in Cairo Press, 1986); Mustafa Fiqqi, *Al-Aqbat fi al-siyasa al-Misriyya* (Cairo: Dar al-Shuruq, 1985). For a more concise discussion see Ibrahim, *Al-Milal wal-nihal*, pp. 406–446, and tables on pp. 510–514.

3. Carter, *The Copts*, 279–281; Rafiq Habib, *Al-Ihtijaj al-dini wal-sira' al-tabaqi fi misr* (Cairo: Sina, 1989), pp. 107–111.

4. Carter, *The Copts*, pp. 89ff.

5. For further discussion of these developments, see Ibrahim, *Al-Milal wal-nihal*, pp. 446–450. According to Ibrahim, the Copts lost some 75 percent of their jobs and property.

6. Saad Eddin Ibrahim, *The Copts of Egypt* (London: Minority Rights Group, 1996), p. 16. According to this source, by 1977 the Coptic diaspora in the United States and Canada had reached 85,000. Church assessments put it at 65,000 in that year and estimated that by 1995 the number had grown to approximately 300,000 in the United States, 50,000 in Canada, and 35,000 in Australia; see Nabil 'Abd al-Fattah (ed.), *Taqrir al-hala al-diniyya fi Misr, 1995* (Cairo: al-Ahram Center for Political and Strategic Studies, 1996), pp. 216–217.

7. Details in Ibrahim, *Al-Milal wal-nihal*, p. 462; Pennington, "The Copts in Modern Egypt," p. 171. The commission of inquiry submitted detailed recommendations, which, however, were ignored.

8. For a succinct and sophisticated analysis of these issues, see Hamied Ansari, "Sectarian Conflict in Egypt and the Political Expediency of Religion," *Middle East Journal* 38, no. 3 (summer 1984), pp. 397–418. Also, Faraj Fuda, "Al-Fitna al-ta'i-fiyya," in Faraj Fuda et al., *Al-Ta'ifiyya ila ayna!?* (Cairo: Dar al-Misri al-Jadid, 1987), pp. 11–58.

9. Pennington, "The Copts in Modern Egypt," pp. 167–168.

10. Details and text in Ibrahim, *Al-Milal wal-nihal*, pp. 549–550; 'Abd al-Fattah, *Taqrir al-hala al-diniyya*, pp. 87–88.

11. Details in Shimon Shamir and Ran Segev, "The Arab Republic of Egypt," *Middle East Contemporary Survey (MECS)*, vol. 1 (1976–1977), p. 298; Israel Altman, "The Arab Republic of Egypt," *MECS*, vol. 4 (1979–1980), pp. 335, 344.

12. Quoted by Nabil 'Aziz 'Abd al-Malik, "Huquq al-aqbat al-insaniyya wal-wahda al-wataniyya al-Misriyya fi daw al-i'lanat al-'alamiyya li-huquq al-insan wal-aqalliyyat," in Ibn Khaldun Center, *Al-Milal wal-nihal wal-a'raq, al-taqrir al-sanawi al-thani* (Cairo: Ibn Khaldun Center, 1995), p. 127.

13. For a discussion of Coptic complaints, see 'Abd al-Malik, "Huquq al-aqbat," pp. 122–132; John Eibner (ed.), *Church Under Siege* (Zurich: Institute for Religious Minorities in the Islamic World, 1993). Ibrahim, *Al-Milal wal-nihal*, pp. 515–517, pro-

duces tables showing Christian representation in Egyptian parliaments and cabinets from 1952 on. According to these tables, between 1952 and 1980 (with one short-lived exception in 1970–1971) Copts always occupied one ministerial position only. In 1980 a second Copt minister (with the somewhat lower position of minister-of-state) was appointed. See also Sulayman Shafiq, "Al-Aqbat wa-azmat al-muwatana," in Ibn Khaldun Center, *Al-Milal wal-nihal . . . al-taqrir al-sanawi al-thani,* pp. 213–215.

14. Details in 'Abd al-'Azim Ramadan, *Jama'at al-takfir fi Misr* (Cairo: al-Hay'a al-Misriyya al-'Amma lil-Kitab, 1995), pp. 275–277.

15. Ansari, "Sectarian Conflict," pp. 403–404.

16. Sadat's speech, *al-Ahram,* 15 May 1980, and further in Altman, "The Arab Republic of Egypt," *MECS,* vol. 4 (1979–1980), pp. 329–332. Sadat's speech came after a visit to the United States, where he was embarrassed by noisy protests by members of the Coptic diaspora. See also Ramadan, *Jama'at al-takfir,* pp. 303ff; Hala Mustafa, *Al-Dawla wal-harakat al-Islamiyya al-mu'arida bayna al-muhadana wal-muwajaha* (Cairo: Markaz al-Mahrusa, 1995), pp. 267–279.

17. Ibrahim, *The Copts of Egypt,* pp. 18–19. See also note 16.

18. Ibn Khaldun Center, *Humum al-aqalliyyat, al-taqrir al-sanawi al-awwal* (Cairo: Ibn Khaldun Center, 1993), pp. 47–48.

19. "Misr: fitna bi-thiyab al-tha'r," *al-Watan al-'Arabi,* 3 July 1992, pp. 24–25.

20. Ibrahim, *Al-Milal wal-nihal,* p. 473. For details and a discussion of the incident and its implications, see Ansari, "Sectarian Conflict," pp. 408–413.

21. Quoted in Ansari, "Sectarian Conflict," p. 415.

22. Details in Ami Ayalon, "The Arab Republic of Egypt," *MECS,* vol. 11 (1987), pp. 334–335.

23. *Al-Jumhuriyya* (Cairo), 4 March 1990; *al-Akhbar,* 8 March 1990; AFP, 10 March—Foreign Broadcasting Information Service: Near East and South Asia. Daily Report (DR), 11 March, 1990; *Akhir Sa'a,* 14 March 1990; *al-Ahram,* 15, 22, 27 March 1990; MENA, 25 March 1990; *Middle East International,* 8 June 1990.

24. *Le Monde,* 25 September 1991, 10, 28 December 1992; *Misr al-Fatat,* 7 October 1991; *New York Times,* 22 October 1991; *al-Ahram Weekly,* 31 October 1991; MENA, 8 December—DR, 9 December 1992; *al-Wafd,* 13 December 1992.

25. Details in Ami Ayalon, "The Arab Republic of Egypt," *MECS,* vol. 16 (1992), pp. 366–372; *MECS,* vol. 17 (1993), pp. 284–288; *MECS,* vol. 18 (1994), pp. 261–265.

26. Ibrahim, *Al-Milal wal-nihal,* pp. 522–523. Also Ibn Khaldun Center, *Humum al-aqalliyyat,* pp. 38, 40–41; Ibn Khaldun Center, *Al-milal wal-nihal . . . al-taqrir al-sanawi al-thani,* p. 235.

27. Rafiq Habib, *Al-Masihiyya al-siyasiyya fi Misr* (Cairo: Jaffa, 1990); Habib, *Man yabi' Misr? al-dawla, al-nukhba, al-kanisa* (Cairo: Misr al-'Arabiyya, 1994), esp. pp. 99–124; Ghali Shukri, a series of reports in *al-Watan al-'Arabi* starting from 21 January 1994; *al-Majalla,* 2 October 1994; *al-Wasat,* 5 December 1994; Sa'd al-Din Ibrahim, *The Copts of Egypt,* pp. 21–22.

28. See, for example, Interior Minister 'Abd al-Halim Musa in MENA, 6 May—DR, 8 May 1990.

29. At the time of Sadat's death, the Egyptian cabinet uncharacteristically included three Copt ministers, of whom one had been appointed two weeks previously and another in May 1980. Mubarak initially retained this number, but he brought it down to two within less than a year.

30. The Ibn Khaldun Center is an independent research institute whose main concern is the social, political, and cultural development of Egypt and the Arab countries, with special emphasis on issues of democracy and civil rights. It was set up in 1988

but became particularly active following the 1990–1991 Gulf crisis and war, which drew much international attention to questions of civil society in the Arab world. The center has been chaired since its foundation by Professor Sa'd al-Din Ibrahim of the American University in Cairo. Its monthly mouthpiece, *Civil Society* (and its Arabic version, *Al-Mujtama' al-madani*), is a bold promoter of liberal, secular-oriented, and democratic views.

31. 'Abd al-Hamid Safwat, "Mu'tamar al-aqalliyyat bayn al-ithara wal-mawdu'iyya," in Ibn Khaldun Center, *Al-Milal wal-nihal . . . al-taqrir al-sanawi al-thani,* pp. 182–186, presenting a systematic and critical textual analysis of Haykal's essay. According to Safwat's count, over 80 percent of it dealt with irrelevant matters.

32. Bishri to *Al-Watan al-'Arabi,* 6 May 1994, p. 30.

33. Ibn Khaldun Center, *Al-Milal wal-nihal . . . al taqrir al-sanawi al-thani,* p. 1 of the English part. In the Arabic part, p. 9, he mentions a total of 200 articles and other pieces published in April–May 1994.

34. Safwat, "Mu'tamar al-aqalliyyat," pp. 169–186, analyzing the contents of 142 reports, articles, and interviews on the subject appearing in Egypt between 8 April and 14 May 1994.

35. Haykal in *al-Ahram,* 22 April 1994.

36. According to Safwat's count, only thirteen articles, or 9 percent of the total pieces examined in his study, supported the idea.

37. *Civil Society,* May 1994, pp. 3, 14. The controversy occupied much of the May and June issues and to a lesser extent subsequent issues.

38. *Civil Society,* May 1994, back cover. See also Safwat, pp. 178–180.

39. Ibn Khaldun Center, *Al-Milal wal-nihal . . . al-taqrir al-sanawi al-thani,* pp. 24–28 and 72–73 of the English part; pp. 113–136 of the Arabic part.

40. *Al-Hayat* (London), 29 April 1994; Marlyn Tadros, "A Case of Fear, Ignorance and Passivity," in Ibn Khaldun Center, *Al-Milal wal-nihal . . . al-taqrir al-sanawi al-thani,* p. 27.

41. See, for example, William Sulayman Qilada, Nabil Murqus, Samir Murqus, and others in *al-Watan al-'Arabi,* 6 May 1994, pp. 31–33. Also *al-Wasat,* 2 May 1994, pp. 26–28.

42. Shenuda's interview in *al-Musawwar,* 29 April 1994. See also *al-Hayat* (London), 25 April 1994.

43. MENA, 25 February—DR, 27 February 1996; *Civil Society,* June 1996, pp. 12–13; April 1997, pp. 4, 7; *al-Hayat,* 16 February 1997; *al-Wasat,* 24 March 1997.

44. *Al-Quds al-'Arabi,* 16 April 1997.

45. Mustafa Mashhur, General Guide of the Muslim Brotherhood, in an interview to *al-Ahram Weekly,* 3 April 1997.

46. *Al-Wasat,* 21 April 1997.

47. Usama Salama in *Ruz al-Yusuf,* 21 April 1997. See also the response by Sa'd al-Din Ibrahim in the following issue of that journal, and *Civil Society,* August 1997, pp. 11–12.

48. Robert Springborg, "Egypt: Repression's Toll," *Current History* 97, no. 615 (January 1998), pp. 35–36.

49. 'Abd al-Fattah, *Taqrir al-hala al-diniyya,* pp. 316–317. For a detailed discussion of the Copts and the 1995 elections, see esp. pp. 307–326. Also Muhammad Ahmad Khalfallah in *al-Ahali,* 20 December 1995. Of the seventy-seven Copts who ran for election, thirteen were nominated by other political parties and the rest competed independently.

50. Muris Sadiq in *al-Ahali,* 30 December 1995.

4

Religion and Conflict in Sudan: A Non-Muslim Minority in a Muslim State

Yehudit Ronen

Geographically and societally diverse, Sudan is a veritable kaleidoscope of religion, race, language, and other basic factors. Located at the crossroads of the Middle East and sub-Saharan Africa, it borders on nine countries of the two regions—Egypt, Libya, Chad, the Central African Republic, Zaire, Uganda, Kenya, Ethiopia, and Eritrea. Given its long border along the Red Sea, Sudan enjoys geographic proximity to the Arabian Peninsula. Stretching more than 2.5 million square kilometers, Sudan is the largest country in Africa and the Middle East. These geographical features, in addition to Sudan's largely artificial international boundaries—demarcated arbitrarily during the colonial era in complete disregard of racial, religious, and linguistic affiliations—created a particularly heterogeneous community. More specifically, it made the country a microcosm of the Arab Muslim world and sub-Saharan Africa.

Furthermore, every large migration, whether due to an external demographic push into Sudan or internal resettlement after natural (or man-made) disaster, further enriched and rearranged the Sudanese human makeup. The Sudanese experience, therefore, is one that contains a great "fluidity of identity." Local and personalized group identities are integrated into broader identities that are complex and often overlap in "confusing ways."[1]

Sudan's diversity is so great that the various tribal and regional systems have been said to "have in common only nominal unity within a formal government structure."[2] But it has also been pointed out that this "unity in diversity" that gives Sudan its special character and that the interaction of all the various elements creates the special mood of Sudan.[3] In any case, as 'Ali A. Mazrui put it, Sudan turned out to be an area of "multiple marginality," comprising many diverse human settings yet central to none.[4]

Against this background, one may better understand the deep religious, ethnic, and cultural schism that has unceasingly plagued Sudanese society and state, dominating even the political and socioeconomic spheres. The principal rift lies between the country's two largest and most starkly dissimilar human blocks: the Arab Muslim majority, concentrated in the north-center of the country, and the sub-Saharan African minority, which includes Christians and animists, who live mostly in the south.

At the time of independence, the Arab Muslim community constituted less than 60 percent of the population.[5] The elite of this community, as the sole effective player in the national political arena, considered itself the only legitimate ruler. This monocentrism drew additional strength from the legacy of Muhammad and the Arab Muslims' historical experience. Naturally, this elite's experience of national struggle against British-Egyptian condominium rule, and its realization of the right to self-determination, strengthened its collective consciousness, further enhancing its national solidarity and, consequently, its hegemonic inclinations.

In contrast, the large non-Arab and non-Muslim minority in the south lacked cultural, religious, or political coherence. This geographically dispersed population was plagued by ethnic loyalties and regional and economic rivalries. Furthermore, the Christians and animists of the south, though all of sub-Saharan African origin, did not share a common language. Most spoke not Arabic but one of the many vernacular, mostly African, languages, or English. These linguistic and ethnic features, although not intrinsically unifying, underscored the south's orientation as an integral part of the sub-Saharan black African continent. The north diverges here, in that it has traditionally perceived itself as a vital, inseparable part of the Arab Muslim Middle East. Consequently, then, it is both appropriate and convenient to refer to members of the non-Muslim, non-Arab minority and members of the ruling Muslim Arab majority as southerners and northerners, respectively.

In the middle lives another non-Arab and (partly) non-Muslim minority—the Nuba sub-Saharan African people. While many are animists, large groups have converted to Islam or Christianity. This community of about one million people lives in the mountains of southern Kordofan, in the center of the country, between the Arab Muslim north and the non-Arab and non-Muslim south.[6] The true ethnic, cultural, and religious boundary between non–Muslim sub-Saharan Africa and the Muslim Arab world runs through the Nuba Mountains, not, as commonly believed, along the informal border between the north and the south of Sudan. Notwithstanding the Nuba minority's significant position in the ethnic, religious, political, and military makeup of Sudan, it and other non-Arab (but Muslim) minorities are outside the scope of this discussion.

This chapter will focus on and analyze the case of the non-Muslim and non-Arab minority in the south—one of the most crucial and explosive issues on the public agenda of the Sudanese state, regime, and society. It will examine the roots of the structures and ideas that shaped the ethnopolitics of Sudan.[7]

Strong Conflict of Identities:
North Versus South

The formal transformation of Sudan into a full-fledged Islamic republic on the eve of 1991 exacerbated the already thorny relationship between the non-Muslim minority in the south and the ruling Muslim majority in the north.[8] Yet the new Islamization act, which formally excluded the south, was not the result of any new dramatic policy shift. The reimplementation of the shari'a Islamic law was merely another reflection, albeit a most conspicuous one, of the deeply rooted Muslim Arab identity of the governing majority in Khartoum, and of its conviction that the postcolonial state should be molded in accordance with Islamic principles. This position drew its legitimacy from the prophet's legacy regarding the superiority of *Dar al-Islam* (the Muslim society) over *Dar al-Harb* (the non-Muslim society) and the consequent holy duty of the Muslim Arab majority to incorporate the non-Muslim minority into its ranks.

Moreover, Sudan's Muslim Arab identity is deeply anchored in its pre-independence history. Dating back to the Turko-Egyptian era of 1821–1881, it was significantly strengthened under the Mahdist jihadist state during the years 1881–1898. Although direct Arab and Islamic pressure on minority groups subsided during the Anglo-Egyptian condominium of 1899–1955, it was during this period that the Arab Muslim identity of "the state in formation" was consolidated. Naturally, therefore, when Sudan gained independence in 1956, the Arab Muslim elite, which was the only effective player on the local stage, defined the state's identity as Islamic-Arab. All succeeding Sudanese regimes, whatever their ideological and political orientations, adopted this definition.

In the southern community, however, it was only on the eve of independence and in its aftermath that a native leadership began to emerge and that a distinct southern identity began to develop along with local and ethnic identities. This was the cumulative result of long exposure to both British rule and domination by the Arab Muslim north.

The British referred to the south as a distinct political, economic, administrative, and cultural unit, separate from the north but still a part of the overall Sudanese territory. The British had even considered uniting south Sudan with its Ugandan or Kenyan colonial possessions, or granting it a unique status within the British Empire. Consistent with their perception of the south's distinctness, the British promoted, only in the south, the spread of Christianity and the English language. They even enacted a formal separation policy, preventing northerners and others from entering the south and forbidding southerners to bear Arab names or to wear Arab clothing. The British even declared Sunday the official day of worship in the south, replacing Friday, which had been the day of rest throughout Sudan. The British contributed significantly to the south's ethnic and religious character and to the building of a young, educated, though relatively small, southern elite. Their policies provided this elite with a basic common ground and, most important, a means of communication among themselves and with the north.

The Arab Muslim north contributed more to the southern Sudanese identity than Britain. As Sarah Voll and John Voll pointed out, the sense of southern identity, over and above local group identity, has developed "especially as a product of north-south tensions and interactions."[9] Indeed, it was primarily the unrelenting effort of the northern elite to realize its own self-determination, a process in which the south was not a partner, and the north's aspirations to control the state's power centers that provoked and later fueled the south's antagonism and sense of collective belonging. The south perceived as a serious threat the north's determination to monopolize political and economic resources and dictate the state's cultural and religious identity. This, in turn, rallied the south, turning it into a community of shared grievances, thus providing it with a negative basis for unity, rather than a positive common denominator. The south feared the impending Arab Muslim domination, anxious lest a new colonial regime prove worse than its predecessor. Recalling the atmosphere of the eve of independence from British rule, the southern Sudanese novelist and scholar, Francis Mading Deng, wrote about "fears of the impending return to the days of the slave trade when the Arabs of the north had raided African tribes to the south for slaves."[10]

A succession of actions by the north further heightened the south's anxiety and lent additional credibility to its concern. An important conference that convened in Cairo in 1952 to discuss the form of self-government for Sudan was symptomatic. British, Egyptian, and north Sudanese participated in the conference; the south was not represented. The southern elite responded with an ethnic mobilization to secure the south's share in the spoils of the colonial legacy. It was at that stage that the process of "supertribalization," as Bayo Adekson terms it, or what might more appropriately be termed "superethnization," began to unfold.[11]

But the ruling Arab Muslim majority, motivated and even intoxicated by its sense of power, largely ignored this rising tide of indignation and maintained its hegemony. The south protested violently, first in a confined military uprising in 1955, and several years later in a long armed struggle that gradually escalated to civil war. This, in turn, sharpened what Huntington called the "we/they distinction," so vital in understanding communal conflicts.[12]

As the armed conflict raged throughout the 1960s and early 1970s, the south presented to the central government in Khartoum a wide range of demands aimed at settling the country's chronic strife. The list of demands included a call to incorporate the south into the state's political and economic systems, and a call for a de jure and de facto recognition of its special religious and cultural position, providing it with some regional autonomy. Most radical was the demand to separate the south from the Sudanese mother state. But the very narrow base for this demand in the south itself, combined with outright rejection by the north and by the Organization for African Unity (OAU), which sanctified the state's boundaries, all led to the rapid, although not final, withdrawal of this demand from the south's agenda.

Meanwhile, successive Sudanese governments persisted in maintaining tight control over state power and identity. They did, however, make some attempts to involve the south in the state's political institutions and to allow it a share of its economic resources. Nevertheless, these were basically symbolic gestures that failed to defuse the south's bitterness.

By 1972, after more than a decade of bloodshed, the two warring sides had reconciled themselves to the limits of their power. Recognizing their inability to win on the battlefield, they accepted a political compromise. This took the form of a peace agreement that endowed the south with regional self-government within a unified state. The "regional self-government" arrangement was aimed at providing both sides with a political and constitutional model for coexistence, notwithstanding their enduring enmity, different basic characteristics, and conflicting interests.

It was not long before strong tensions re-emerged. Toward the end of the 1970s, southern circles became increasingly frustrated over the central government's nation-building, or national unity, policy, with its declared aim of integrating the non-Muslim and non-Arab southern minority into the power centers of the state. This policy failed to satisfy the south's aspirations. The north's self-interested policy of "unity in diversity," on its own rigid terms, clashed with the south's growing pressure for a greater and unconditional share of the state's economic resources and political management, fueling the conflict. In effect, the nation-building process had achieved the opposite of its intent, forming subidentities and sharp divisions rather than a united Sudanese society. Growing political and economic pressure upon the regime and social and economic pressure upon the whole of Sudanese society further intensified the strain and animosity between and within the societies of the south and the north. In the early 1980s Sudanese president Ja'far Muhammad al-Numayri, in power since 1969 and the leader who had signed the peace agreement with the south, shifted emphasis from the country's management to religious and personal affairs, mainly as a result of accumulating political fatigue, further eroding these relations. Though stated in a different context, Alfred Cobban's reference to a society's transition from "state making to . . . state breaking," seemed to be increasingly applicable to Sudan.[13]

Religion in North-South
Relations and State Politics

For years, conventional wisdom held that the religious factor, namely the enforcement of Islam, had played a crucial role in rekindling and fueling the south-north war. Although this assumption wrongly ignored or minimized other important sources of strong mutual enmity (such as sharply conflicting political interests, acute economic inequalities, the lingering sense of deprivation in the south, different cultural and ethnic affiliations, and diverse social structures), nothing quite touched the nerves of both communities like the religious issue. Not surprisingly, therefore, religion tops the country's public agenda, often serving as a litmus test for other, no less important, aspects of south-north relations. Thus, the prominence of the religious issue on the south-north, or minority-majority, axis and on Khartoum's political stage, and its eclipsing, albeit unjustly, of other critical bones of contention, justifies a special discussion.

In early September 1983—several months after the re-eruption of the war in the south—Numayri imposed the shari'a Islamic law as the core of a new legal system throughout Sudan. It was the first time in the short history of the state that such a move had been made. The president embarked on a series of demonstrative actions to dramatically inculcate the Islamization spirit to the public and reap political gains at the same time. Most interesting of these was the release of 13,000 prisoners who had not been convicted in accordance with Islamic law. Though approximately 3,000 non-Muslim southerners were among those released, this amnesty did not ease the south's chronic anxiety regarding the Islamization process.[14] Wishing to head off the shari'a law, while at the same time manipulating it to mobilize moral and political support for its cause within secular circles in Khartoum, in sub-Saharan Africa, and especially in the West, the south forcefully announced its opposition to the shari'a implementation. To shore up their opposition, southerners staged demonstrations in Juba and other places in the south. Southern students at Khartoum University—one of the south's most politically conscious elites—went further by accusing Numayri of "selling the country to the Muslim Brothers [who] have been pointing their fingers at the south," saying that the south's "existence as a distinct entity with African cultures, beliefs and morals poses a danger to national unity and a stumbling block to the expansion of Arab neo-colonialism in Africa."[15] The southerners' fears of the powerful Muslim Brothers were understandable in view of the latter's prominence in Sudanese politics, Numayri's political dependence upon them during the first half of the 1980s, and their demand to turn Sudan into an Islamic state.

Aware of the south's importance as a source of backing for the regime, as evidenced by its significant support of Numayri during the serious coup attempt of July 1976, the Sudanese president tried to soothe the southerners' tempers. Though never doubting the righteousness and legitimacy of the imposition of shari'a, he stated:

> we shall maintain the rights of non-Muslims who will enjoy peace, protection and benevolence. We will not tolerate any violation of the non-Muslims' rights or any violation of their personal freedom or of the principles of justice and equity. . . . We will not allow incitement of religious antagonism and conflicts. . . . We will maintain coexistence of Muslims with all believers in other holy books.[16]

In an October 1983 statement, the president's office emphasized to the south that "non-Muslims are not subjected to punishments outlined in the new penal code for offences such as drinking alcohol, adultery, and adultery libel. . . . Penalties for those offences are imposed only on Muslims." However, the statement added that "the new penal code has prohibited alcohol drinking for Muslims and intoxication and causing disturbance for *all people irrespective of their religions.* Dealing in alcoholic drinks is *also prohibited for both Muslims and non-Muslims*" (emphasis mine).[17] The ambivalence in the president's statements, combined with the Muslim Brothers' demand that Islamic laws be enforced "on all Sudanese citizens, even on the non-Muslim minorities, with no exception," further alarmed the south.[18] The first amputations to be carried out according to the shari'a law, in 1983–1984, and the case of an Italian Christian citizen who was flogged, fined, and imprisoned on the charge of dealing in alcoholic drinks in late spring 1984, intensified anxiety in the south.[19]

Sharp dissent over the implementation of shari'a law soon became the driving force of war between the south and the north. Yet both sides were fully aware that the underlying cause of hostilities went much deeper.

In a way, it was the south that, in spring 1984, accentuated the religious issue, eclipsing other, more crucial sticking points between the two communities. The south found this issue morally and politically expedient in furthering its cause against the north.

The political and military force leading the south's renewed struggle against the north in 1983 was the Sudanese People's Liberation Movement and Army (SPLM/SPLA). Led by John Garang De-Mbior of the Dinka (the largest ethnic group in the south), the SPLM/SPLA originally defined itself as a unionist movement dedicated to the creation of a secular, united Sudan. The only significant representative of the south, it clearly wished to resolve the conflict within the Sudanese political sphere. Garang's movement, later known mainly as the SPLA, has since raised the flag of a national struggle, involving all Sudanese, irrespective of religion.

Despite its frequently stressed opinion that religion must no longer be used for political aims, the SPLA itself continued to wave the banner of religion while fighting Khartoum. The SPLA accused Numayri's government of lies regarding the nonapplication of Islamic penalties to Christians. In spring 1984, for example, it claimed that "four Christians from the south were among those who had their hands cut off in Khartoum."[20] Numayri's statement that "the state has the right to punish the wrongdoers whether they are Sudanese, foreigners, or non-Muslims," further agitated the south but also served to justify its struggle against the north.[21]

After the overthrow of the Numayri regime in April 1985, the Islamization process was plainly neglected. During the one-year transition rule of General 'Abd al-Rahman Muhammad Hasan Siwar al-Dhahab, the shari'a controversy was virtually, though not formally, shelved, due mainly to the new leadership's preoccupation with consolidating its power, coping with the immediate, distressing economic problems, and stabilizing Khartoum's political arena. Nevertheless, the south continued to demand, among other things, the immediate formal repeal of the shari'a law as a condition for opening any dialogue with Dhahab, and that Khartoum refer to the armed conflict as the "problem of Sudan" instead of "the so-called problem of southern Sudan."

On another level, talks were held toward the end of Dhahab's rule between the SPLA and the Alliance of National Forces for the National Salvation of Sudan—a grouping representing the professional elite and various political parties that emerged on the political scene on the eve of Numayri's overthrow. The talks produced an agreement, known as the Koka Dam Declaration, in March 1986. Among its points was the agreement to repeal the 1983 shari'a law and all other laws that restricted freedom. Another noteworthy demand was the abrogation of military pacts concluded between Sudan and Libya, and Sudan and Egypt, which the declaration's signatories thought impinged on Sudan's national sovereignty.[22] For some obscure reason, the SPLA failed to include the south's otherwise explicit demand for a greater share in the national economic and political pie. In any case, it was clear once again that the shari'a issue was neither the sole nor primary source of antagonism between the two communities. Reached on the eve of a new government in Khartoum, the Koka Dam agreement, as well as the shari'a dispute, lingered on into the next political era.

During Sadiq al-Mahdi's democratic government (1986–1989), the struggle over the status of the shari'a took a new turn. Once polarized along the south-north axis, the dispute had spread laterally to entangle the politics of the north. In effect, it became the focus of Khartoum's political life, obscuring other major domestic issues, including the most alarming economic turmoil and the war in the south. The centrality of the shari'a issue stemmed not from its religious significance but from its political impact on the state's leadership.

Mahdi, the democratically elected prime minister and veteran leader of the strongest political force, the Umma Party (UP), inherited the Koka Dam agreement. Though he praised it, he could not meet the agreement's demands. Repealing the shari'a law would have been costly in both the short and long term. Such an action would have most probably provoked the militant National Islamic Front (NIF), led by Hasan 'Abdallah al-Turabi. A breakaway faction of the Muslim Brothers in the aftermath of Numayri's downfall, the NIF had become the third most significant force in Khartoum's politics, persistently demanding the reinforcement of the shari'a nationwide. Moreover, he could hardly afford to cancel the military agreements with Egypt and Libya while Ethiopia was increasingly supporting the SPLA.

While Mahdi did not dare take any formal steps to change the virtually stalemated status of the shari'a law, by his inaction he further neutralized the Islamization policy. In spite of strong pressures, he did not endorse the agreement signed by the southern SPLA and the Democratic Unionist Party (DUP, the second most significant force in Khartoum's politics) in November 1988. This agreement emphasized the two sides' eagerness to convene the national constitutional conference on 31 December 1988, on condition, above all, that the government formally freeze the implementation of the controversial shari'a law until that time. Mahdi knew that meeting this condition would infuriate the NIF. The latter opposed the SPLA-DUP agreement and insisted upon the immediate reinforcement of the shari'a law. NIF leaders repeatedly declared their determination to continue "the battle" until the Mahdi government's fall "or until it changes its decisions to obstruct the shari'a."[23] All in all, Mahdi's government was helpless against the NIF, as it was on all other domestic fronts. On 30 June 1989, Brigadier General 'Umar Hasan Ahmad al-Bashir launched a military coup and seized power in Khartoum.

Soon after seizing power, Bashir announced his objection to the Koka Dam and SPLA-DUP agreements. In other words, he unequivocally objected to the repeal of the shari'a law. Instead, he offered to hold a nationwide referendum on the divisive issue of the shari'a if the problem could not be resolved through negotiations. The SPLA flatly rejected Bashir's offer, stating that "it is blasphemous to say that God's laws should be judged by human beings."[24] This argument did not necessarily reflect the SPLA's real stand. It might have been merely a tactic to eliminate the referendum idea. In any case, a fair plebiscite seemed impossible, owing to more than the chaos in the south. Because more than half of the Sudanese population were Muslims, the results of a referendum were predictable, that is, to the non-Muslim south's clear disadvantage. Nevertheless, an attempt was made to negotiate in Addis Ababa in mid-August 1989, but the negotiations promptly broke down, in part over the inflexible views on the shari'a issue. The SPLA consequently stated that the collapse of the talks exposed the real nature of the new rulers, being "Muslim fundamentalist."[25]

In 1990, a more self-confident regime felt free to expose its militant Islamic orientation, virtually identical to that of the NIF. Turabi even stated that his party had engineered Bashir's coup and that the NIF would devote itself to turning Sudan into a strictly Islamic state.[26] The government soon adopted an

Islam-inspired punitive policy, as evidenced by several executions for illegal currency, drug dealings, and floggings. In addition, alcohol was banned; shops and public buildings were closed during *jum'a* (Friday) prayers; government banks were ordered to conduct business only with Islamic banks; women's employment was allegedly limited mainly to the welfare field; segregation of the sexes in public transport was instituted; and Sudan's traditionally liberal, secular civil servants were systematically replaced by NIF activists. Masses of NIF affiliates joined the army, reflecting the increased role of Islam in public life. The imposition of Islam on many facets of public and private life accommodated the core assumption of the Sudanese Islamic movement that only through strict and uncompromising adherence to Islamic principles can society achieve social and economic progress and political autonomy. As expected, the regime in Khartoum refused to consider a repeal of the shari'a law. The south continued to demand the repeal of the shari'a as the prerequisite for any negotiation.

In early 1991, more determined than its predecessors to fortify the state's Muslim Arab identity, the Bashir regime reinforced the shari'a law, suspended since Numayri's overthrow. Trying not to aggravate tensions with the non-Muslim south—a thorn in the regime's side—Bashir stated that the legal system in the south would remain unchanged "in the meantime."[27] However, Bashir did not specify how long this would be, nor did he clarify whether the shari'a would apply to the non-Muslims, mostly southerners, living in the north (roughly estimated at two million to three million).

Encouraged by Turabi's NIF, Bashir and his media projected the impression that the country was entering a new, promising phase. They depicted the people as being swept up by a powerful Islamic wind. Stirring *Mubaya'at* (oath-of-allegiance ceremonies) for *qa'id al-Umma* (the leader of the Islamic nation) swept the country and heightened the euphoric atmosphere of Islam ascendant. The reimplementation of the shari'a had turned the Sudanese state from one merely governed by a Muslim majority to a full-fledged, formally Islamic one—a dramatic change of status both de jure and de facto. The change clearly came at the expense of the non-Muslim minority in the south. It also minimized those universal elements of the modern nation-state that generally accommodate minorities and, in this case, had benefited secular Muslim circles in the north. Hence, Islamicizing the country once again threatened the sensitive religious status of the south.

Meanwhile, new developments affected the south-north axis. In mid-1991, the SPLA lost its sole source of political and military backing, the Ethiopian regime of Mengistu Haile Mariam. This was a serious blow, as the SPLA lost its headquarters in Addis Ababa, its rear bases, and its supply routes. It could no longer broadcast from its radio station on Ethiopian territory. Hundreds of thousands of southern Sudanese refugees fled Ethiopia, as did the top SPLA officials, including Garang who escaped to Kenya. This dramatic turn of events rapidly weakened the SPLA's position. The ensuing power struggle and ideological and ethnic rivalries plagued the southern movement, significantly reducing its ability to fight Khartoum in general, and the repeal of the shari'a law in particular. During the first half of the 1990s, the effectiveness of the shari'a law had become a fait accompli, but Garang's SPLA had no choice but to shift emphasis from this issue to the more immediate struggle for political survival.

The South's Call for Self-Determination

The shari'a controversy reappeared from time to time on the south-north agenda of talks; however, neither side changed its position. During the Abuja (Nigeria) negotiations of 26 May 1992 to 5 June 1992, for example, Khartoum pledged to exempt the non-Muslim south from the shari'a law. This did not satisfy the south, whose representatives insisted that the political structure of the country should be "based on multi-party democracy, secularism and equality of all people before the law," not on religious law. Failing this, Garang's mainstream SPLA warned, it would seriously consider self-determination.[28] The breakaway SPLA faction under Riek Mashar's leadership appeared even more radical at that stage, professing that the only solution to the south-north conflict was secession. In September 1994, Mashar's faction went so far as to rename itself the South Sudan Independence Movement (SSIM), with its military arm to be called the South Sudan Independence Army (SSIA).

It bears mention here that secessionist demands do not necessarily lead to separation. They may instead pave the way to a redefinition of the relationship with the central government, on the basis of a greater share in the state's power. A case in point involves the Anya-Nya, the southern movement that fought the northern "Arab enemy" throughout the late 1960s and early 1970s. Initially it declared the right of self-determination as the clear and straightforward goal of its struggle but eventually compromised on the formula of regional self-government for the south in 1972.[29]

Since late 1993, however, the SPLA's call for the right of self-determination has steadily gained momentum, precipitating a growing political radicalization in the south. The declaration signed in Washington in October 1993 under the formal aegis of the United States by the SPLA clearly attested to this trend. It stressed, for the first time since the rekindling of the war a decade earlier, "the right of self-determination for the people of Southern Sudan, Nuba Mountains and marginalized areas."[30]

Garang's call for self-determination in late 1993 and early 1994 raised the question of motive: Did it indicate that he was abandoning the long-held preference for the reunification of the south with the rest of the country if certain conditions were met? Or was the new position merely a tactic aimed at improving Garang's political standing in the south, in his own movement and vis-à-vis Khartoum? After all, it was the principle of self-determination that was winning increasing popularity for Mashar's splinter group, possibly prompting Garang to adopt the same principle in order to regain political support in the south. Moreover, by advocating self-determination, Garang moved closer politically and ideologically to the splinter faction, hoping thereby to eliminate, or at least reduce, his rival's political attractiveness and motivation to continue opposing him. Adopting self-determination could also placate critics in Garang's own faction, who pressed for a radical secessionist stand. Garang may have also hoped that this ideological turnabout would increase the pressure on Khartoum. His movement's growing radicalism would presumably draw a more conciliatory tone from the regime at the negotiation table. At the same time, however, one cannot dismiss the possibility that Garang's newly professed self-determination principle marked a real ideological shift and revised perception of the south-north conflict.

As time elapsed, and despite Garang's sporadic statements throughout 1995 that the SPLA was not fighting for "a separatist state" but for "a united Sudan," the SPLA seemed to increasingly lean toward the self-determination option in the meaning of secession.[31]

Throughout 1994–1995, Garang continued to wave the banner of self-determination while Khartoum reiterated its refusal to negotiate that demand. Garang's SPLA and a wide spectrum of the northern opposition produced a declaration of political agreement in Asmara, Eritrea, in December 1994, wherein all parties agreed that the self-determination principle would have to be the basis of any long-term political solution to the south-north conflict.

In June 1995 those same parties met again in Asmara for a weeklong conference. There they declared their commitment to the future implementation of the right of self-determination for all the people of Sudan, not only for the southern population but also the people of Abyei District, the Nuba Mountains, and the Igessina Hills—mostly of sub-Saharan African origin and partly of non-Muslim affiliation. Thus, the south retained the option of either voting for separatism or maintaining the confederal pattern of relations with the central government in Khartoum at a future referendum. They intended this confederation to be implemented at the end of an interim period of no more than four years from the anticipated fall of Bashir's regime. During this interim period, the agreement further stressed, Sudan would be ruled on the basis of decentralization. The south "will have a confederal relationship with the central government in Khartoum, while the regions of northern Sudan will have a federal relationship with the center," it proclaimed.[32]

The SPLA call for self-determination was apparently influenced by the case of neighboring Eritrea, which won independence in 1993 after a long armed struggle. Southerners pointed to Eritrea's success as an obvious precedent for southern Sudan. The saliency of ethnicity and other related topics in reshaping the political life and the status of the state in Eastern Europe at the end of the 1980s and early 1990s, led by the collapse of the Soviet Union, enhanced the appeal of the self-determination option to the southern Sudanese. As one might expect, Bashir's government has categorically rejected self-determination for the south, regarding it as a slippery slope that would inevitably lead to the division of Sudan.

Whatever its underlying causes, this shift in the SPLA's position illustrates that political, rather than religious motivations have driven the south-north conflict. Below the surface lies a broad cluster of issues pertinent to pluralistic societies undergoing a process of national integration. Still, the centrality of Islam to all Sudanese regimes should not be underestimated, nor the divisive impact of having an overwhelmingly Muslim north and non-Muslim south. Islam has been the common denominator for the otherwise diverse northern population, whereas opposition to Islamization served as a primary rallying point for the non-Muslim, extremely heterogeneous society of the south.

In the mid-1990s Bashir's regime was enthusiastically furthering its radical Islamic ideological goals by applying the shari'a law to nearly all aspects of life. This, combined with repeated statements that the implementation of Islamic law was nonnegotiable, made academic the issue of whether the process was legitimate.

To sum up, the minority-majority, or south-north, conflict is essentially a struggle between two starkly different societies to define the state's identity and, as far as the south is concerned, to maintain its own in the face of the rising tide of Islam. Chronic stratification, primarily in the realm of political and economic power, has fostered and prolonged the conflict.

It could be defined as a struggle between Africanism and Arabism, or in the words of a southern Sudanese scholar, a conflict between "two identities with differing perspectives on the universe."[33] Nevertheless, the religious component of identity is central to both.

Charles W. Anderson, a scholar who examined crises in religiously pluralistic societies, concluded that religion, though often not the primary cause of a conflict, might "by positing a divine imperative for communal identity, remove differentiation from the plane of human rationality or debate. Then, conflict can become invested with a mandate from heaven and be pursued as a holy duty."[34] It seems, to a great extent, that this was the case in Sudan in the 1990s.

Notes

1. Sarah Potts Voll and John Obert Voll, *The Sudan: Unity and Diversity in a Multicultural State* (Boulder, Colo.: Westview, 1985), p. 7.

2. Harold D. Nelson, *Area Handbook for the Democratic Republic of Sudan* (Washington, D.C.: Government Printing Office, 1973), p. 1.

3. Voll and Voll, *The Sudan,* p. 1.

4. 'Ali A. Mazrui, "The Multiple Marginality of the Sudan," in Y. F. Hasan (ed.), *Sudan in Africa: Studies Presented to the First International Conference Sponsored by the Sudan Research Unit,* 7–12 February 1968 (Khartoum: Khartoum University Press, 1971), pp. 240–255.

5. Oliver Albino, *The Sudan: A Southern Viewpoint* (London: Oxford University Press, 1970), pp. 3–4, quoting Sudan's 1956 population census. The southerners constituted 30 percent of the total population of 10,231,507. According to various estimates, this proportion is still valid.

6. *Sudan: Country Report,* no. 4 (London: The Economist Intelligence Unit, 1992).

7. For a comprehensive discussion of ethnopolitics in the Middle East, see Gabriel Ben-Dor, "Ethnopolitics and the Middle Eastern State," in Milton J. Esman and Itamar Rabinovich (eds.), *Ethnicity, Pluralism, and the State in the Middle East* (Ithaca, N.Y.: Cornell University Press, 1988), pp. 71–92.

8. For more details on Sudan's transformation, see Yehudit Ronen, "Sudan," *Middle East Contemporary Survey (MECS),* vol. 15 (1991), pp. 643–644.

9. Voll and Voll, *The Sudan,* p. 7.

10. Francis Mading Deng, *The Cry of the Owl* (New York: Lilian Barber Press, 1989), p. 45.

11. Bayo J. Adekson, "Ethnicity, the Military, and Domination," *Plural Societies* 9, no. 1 (spring 1978), p. 100. For another interesting discussion on the role of ethnicity in mobilizing postcolonial societies in Africa to "fight" for their share in the state's resources, see, for example, Pierre van den Berghe, "Ethnicity: The African Experience," *International Social Science Journal* 23, no. 4 (April 1971); Nelson Kasfir, *The Shrinking Political Arena: Participation and Ethnicity in African Policies with a Case Study of Uganda* (Berkeley: University of California Press, 1976), chapters 2–3.

12. Samuel P. Huntington, "Civil Violence and the Process of Development," *Adelphi Papers,* no. 83 (1972), pp. 10–11.

13. Alfred Cobban, *National Self-Determination* (Chicago: University of Chicago Press, 1944), p. xi.

14. *Al-Nahar Arab Report and Memo* (Beirut and Zurich, weekly), 10 October 1983; *Al-Majalla* (London, weekly), 8–14 October 1983.

15. *Africa Now* (London, monthly), November 1983.

16. Sudanese News Agency (SUNA, Khartoum official news agency), 13 October—Foreign Broadcasting Information Service: Near East and South Asia, Daily Report (DR), 14 October 1983, Numayri's speech to the nation.

17. SUNA, 17 October—DR, 18 October 1983.

18. A statement by Dr. Hasan 'Abdallah al-Turabi, veteran leader of the Muslim Brothers, in *al-Sahafa* (Khartoum, daily), 2 October 1983. Since the advent to power in a military coup of the Bashir regime, Turabi has been considered the force behind the throne. In 1996 he was elected speaker of the National Assembly.

19. *Al-Siyasa* (Kuwait, daily), 1 June 1984.

20. A statement by Joseph Oduho, a senior southern politician, in Paris, *Le Monde* (Paris, daily), 27 April—DR, 3 May 1984.

21. SUNA, 20 July—DR, 23 July 1984.

22. For the full text of the declaration, see Sudanese People's Liberation Army (SPLA), 28 March—British Broadcasting Corporation, Summary of World Broadcasting (SWB): The ME (Middle East) and Africa, 1 April 1986.

23. Al-Fatih 'Abdun, a central NIF figure, *al-Sharq al-Awsat* (London, Jidda, and Riyadh, daily), 4 May 1989.

24. Yehudit Ronen, "Sudan," *MECS,* vol. 13 (1989), p. 620.

25. Radio SPLA, 3 September—DR, 7 September 1989.

26. *Al-Qabas* (Kuwait, daily), 26 March 1990, interview with Hasan 'Abdallah al-Turabi.

27. *Al-Inqadh al-Watani* (Khartoum, daily), 5 January 1991.

28. *Sudan Democratic Gazette* (London, monthly, close to Garang's SPLA), July 1992.

29. *Anya-Nya: What We Fight For,* Anya-Nya Armed Forces, South Sudan Liberation Movement, 1972, p. 10.

30. For the text of the document, see *Sudan Democratic Gazette,* November 1993.

31. The Beirut-based daily *al-Safir,* 23 June 1995, and Middle East Broadcasting Corporation Center (MBC) TV, 10 November—SWB, 13 November 1995.

32. *Sudan Democratic Gazette,* August 1995.

33. Dunstan M. Wai, *The African-Arab Conflict in the Sudan* (New York: Africana Publishing Company, 1981), p. 1.

34. Charles W. Anderson, Fred R. Von der Mehden, and Crawford Young (eds.), *Issues of Political Development* (Englewood Cliffs, N.J.: Prentice-Hall, 1967), p. 26.

PART TWO

The Levant

5

The Palestinians in Jordan: Demographic Majority, Political Minority

Asher Susser

The Palestinians in Jordan differ in many respects from other minorities in the Arab world. First of all, numerically they are not a minority. It is now generally accepted that they constitute just over half of Jordan's population. Politically, however, in terms of their representation in the power structure of the state, they are a minority.

The Palestinians are neither a religious minority like the Copts in Egypt and the 'Alawis in Syria nor an ethnic minority like the Kurds in Iraq. The Palestinians, like their Jordanian compatriots, are Arabs. Most are Sunni Muslims, and only a small minority (less than 10 percent) are Christian Arabs (mainly Greek Orthodox).

The Palestinian-Jordanian cleavage is a twentieth-century phenomenon. It is a product of state formation and modernization in the Middle East in the aftermath of the dissolution of the Ottoman Empire, and of the Jewish-Arab conflict in Palestine and the broader Arab-Israeli conflict. Compared to the intra-religious cleavage between Sunnis and Shi'is, the inter-religious one between Muslims and Christians, and ethnic differences between Kurds and Arabs—all of which go back centuries—the Palestinian-Jordanian cleavage has relatively shallow historical roots. Moreover, the modern-day nationalist cleavage is mitigated by the traditional or primordial common identities of the religious community that have not been superseded by the more modern territorial-state identities. In some important social spheres, the primordial attachments still reign supreme.

Corporate identities along religious and ethnic lines continue to serve as important social distinctions, and in this respect, Jordanians and Palestinians hardly differ. It is therefore very common, for example, for Jordanians and Palestinians to intermarry. Jordanian and Palestinian Muslims intermarry fre-

91

quently, as do Jordanian and Palestinian Christians. Muslims marrying Christians, however, remains rare.

All the same, the modern-day cleavage of national identity has assumed considerable political importance in Jordan. The historical experience of Jordanians and Palestinians, though linked, has been markedly different, producing divergent senses of national consciousness. It was the Arabs of Palestine who bore the brunt of the confrontation with Zionism, and it was their traumatic defeat in 1948, the loss of their homeland, and their dispersal that were the crucial formative components of their unique collective historical experience and identity.

For the most part, the new states that emerged in the Middle East in the aftermath of World War I were rather artificial creations. Nevertheless, a sense of territorial identity and loyalty to the state has developed over the years as new "nation-states" have come into being, with the formation of state institutions, bureaucracies, and political and military elites. This is as true of Jordan and the Jordanians as it is elsewhere in the Arab world. The Palestinians, however, are in a category unto themselves. They have developed a sense of territorial nationalism as a direct consequence of the loss of their political patrimony, rather than as a result of their uninterrupted and independent control of it, as is the case of the Jordanians and other Arab peoples. This does not make their territorial identity any less devout or genuine. If anything, it is often only more so and has frequently been in conflict with that of their Jordanian compatriots.

The political and socioeconomic components of the Jordanian-Palestinian cleavage have, however, evolved over the years. There has always been an imbalance in the power structure in favor of the original East Bank Jordanians. But this preference for East Bankers has not always had the same reasoning nor served the same purpose. Initially, the relative (never absolute) exclusion of Palestinians was, in essence, a defensive function of the mistrust toward the defeated and disenchanted Palestinian community. The Palestinians had a litany of grievances against the Hashemite monarchy, primarily because of its policies and military performance in the conflict with Israel. In later years the relative exclusion continued, but increasingly as an expression of a distinctive and assertive Jordanian national identity, or "Jordanianism."

Competing and discordant national identities are not the only components of the cleavage between Jordanians and Palestinians. Other social and political processes, some mitigating and others not, have affected the evolving relationship between the two communities. For decades the crux of the Jordanian-Palestinian divide was rooted in the divergent interests and policies of the Jordanian state and the Palestinian national movement in the Arab-Israeli conflict. More recently this divergence has all but disappeared, as Jordan and the Palestine Liberation Organization (PLO) have already come to terms with Israel, or are in the process of doing so. Concurrently, however, as one major cause for divergence has receded, another has surfaced to take its place. Inter-communal tensions are becoming increasingly evident in the socioeconomic domain, where Palestinian predominance in the private sector of the Jordanian economy is beginning to have a fractious effect.

Imbalance of Power

The Palestinian-Jordanian relationship was hardly ever smooth sailing. Politically, the Palestinians were not really fully integrated as Jordanians. Their demographic weight has never been accorded proportional representation in the institutions of state.

After the annexation of the West Bank the Palestinians had a two-thirds majority in the kingdom. Palestinians constantly migrated from the West Bank to the East Bank (the administrative and economic center), and in the wake of the 1967 war another 300,000 Palestinians left the West Bank and Gaza for the East Bank. In the East Bank alone the Palestinians totalled approximately half of the population. Since the return to Jordan of another 230,000 to 300,000 Palestinians from the Gulf in 1990–1991, they are now definitely a majority of just over half.

Although they are a majority, there have traditionally been few Palestinians in the upper decisionmaking echelons. The key personalities of the royal court, with few exceptions, are disproportionately drawn from the Hashemite family itself and from prominent Transjordanian Muslim families, tribes, and clans.[1] From the time of the annexation of the West Bank (a term coined by the Jordanians to de-emphasize its Palestinian character) to the Rabat resolutions of 1974, which recognized the PLO as the sole legitimate representative of the Palestinian people, about half the ministerial portfolios in Jordanian cabinets went to Palestinians. Since 1974, the ratio has dropped to around one-fifth. Moreover, only in exceptional cases did Palestinians assume the key posts of prime minister, interior minister (with responsibility for the domestic security organs), or information minister.[2] Since 1948 a number of Palestinians have served as prime ministers, but only for very brief interludes, during crises with the Palestinians or in caretaker cabinets.[3] All their terms combined amount to barely one year. The last of these was Tahir al-Masri, who served as prime minister from June to November 1991. His appointment was not at a time of crisis with the Palestinians nor was his a caretaker government. He might have lasted longer in office had it not been for the virulent opposition to his premiership amongst the East Bank stalwarts of the Jordanian establishment.[4]

The disproportionate distribution of political power is most readily apparent in the structure and personnel of the armed forces and the domestic security organs—the mainstay of the regime. Since the 1930s, East Bankers, and especially the Bedouin, have formed the backbone of the army combat units. Since the annexation of the West Bank, Palestinians have served in the armed forces, at times even in large numbers, but usually not in crack infantry units or in the armored corps, which have predominantly comprised Bedouin soldiers. This is all the more so in the command structure of these formations.[5]

In the early 1970s, after the civil war, the number of Palestinians in the army was reduced from around 40 percent to about 15 percent. After the introduction of conscription in 1976 the ratio rose again to approximately 30 percent. Conscription increased the number of Palestinians in the army but did not significantly alter the composition of the combat units. The training and service programs for conscripts differed from that of the career soldiers. Most of the conscripts served in office jobs and did not choose military careers once their two years of service were concluded.[6]

When conscription was introduced in 1976, Jordan was experiencing economic prosperity. However, in the late 1980s the country entered a protracted economic crisis, one of the results of which was the decision to trim the military. King Husayn called for reorganization of the armed forces with an eye to quality rather than quantity.[7] In early 1992, as part of the new cutback policy, conscription was suspended. Despite the obvious economic constraints, it is not unlikely that there were political concerns as well, primarily the desire to keep undesirable elements, such as Islamic radicals or suspect Palestinians, out of the armed forces.

Evolution of a Collective Identity

The place of the Palestinians in the Jordanian state, in terms of numbers and relative representation in the ruling elite and the nature of the Jordanian-Palestinian cleavage, should be seen within the broader context of three distinct phases of evolution of the Jordanian collective identity: the period of 'Abdallah's reign, only at the end of which did the Palestinians become part of the state in numbers of far-reaching demographic consequence; Husayn's rule over both the East and West Banks; and, last, the post-1967 era, when Jordan, in almost every practical sense, reverted to being an East Bank state.

Phase One: 'Abdallah and Arabism

In the early years of the Emirate of Transjordan, the founder of the country, the emir 'Abdallah, had no particular penchant for a Jordanian territorialist identity. On the contrary, he tended to emphasize Transjordan's Arab character and highlight Arabism as the driving force of historical consequence, with the Hashemites, naturally, at the helm. For 'Abdallah Transjordan was but a stepping-stone to Greater Syria and not much of a prize in and of itself.[8] 'Abdallah urged his followers not to identify themselves by geographical region but rather as members of the Arab nation, and thus to regard "all the Arab countries [as] the country of every Arab."[9] The ministers in his first government and the officers of the newly formed security forces were, more often than not, Arabs who hailed from other countries, such as Syria, Lebanon, Iraq, or Arabia.[10]

This, however, gave rise to domestic opposition and to what one could cautiously regard as the initial, albeit embryonic, stirrings of local Transjordanian patriotism. Both tribal leaders and "petty bourgeoisie professionals" vented their protest against this rule of outsiders. The slogan of "Transjordan for the Transjordanians" was heard for the first time.[11]

It would be an exaggeration to describe this phenomenon as a coherent form of Jordanian nationalism. No similar objection arose in later years to the many Palestinians who served in the Transjordanian bureaucracy, three of whom, Tawfiq Abu al-Huda (from Acre), Ibrahim Hashim (from Nablus), and Samir al-Rifaʻi (from Safed), alternated as prime ministers through much of 'Abdallah's reign. Their service to the regime, however, was not to the exclusion of Transjordanians. Furthermore, the longstanding historical ties between Transjordan and Palestine and the fact that these Palestinians fully integrated into the Transjordanian establishment probably made their presence more naturally acceptable than that of their non-Jordanian predecessors. Moreover, because of 'Abdallah's vision of Arabism, the early process of state building in Transjordan was not accompanied by the deliberate promotion of a Transjordanian territorial identity. Actually, 'Abdallah disliked the name Transjordan (*Sharq al-Urdunn*). He preferred, at least initially, to refer to this territory as the Arab East (*al-Sharq al-ʻArabi*), which left the Pan-Arab option open. The unified security force established in 1923 was "pointedly not called Transjordanian," but rather *al-Jaysh al-ʻArabi* (the Arab Legion), and this still remains the official name of the Jordanian Army.[12]

'Abdallah's sights were set on expansion, at most in all of Greater Syria and the Hijaz and at least in Palestine. For 'Abdallah the center of the Arab world was Greater Syria (*bilad al-sham*), with Damascus at its core. This was one naturally unified country (*Suriyya al-tabiʻiyya*), the partition of which was uncalled-for and illegitimate.[13]

'Abdallah's vision, if not to say obsession, with respect to Greater Syria, was an unrealistic ambition. It enjoyed no support of consequence in the Arab world, and even his British mentors thought little of it. 'Abdallah's greatest achievement was the stabilization and consolidation of the Jordanian state, no mean feat considering his point of departure. Although for him this remained but a means to an end, for his successors it was to become an end in itself.

By the time of 'Abdallah's assassination in 1951, the Hashemite Kingdom of Jordan (as it had been named since independence in 1946) had been radically transformed. It was no longer the dusty desert principality of 'Abdallah's early years, but a state that had expanded to include the West Bank, had tripled its population, and now had a large Palestinian majority that outnumbered the original East Bankers by two to one.

Phase Two: Husayn and the Unity of the Two Banks

During the first period of King Husayn's reign, from 1953 to 1967, the major effort of the state was directed toward the incorporation of its new Palestinian citizens—refugees and nonrefugees alike—under the banner of Hashemite Arabism. The common Arab identity was to unite Jordanians and Palestinians in one state.

The task of unification and assimilation was fraught with difficulty. The Jordanian state and the Palestinians did not share interests on the most crucial of issues. For Jordan, the post-1948 situation was more than satisfactory. Jordan did not believe in the Arabs' capacity to dislodge Israel and sought above all else to maintain the territorial status quo. Such a policy was anathema to the great majority of Palestinians, who, disgruntled, defeated, and dispersed, wished for nothing more than to overturn the status quo and to have the Arabs turn back the historical clock by eliminating Israel. Their savior, therefore, was 'Abd al-Nasir with his messianic brand of revolutionary, antimonarchist, anti-Israeli, and anti-Western Arab nationalism. The seemingly "anachronistic" Hashemite monarchy could hardly compete with the "progressive" alternative of Nasserism.

The monarchy and its Palestinian subjects were constantly at loggerheads, placing the regime on the horns of an incessant dilemma. While seeking to integrate the Palestinians, the Jordanians did not really trust them. Palestinians were, therefore, only partially integrated into the ruling elite. The Transjordanian political elite reigned supreme as the administrative centrality and economic preference of the East Bank over the West Bank were maintained throughout.

Unlike 'Abdallah, Husayn did not harbor any expansionist designs. Maintaining the integrity of the kingdom in the face of the aggressive Pan-Arab onslaught of 'Abd al-Nasir and his allies, in the Arab world and among the Palestinians, was a tall enough order in itself. As in 'Abdallah's time, Husayn did not initially promote a particularist Jordanian territorial identity, but the context was entirely different. 'Abdallah's brand of Arabism was conceived to justify expansion. For Husayn, Hashemite Arabism, drawing its inspiration and legitimacy from the pioneering role of the Arab revolt against the Ottomans in World War I, was Jordan's defensive alternative to Nasserism and the justification for Jordanian-Palestinian unity in the Hashemite Kingdom, on both banks of the Jordan.

Because Jordanian-Palestinian unity was the essence, it was customary for Husayn to declare that "Jordan is Palestine and Palestine is Jordan." This

formula of unity left no room for a separate Palestinian identity, nor for an especially Jordanian one. Under these circumstances it comes as no surprise
that the promotion of a Jordanian identity was conspicuously absent from the
textbooks of the state-run schools until 1967. Their pedagogic message was
distinctly Arab nationalist.[14]

The revival of Palestinian identity that began to gain currency in the late
1950s and early 1960s in the Arab world and among the Palestinians was, for
the Jordanians, an intolerable threat to the unity of the kingdom. It was diametrically opposed to the fundamental thrust of Jordan's policy of incorporating and assimilating the Palestinians, which required the systematic erasure of
any semblance of Palestinian nationalism or separate identity.

The war of June 1967 was a watershed in this respect, as in so many oth-
ers. The loss of the West Bank, and of Jordan's manipulative control of the
Palestinians there, ushered in a new phase in Jordanian-Palestinian relations.
The Arab-Israeli conflict was "re-Palestinized." The Jordanization of the
Palestinians was arrested and, at the same time, the Israeli occupation provided a rallying cry for a vibrant Palestinian nationalism. The eclipse of Pan-
Arabism, in the wake of 'Abd al-Nasir's shattering defeat, paved the way for
an unprecedented legitimization of territorial nationalism in the Arab world.
The panacea for the Palestinians was no longer Arab salvation but the armed
struggle of the *fida'iyyun,* the backbone of Palestinian national revival. The
impact on Jordan was profound.

The *fida'iyyun,* unable to establish themselves in the Israeli-occupied territories, deployed their forces in Jordan, creating a "state within a state." Jordanian sovereignty was steadily eroded until the inevitable bloody clash of
1970–1971, the civil war between the Jordanian army and the armed forces of
the PLO. The *fida'i* presence had aroused fears among Jordanians that the
Palestinians' hidden ambition might actually be to take over Jordan and transform it into their "alternative homeland" (*al-watan al-badil*). Even after the
Palestinian defeat in Jordan, this anxiety was rekindled in the 1970s and
1980s by the oft-asserted contention by some on the Israeli right that, because
of its Palestinian majority, Jordan was in effect the state of the Palestinians—
in other words, "Jordan is Palestine."

Phase Three: The Evolution of Jordanianism

Jordan's conflict with the Palestinians, and the civil war of 1970–1971 in particular, was more than just a struggle for political supremacy. It was a traumatic, formative experience that accelerated the coalescence and consolidation of the divergent group identities of Jordanians and Palestinians alike. It
widened the distinctive divide between the communities and endowed both
Jordanians and Palestinians with an added sense of national consciousness,
fueled by mutual mistrust and acrimony.

The policy of incorporating or assimilating the Palestinians had met with only limited success. This had ominous consequences for East Bankers. The unification of the East and West Banks and the continuous migration of Palestinians to the East Bank, instead of producing the desired integration, was now perceived by many Jordanians as a threat to their own political patrimony.

King Husayn adopted an ambivalent approach. He made a concerted effort to reinforce the particularist Jordanian loyalty, identity, and sense of statehood, but simultaneously sought to avoid alienating his Palestinian subjects and preserve at least a measure of influence over the Palestinians' political destiny.

In the aftermath of the civil war, many Palestinians were removed from the bureaucracy and the military, thus further reducing their representation in the machinery of state.[15] The king's former slogan, "Jordan is Palestine and Palestine is Jordan," was gradually superseded by "Jordan is Jordan and Palestine is Palestine," culminating in the formal disengagement from the West Bank in 1988.

In contradistinction to 'Abdallah and the first period of Husayn's reign, the regime, as of the early 1970s, initiated a deliberate inculcation of a distinctive Jordanian territorialism, national consciousness, and identity. Jordan was now in constant "search of a usable past" to promote a sense of Jordanianism.[16]

Jordanian territorialism was projected from a secular vision of history that appropriated equally the pre-Islamic and the Islamic and modern Arab history of the land that became Jordan, all embraced as vestiges of a specifically Jordanian heritage. The archaeological marvels of Roman Jarash; Petra of the Nabateans, whom the leadership in Jordan tended especially to portray as the historical predecessors of modern-day Jordanians; the Umayyad desert castles; and the tombs of the companions of the Prophet (*sahaba*) in Jordan are all regularly highlighted and injected into the people's collective consciousness through festivals and other public occasions and commemorated on banknotes and postage stamps.[17] Jordan's newest universities, Yarmuk in the north and Mu'ta in the south, established in the 1970s and 1980s, both bear the place names of historic battles waged by Islamic forces in the early seventh century on the land of Jordan against the Byzantines (in 629 and 636). All these are revived and reconstructed as an exercise in the "invention of tradition" to bolster the territorial state and to "transform it into a 'community of memory,' i.e., a nation state."[18]

Jordan's new national charter, endorsed in 1991, opens with an elaboration on the theme of Jordan throughout the ages as a wellspring of civilization, development, and prosperity, obviously formulated to dispel the notion that Jordan is an artificial creation with no real historical roots. As the charter would have it, the conscious identity of the Jordanian people was not a product of the creation of the Jordanian state, but rather a forerunner to its formation and a factor in the British failure in 1920 to "tear apart the unity of the Jordanian people" by establishing separate local governments on the East Bank for the areas of Irbid, Salt, and Karak.[19] The suggestion was that the establishment of the state was actually an act of self-determination rather than a consequence of British colonial mapmaking.

In Husayn's pronouncements, Jordan, in and of itself, is presented as a model of tolerance and political pluralism worthy of emulation.[20] Jordan is not a stepping-stone of last resort to other, greater domains, but a model in its own right for Jordanians to be proud of and for other Arabs to follow.

The promotion of Jordanian consciousness was not just a counterweight to Palestinian national fervor. It was equally intended by the monarchy to convince the Israeli right of the futility of the "Jordan is Palestine" theory. Forcefully refuting this notion, Crown Prince Hasan observed that Jordan was "not [a] waste land," nor was it the "alternative repository for the Palestinian people."[21]

Tribalism, Jordanianism, and the State

The promotion of Jordanianism has gone hand in hand with the integration of the tribes into the machinery of the state. Jordanian society has developed with an almost built-in functional cleavage, whereby the Jordanians have come to dominate the bureaucracy, the military, and domestic security, that is, the running of the state, whereas the Palestinians have attained predominance in the private sector, the financial markets, and the economy in general. Since the early years of union between the East and West Banks, Palestinians have complained about their underrepresentation in government. However, in more recent years, as the economy has faltered and the government has been induced to cut back on its own spending, it has been those on the government payroll (i.e., mainly Jordanians) who have begun to feel disadvantaged compared to many of their Palestinian compatriots.

This cleavage is deeply rooted in Jordan's political and social history. One of the most important and lasting achievements of 'Abdallah's reign was the integration of the Bedouin into the state, first and foremost through recruitment into the Arab Legion.[22] In a revolutionary turn of events, those whose traditional lifestyle had been antithetical and even hostile to any form of both centralized control and law and order were transformed into the backbone of the state.

Service in the Arab Legion contributed decisively to the transformation of tribal allegiance to loyalty to the commanding officer and ultimately to the monarch. It was the king who now took over the role of "the shaykh of shaykhs"—the supra-tribal leader.[23] The Hashemite kings of Jordan, 'Abdallah and Husayn, who trace their lineage to the Prophet, could double as religious leaders or bearers of the religious heritage, thus further augmenting their appeal to tribal soldiers.[24]

The preferential enlistment of the Bedouin not only provided poor people with career opportunities. It also served to consolidate the legitimacy of the state and to create a patron-client relationship,[25] superbly characterized as the "quintessential monarchical/tribal-military axis."[26]

As Philip Khoury and Joseph Kostiner have indicated, the process of state formation in the Middle East has led to the weakening of tribal authority and the erosion of old tribal loyalties. This has resulted in the emergence of new groupings that retain certain tribal characteristics but are also significantly "shaped by other factors, including class, ethnicity and even nationalism."[27] This is all especially true in Jordan.

The tribe as liaison between the individual and the state has given way to the state itself, which has direct access to the individual tribesmen through the wide range of services it offers. Concomitantly, the settled tribes have developed a greater vested interest in the state,[28] further reinforced by the central role the state plays in the allocation of financial resources.[29]

Consequently, new forms of tribal identity, as opposed to common perceptions of traditional tribalism, are far from antithetical to the state. On the contrary, the Bedouin have become full participants and are, generally speaking, strongly committed to the continuity and welfare of the state.[30]

Two historical processes have thus coalesced in the past generation: the evolution of Jordanianism and the integration of the tribes. In the process, it is the tribes who have become the standard-bearers of Jordanianism. According to one prominent Jordanian, "Tribalism has now changed into Jordanianism."[31] In the words of another, the youth of the East Bank have, in the last decade or so, begun to perceive their affiliation to the state as a means of "protection against the Palestinian danger. . . . The state to them is the tribe of the Jordanians versus the tribe of the Palestinians."[32]

Moreover, the state itself has consciously promoted Jordan's tribal heritage as "a symbol of Jordan's distinctive national identity . . . vis-à-vis its most distinctive other, Palestine."[33] Yet Jordanian national identity is not only a "reactive delineation against others" but is also evolving toward a positive identification with the institutions, the monarchy, the army, and the political system.[34]

Because of their symbiotic relationship with the state, the tribes have declined as autonomous power structures. Yet tribalism or tribal solidarity is still deeply entrenched in Jordan's social fabric.[35] "Family and tribe remain two of the strongest institutions in Jordanian society."[36] This has significant ramifications for Jordanian-Palestinian relations. Because the bureaucracy is preponderantly staffed by East Bankers, kinship-based patronage naturally favors other East Bankers at the expense of the Palestinians. The Jordanianized bureaucracy, or "bedoucracy" as it has been called, perpetuates itself.[37] The ability of East Bankers to obtain favors and jobs under these circumstances is far greater than that of their Palestinian compatriots, though no deliberate policy of discrimination may be intended by the monarchy itself. In practice, however, an alliance has evolved between the state and its machinery and one of the two communal groups in the country.[38]

Jordanianism and the Palestinians

The calculated promotion of Jordanian national identity, resting on the alliance with the East Bankers, was problematic in that it was not intended by the monarchy to exclude the Palestinians of the East Bank. This, of course, entailed much internal contradiction.

Jordan's Palestinian policy has gradually evolved since the early 1970s. 'Abdallah, and Husayn in his early years, sought to inherit and assimilate Arab Palestine and its people as Jordanians under the canopy of Hashemite Arabism. After 1967, however, with the steady consolidation of the Palestinian national movement, Husayn, unable to stem the tide, conceded. Jordan's role was downgraded from inheritor to mere partner. This was the essence of the ideas of federation, first proposed by Husayn in 1972, and subsequently of confederation between Jordan and a future Palestinian entity or state. Jordan had come to terms with the reality that it would not be able to restore the status quo ante in the West Bank.

The Jordanians, however, had no intention of conceding their patrimony on the East Bank. Considering the historical ties between the two banks and the demographic reality on the East Bank, this was not free of difficulty and potential irredentism. Husayn therefore was determined to simultaneously bolster a sense of Jordanianism and avoid being marginalized in the Arab-Israeli peace process by maintaining a measure of influence and input on the Palestinian track. He consequently never excluded the possibility of forming some special relationship with the Palestinian entity or state of the future, as an essential means of securing the kingdom on the East Bank. Husayn asserted repeatedly that Jordan's Palestinian citizens on the East Bank were Jordanians in every sense, fully equal to their East Banker compatriots (even though in practice they were not), and owed their unswerving allegiance to king and country. This had always been the official position, but it was even more emphatically so after the signing of the Oslo accords in the summer of 1993.

Anxious that Palestinian advances toward statehood might erode East Bank Palestinian loyalties, or alternatively spur anti-Palestinian sentiment among East Bankers, Husayn made every effort to curb a fractious rise of intercommunal tension. In the aftermath of the Oslo accords, Husayn constantly restated his time-honored formulas on Jordanian-Palestinian unity that had been the king's staple political lexicon for decades. All the people of Jordan, he professed, were members of one family, united just like the *ansar* (the Prophet's supporters in Medina) and the *muhajirun* (the Prophet's Meccan companions, who migrated with him to Medina) in the early days of Islam. Now, however, when addressing the nation, he notes especially that he is speaking to the Jordanian people "of whatever descent and origin" and warns very firmly that anyone who tampers with this national unity will become his "enemy until doomsday."[39]

Despite the king's warnings, Jordan's more liberalized political system of recent years was exposed to ultra-nationalist Jordanian rumblings that freely entered the public discourse. A Transjordanian right-wing nationalist movement, cynically referred to by its critics as the Jordanian Likud (*al-Likud al-Urdunni*), was clearly taking shape. Its spokesmen were uninhibited in their contention that "Jordan for the Jordanians" had to be protected from possible Palestinization. They were quite explicit in their view that the Palestinians in Jordan (all or many of them) should return (i.e., not as a matter of choice) to Palestine when Palestinian self-rule became a reality. Latent tensions between Jordanians and Palestinians resurfaced with a "saliency unheard of since the dark days of Black September [1970]."[40]

The origins of this school of thought were indeed in the early 1970s, provoked first by the civil war and then by the Rabat resolutions, but they were considerably more restrained at the time.[41] After all, the resolutions of the Rabat Arab summit of 1974, recognizing the PLO as the sole legitimate representative of the Palestinian people, were only a theoretical challenge to Jordan. They had no immediate operational content. The Oslo accords were another story altogether. Now some of the ultra-nationalists were seriously campaigning for the disenfranchisement of the Palestinians, who only "pretended to be Jordanians."[42] Needless to say, these positions are flatly opposed by the monarchy, nor are they shared by most East Bankers. But this kind of intercommunal tension has not abated. In recent years it seems to have even been exacerbated by the functional cleavage that divides Jordanians and Palestinians.

The Palestinians, the Economy, and the Monarchy

Because state policy has always been to absorb the Palestinians, and because their place was generally not to be found in the employ of the government, they have established their prominence in the economy. Economically, Palestinians have been very well integrated into the state and the fabric of society, and many have willingly thrown in their lot with the Jordanian kingdom.

Some Palestinians, especially refugee-camp dwellers (about 20 percent of the total refugee population and some 10 percent of the total Palestinian population in Jordan) are still reluctant to renounce their affiliation to Palestine. This "deliberate non-assimilation of Palestinians, as part of their identity building," provokes mirror-image reactions among Transjordanians.[43] It is these Palestinians (mostly 1967 refugees) whom many Jordanians, the government included, would like to see return to the Palestine of the future.

As for the rest of the Palestinians, many—especially among those who arrived in 1948–1949—have made it to the middle, upper-middle, and upper classes of Jordanian society and have by now acquired a real stake in the continued stability and security of the regime.[44] Significant segments of this Palestinian community were alienated from the PLO because of the civil war, and in recent years a variety of regional changes has reinforced this trend of Palestinian acceptance of and loyalty to the monarchy and the Jordanian state.[45]

A "sea change of sorts has occurred."[46] First of all, the major irritant in Jordan's relations with its Palestinian citizens has been mitigated considerably. In the more distant past, Jordan's relative moderation toward Israel was perceived by the Palestinians as inimical to their most basic interests and aspirations. However, in an era of Middle East peacemaking, in which the PLO is as much of a full participant as Jordan, this is no longer so. Moreover, in recent years a number of Husayn's major policy decisions have further endeared him to his Palestinian subjects: the disengagement from the West Bank in 1988, the political liberalization set in motion in 1989, and Jordan's stand alongside Iraq in the Gulf War.[47] Jordan's peace with Israel and the subsequent shift away from Iraq, though less popular, have not markedly altered the generally favorable appraisal of many Palestinians of their lives as Jordanians. Certainly in comparison to the lot of Palestinians elsewhere, their experience in Jordan under King Husayn has, for the most part, been secure, benevolent, prosperous, and difficult to improve upon elsewhere in the Arab world, including in an independent Palestine. This is so much the case that even the younger generation of Palestinians is far more "likely to express loyalty to Jordan, or at least Husayn, than ever before."[48]

The Functional Cleavage and East Banker Apprehension

Ironically, this greater Palestinian willingness to integrate is not always met with a welcoming embrace by East Bankers. Many East Bankers remain suspicious of the Palestinian presence. Palestinian loyalty to the Jordanian state is still questioned. East Bankers consequently harbor anxieties with respect to both the Palestinian demographic weight and their prominence in the economy.

A study published in Jordan in early 1995 on the Jordanian-Palestinian cleavage revealed a series of perceived impediments to the advancement of domestic cohesion.

In the opinion of citizens of Jordanian origin, the obstacles were as follows:

1. The concentration of the private business sector in the hands of citizens of Palestinian origin;
2. Fear of the increasing number of Palestinians (based not on anxieties about their natural increase but on concerns about regional developments that might lead to large-scale Palestinian migration to Jordan—induced, for example, by Israeli actions or refugee resettlement from Lebanon);
3. The dual loyalty of the Palestinians;
4. The Palestinians' ingratitude toward Jordan despite the privileges and benefits accruing from longstanding Jordanian citizenship.

In the opinion of their Palestinian compatriots the obstacles were as follows:

1. The domination of government jobs by citizens of Jordanian origin;
2. Underrepresentation of Palestinians in government and in Parliament;
3. The allocation of "sensitive" posts exclusively to Jordanians;
4. The preferential treatment accorded to Jordanians by the bureaucracy in all spheres.[49]

The functional cleavage, whereby the Jordanians control the machinery of state and the Palestinians are predominant in the economy, has clearly evolved as a fundamental feature of Jordanian society and a "main source of the fears, anxieties and concerns of Jordanians and Palestinians."[50] In recent years this cleavage has even been exacerbated.

Political liberalization has afforded the Palestinians a more influential voice in Jordanian politics. Economic liberalization, however, tends to cut back on the size and allocative nature of the state sector. Both processes have potentially negative consequences for a sizeable proportion of East Bank Jordanians.[51] The return of 230,000 to 300,000 Palestinians to Jordan from the Gulf after the Iraqi invasion of Kuwait and the Gulf War (1990–1991) introduced additional strain into the already sensitive equation. Most Jordanian migrant workers were of Palestinian extraction. Their departure reduced competition in the local job market and lessened the potential for tension or conflict.[52] Now, however, many of the returnees from the Gulf, who accumulated sufficient wealth, have established their own businesses in Jordan. They are considerably better off than Jordanians who continued to work for the government, particularly as a result of the cutbacks in government spending.[53]

Jordanians have other concerns as well. The peace treaty with Israel may result in a further downgrading of the public sector, manpower reductions in the military, and yet additional economic gain for the private sector, once more turning the East Bankers into the "economic, political and social losers."[54]

In April 1989 and again in August 1996 riots broke out in Jordan, following price hikes for basic commodities. In both cases the core of the troubles was in the more tribal south, always the bedrock of support for the regime. The Palestinians took no part in the incidents on either occasion. It would be a gross exaggeration to suggest a serious crack in the historical association and fundamental loyalty of the more tribal south to king and country. But the ramifications of the functional cleavage in an era of economic uncertainty is taking a toll that requires the regime's attention.

The intercommunal tension is palpable. At the same time, however, according to the study quoted previously, most Jordanians, both originally Jordanian and of Palestinian origin, support some form of union between Jordan and Palestine in the future (see Appendix at the end of this chapter). There is still a constituency of Jordanians who regard confederation with trepidation, fearing being overwhelmed by Palestinian numbers and economic power. However, they represent a minority.

Conclusion

Overall support for some form of union tends to reaffirm the relative historical shallowness of the communal cleavage. It is political, social, and functional, not ethnic or religious, and therefore not of the primordial nature that has withstood the challenges of modernization and remained a divisive factor in other Arab states. The cleavage in Jordan is actually a consequence and product of modernization and the concomitant political, social, and economic changes, all relatively new, that have preserved the ethnic and religious Arab and Muslim cultural ties and common heritage that unite Jordanians and Palestinians more than they divide them. Moreover, Jordanians and Palestinians, much more than any other two Arab peoples, are tied together by an uncommon web of historical affinity and intimacy. The historical ties between the East and West Banks have existed for centuries. They were deeply influenced by the lay of the land, which made social, commercial, and administrative ties along an east-west axis far more natural than along the north-south one. Thus, the relations between the Hawran in the north and adjacent Palestine to the west were far closer than those between the Hawran and the Balqa to the south. Relations between the Hawran and the Karak region farther to the south were almost nonexistent. Similarly strong or even stronger social and commercial ties linked Salt with Nablus, the Balqa with Jerusalem, and Karak with Hebron and Gaza.[55]

Furthermore, Jordan and the Palestinian national movement are both products of the British Mandate for Palestine, and their respective fates have been molded inseparably by the struggle for Palestine and the Arab-Israeli conflict and its consequences.

As two seasoned Jordanian observers (one Palestinian and the other Jordanian) have noted, "It would be a historical anomaly, and an almost impossible nation-building challenge, for Jordan and Palestine to try to develop as independent states separated by the sorts of borders and socio-economic barriers that define relations amongst most Arab countries." Jordanians and Palestinians were "more like Siamese twins." They had never been separated and to do so would "spell an end to both: culturally, nationally and economically, but foremost of all, politically."[56]

Distinctive, authentic Jordanian and Palestinian identities have evolved, and both communities earnestly desire to preserve them. Yet the majority in both communities believes that some form of special relationship will have to link them in the future. Historical ties, geographic proximity, and demographic realities are difficult to ignore.

Indeed, Jordan's national charter, while fully cognizant of the distinctive Jordanian and Palestinian identities, simultaneously elaborates upon the extraordinary historical association between Jordan and Palestine. This, the charter asserts, makes some future unionist relationship between the states of Jordan and Palestine inevitable, provided that Jordanian national unity (i.e., between Jordanians and Palestinians on the East Bank) is maintained and that there is no contradiction between the Palestinian and Jordanian identities. Needless to note, this is easier said than done, but it is by no means unattainable.

Appendix 5.A Breakdown of the Type of Future Relationship Desired Between Jordan and Palestine, by Country of Origin (percentages)

Type of Link	National Sample			Opinion-makers' Sample			Refugee Camp Sample
	Jordan	Palestine	Total	Jordan	Palestine	Total	Total
Merger	30.4	37.8	34.20	26.4	32.8	29.6	44.4
Federation	17.0	20.5	18.75	15.0	21.1	18.0	15.4
Confederation	18.4	20.7	19.55	19.0	21.1	20.0	11.8
Leave decision for the future	6.6	6.0	6.30	14.6	15.8	15.2	5.4
Other	5.0	6.5	5.80	4.0	3.2	3.6	9.7
Opposed to any link	17.7	6.7	12.10	18.2	4.0	11.2	9.7
Don't know	4.9	1.8	3.30	2.8	2.0	2.4	3.6
Total	100.0	100.0	100.00	100.0	100.0	100.0	100.0

Source: Public opinion poll conducted by Center for Strategic Studies, University of Jordan, as published in *al-Dustur*, 8 February 1995.

Notes

1. Schirin Fathi, *Jordan: An Invented Nation? State-Tribe Dynamics and the Formation of National Identity* (Hamburg: Deutsches Orient-Institut, 1994), p. 127.

2. Uriel Dann, "Regime and Opposition in Jordan, 1949–1970," in Menahem Milson (ed.), *Regime and Society in the Arab World* (in Hebrew) (Jerusalem: Van Leer Institute, 1977), pp. 128–159.

3. This does not include former Palestinians like Tawfiq Abu al-Huda or Samir al-Rifa'i, who also served under 'Abdallah well before 1948 and were regarded as Jordanians by all and sundry.

4. Asher Susser, "Jordan," *Middle East Contemporary Survey (MECS),* vol. 15 (1991), pp. 491–494.

5. Arthur Day, *East Bank/West Bank: Jordan and the Prospects for Peace* (New York: Council on Foreign Relations, 1986), p. 80; Frederick Peake (Peake Pasha), *A History of Jordan and Its Tribes* (Coral Gables, Fla.: University of Miami Press, 1958), pp. 251–253.

6. Day, *East Bank/West Bank,* pp. 79–80.

7. *Al-Dustur,* 20 June 1991.

8. Kamal Salibi, *The Modern History of Jordan* (London: I. B. Tauris, 1993), p. 95.

9. Ibid., p. 93.

10. Ibid., pp. 93–94.

11. Mary Wilson, *King Abdallah, Britain and the Making of Jordan* (Cambridge: Cambridge University Press, 1987), pp. 64–65; Fathi, *Jordan: An Invented Nation?* pp. 92–94.

12. Salibi, *The Modern History,* p. 94.

13. Israel Gershoni, "The Arab Nation, the Hashemite Dynasty and Greater Syria in the Writings of 'Abdallah," part 2, *Hamizrah Hehadash* (in Hebrew) 25, no. 3 (1975), pp. 165–170.

14. Michael Winter, "The Arab Self-Image as Reflected in Jordanian Textbooks," in Asher Susser and Aryeh Shmuelevitz (eds.), *The Hashemites in the Modern Arab World* (London: Frank Cass, 1995), pp. 207–220.

15. Asher Susser, *On Both Banks of the Jordan: A Political Biography of Wasfi al-Tall* (London: Frank Cass, 1994), pp. 156–157.

16. Emmanuel Sivan, "The Arab Nation-State: In Search of a Usable Past," *Middle East Review* 19, no. 3 (spring 1987), pp. 21–30.

17. Fathi, *Jordan: An Invented Nation?* pp. 71–72. An examination of Jordanian postage stamps, from the foundation of the emirate to the present, clearly shows the shift of emphasis from general Arab to Jordanian-Palestinian and then to more purely Jordanian themes. See Stanley Gibbons Stamp Catalogue, part 19, *Middle East,* 5th ed., 1996, pp. 272–318.

18. Sivan, "The Arab Nation-State," p. 28.

19. Text of the national charter as published in *al-Dustur,* 30 December 1990.

20. Asher Susser, "Jordan," *MECS,* vol. 17 (1993), p. 452.

21. Asher Susser, "Jordan," *MECS,* vol. 12 (1988), pp. 601–602.

22. Uriel Dann, *Studies in the History of Transjordan, 1920–1949: The Making of a State* (Boulder, Colo.: Westview, 1984), p. 10; Riccardo Bocco and Tariq Tell, "Pax Britannica in the Steppe: British Policy and the Transjordanian Bedouin, 1923–39," in Eugene Rogan and Tariq Tell (eds.), *Village, Steppe and State: The Social Origins of Modern Jordan* (London: British Academic Press, 1994), pp. 108–109; Laurence Axelrod, "Tribesmen in Uniform: The Demise of the Fida'iyyun in Jordan, 1970–71," *Muslim World* 68, no. 1 (1978), p. 44.

23. Fathi, *Jordan: An Invented Nation?* pp. 96–97, 127; Linda Layne, "Tribesmen as Citizens: 'Primordial Ties' and Democracy in Rural Jordan," in Linda Layne (ed.), *Elections in the Middle East: Implications of Recent Trends* (Boulder, Colo.: Westview, 1987), p. 128.

24. Axelrod, "Tribesmen in Uniform," p. 27.

25. Ibid, p. 26; Laurie Brand, "In the Beginning Was the State . . .: The Quest for Civil Society in Jordan," in Augustus Richard Norton (ed.), *Civil Society in the Middle East* (Leiden, Netherlands: E. J. Brill, 1995), pp. 144–153.

26. Axelrod, "Tribesmen in Uniform," p. 26.

27. Philip Khoury and Joseph Kostiner (eds.), *Tribes and State Formation in the Middle East* (Berkeley: University of California Press, 1990), p. 3.

28. Fathi, *Jordan: An Invented Nation?* pp. 165, 179–180.

29. Yezid Sayigh, "Jordan in the 1980s: Legitimacy, Entity and Identity," in Rodney Wilson (ed.), *Politics and the Economy in Jordan* (London: Routledge, 1991), p. 174.

30. Layne, "Tribesmen as Citizens," pp. 125, 135–136.

31. Ahmad 'Uwaydi al-'Abbadi (an East Banker of tribal origin), quoted in Fathi, *Jordan: An Invented Nation?* p. 259.

32. 'Adnan Abu 'Awda (of Palestinian origin), quoted in Fathi, *Jordan: An Invented Nation?* p. 264.

33. Linda Layne, *Home and Homeland: The Dialogics of Tribal and National Identities in Jordan* (Princeton, N.J.: Princeton University Press, 1994), p. 103.

34. Fathi, *Jordan: An Invented Nation?* p. 238.

35. Ibid., pp. 179–180.

36. Brand, "In the Beginning," p. 180.

37. Fathi, *Jordan: An Invented Nation?* p. 185.

38. Brand, "In the Beginning," p. 184.

39. Asher Susser, "Jordan," *MECS,* vol. 17 (1993), pp. 471–472; vol. 18 (1994), p. 438.

40. Susser, *MECS,* vol. 18 (1994), p. 438.; *al-Majalla* (London weekly), 30 June 1996.

41. Fathi, *Jordan: An Invented Nation?* pp. 213–214.

42. *Al-Majalla,* 30 June 1996.

43. Fathi, *Jordan: An Invented Nation?* p. 220.

44. Ibid., p. 221.

45. Sayigh, "Jordan in the 1980s," p. 173.

46. Brand, "In the Beginning," p. 159.

47. Ibid.

48. Ibid.

49. "The Domestic Dimension," Center for Strategic Studies, University of Jordan, 1996, pp. 12–13.

50. "The Domestic Dimension," p. 16.

51. Brand, "In the Beginning," p. 185.

52. Fathi, *Jordan: An Invented Nation?* p. 173.

53. "The Domestic Dimension," pp. 15–16.

54. Brand, "In the Beginning," p. 160.

55. "The Domestic Dimension," p. 5.

56. Rami Khouri and Musa Kaylani, quoted in Asher Susser, "Jordan," *MECS,* vol. 17 (1993), pp. 469–470.

6

From Hegemony to Marginalism: The Maronites of Lebanon

Meir Zamir

The political institutions, administration, infrastructure, and economy that were largely destroyed during the Lebanese civil war have, since 1990, been rapidly reconstructed. At the same time, Lebanon's citizens have been engaging in an intense public debate over the causes of the war and the direction their state should take following the Ta'if Agreement. Lebanon's ability to break free from Syria and rebuild itself as a major commercial-financial and cultural-intellectual center in the Middle East depends largely on whether, in the aftermath of the internecine violence, destruction, and loss of life, the Christians and Muslims can reach a genuine reconciliation. Such issues are being debated particularly among the Maronites, who are undergoing a severe crisis. Lacking leadership, they are deeply divided and overcome by despair and fear of their future in the Lebanese state. Having seen their dream of an independent sovereign Lebanon, for which they had striven for more than a century, disintegrate before their very eyes, they are now being relegated to a marginal status in a country that is rapidly assuming an Arab-Muslim character. Painfully they are coming to terms with the fact that, like their co-religionists in other Arab countries, their future is as a minority in a Muslim state. The hundreds of thousands of Maronites who fled Lebanon during the civil war remain disillusioned with their country, whose name has become synonymous with terror, violence, and religious and sectarian strife. They live in Europe or North America, and content themselves with short family visits in the summer.[1]

The marginal status of the Maronites in what is called "the Second Republic"—namely the Lebanese state after the Ta'if Agreement—stands out in sharp contrast to their political, social, economic, and cultural dominance before 1975. The Maronites, who considered themselves to be the founders of the Lebanese state, assumed the role of guardians of its independence, sovereignty, and Christian character. They demanded and secured for themselves a preeminent position in its political and administrative systems and in the

111

armed forces, initially with French assistance during the Mandate, and later after independence, when they exploited the National Pact of 1943 to retain and even enhance their privileged status. They not only controlled the presidency but also secured the position of commander-in-chief of the army and head of the judicial system. Indeed, their share in the administration was much greater than their proportion in the general population, and they took advantage of their dominance and access to state institutions to increase their power and wealth. The Maronites determined Lebanon's national identity, which distinguished it from Syria and the rest of the Arab world. Together with the country's other Christian communities, they established one of the most advanced educational systems in the Middle East, turning Beirut into a leading cultural-intellectual center. A wealthy Christian bourgeois elite emerged in Beirut that exploited its close ties with the politicians to shape Lebanon's laissez-faire economy, promoting trade, finance, and tourism rather than agriculture and industry. In the 1950s and 1960s, the Christian financiers and traders of Beirut played a major role in transforming Lebanon into the "Switzerland of the Middle East."[2]

During the civil war the Maronites were under siege, fighting to preserve their community's very existence. Their leaders consequently rejected criticism of their role in the war. They portrayed themselves as the victims of foreign forces—whether Palestinian, Syrian, or Israeli—who were seeking to take over Lebanon, and accused the Lebanese Muslims of lacking patriotism and of failing to rise up in defense of their country's independence and sovereignty. But the violent conflicts among the Christians themselves, culminating in the clashes between Michel 'Awn and Samir Ja'ja', helped consolidate Syrian control of the country and nullified Maronite political power. This has forced the Maronites, both in Lebanon and abroad, to re-examine their role, not only in the civil war, but also prior to 1975. Many now blame their militia chiefs and their politicians for having pursued adventurous and irresponsible policies. For their part, the Maronite politicians who were involved in the war have been granting interviews and writing articles and books in which they attempt to justify their policies.[3]

Notwithstanding the present debate over the responsibility of veteran politicians such as Camille Chamoun and Pierre Jumayyil; former presidents such as Suleiman Faranjieh, Elias Sarkis, and Amin Jumayyil; and commanders of the militias and armed forces such as Bashir Jumayyil, Samir Ja'ja', Eli Hubayqa, and Michel 'Awn, to name but a few, for their community's predicament, questions should be asked concerning the Maronites' role in exacerbating the political and socioeconomic problems that have plagued Lebanon since its establishment. Indeed, one can argue that the policies pursued by their politicians and militias during the civil war were determined, to a large degree, by their long-held perceptions of themselves, Lebanon, the Muslims, and the surrounding Arab world. The Maronites' demise was not merely the result of the miscalculations of their leaders during the war; it was rooted in the hegemonic posture they had assumed since independence.[4]

Between Vision and Reality

During Lebanon's first three decades, the gap between what the founding fathers had envisioned for Lebanon and harsh reality widened. The country was controlled by a Christian minority that faced increasing numbers of restless Muslims. Although its Christian leaders professed their allegiance to the Arab world, it was the only Christian Western state in a region dominated by Arab Muslim countries. Lebanon claimed to be the sole democracy in the Arab world, yet its parliamentary system was based on sectarian representation according to a key that automatically guaranteed a governing majority to the Christian minority. With its capitalist laissez-faire economic system, the government was unable to solve the socioeconomic problems manifested in the widening gap between rich and poor. These problems threatened the stability of the state, as they reflected the deep sectarian and geographical division between the predominantly Christian Beirut and Mount Lebanon and the peripheral regions of both south and north Lebanon and the Biqa' Valley, with their large, mainly Shi'i Muslim populations.

As the internal and external threats to Lebanon's stability and to its very existence as an independent sovereign state increased, the Maronites took it upon themselves to defend their country. They were beset, however, by internal rivalry, with their leaders unable to reach a consensus on which direction to take. They rarely distinguished between their own and national interests. Instead of attempting to defuse the political and socioeconomic tension among the Muslims, which was threatening the delicate sectarian balance, they insisted on maintaining the status quo that guaranteed their privileged positions. Instead of strengthening the Muslims' attachment to Lebanon by granting them an equal share in running the state, the Maronites claimed Lebanon almost exclusively for themselves. It was therefore not surprising that the Muslims, together with the radical leftist organizations whose ranks had been swollen by the disillusioned younger generation during the 1960s and 1970s, blamed the Maronite leadership for all of Lebanon's ills. Although politicians and feudal bourgeois elites of other sects also abused state institutions and enhanced their power and wealth through nepotism and clientelism, Maronite politicians became particularly identified with this corrupt system. Indeed, many Muslims believed that the Maronites, under the pretext of a need to be protected from the Muslim majority, were holding the entire Lebanese state at ransom to further their own interests.[5]

Although some Muslim politicians and leftist organizations advocated radical change—including the abolition of political sectarianism and the transformation of Lebanon into a secular or Arab Muslim state—before 1975 the majority favored maintaining it as a prosperous independent state with a pluralistic culture and mix of East and West. They insisted, however, on equality and that Lebanon be truly part of the Arab world. Indeed, those were the declared goals of the National Pact.

The 1943 National Pact, the unwritten agreement between the Maronite Bishara al-Khoury and the Sunni Riyad al-Sulh, has been the focus of controversy for the past half-century, as each side has interpreted it according to its own particular interests. The National Pact was, in fact, a compromise agreement between Christian and Muslim politicians over the division of political power in the independent Lebanese state, based on proportional sectarian representation and on Lebanon's being a part of the Arab world while maintaining its uniqueness. At the time, the pact was viewed as a pragmatic solution, and it enabled Lebanon to gain independence from France, win the recognition of the Arab states, and become a founding member of the Arab League. But it was vague with regard to Lebanon's national identity; and it perpetuated sectarian division and laid the ground for an inefficient and corrupt political system. The Muslims were willing to accept it for a transitional period only, as envisioned by Michel Chiha, its chief ideologist. Fully aware of the destructive potential of intersectarian violence, which had repeatedly beset Lebanon, he saw the pact and its provision for sectarian representation as an intermediate stage in securing a balance between the sects before all the different elements were integrated into one Lebanese nation. His views, however, were not shared by the majority of the Maronites, who not only insisted on maintaining the status quo indefinitely but exploited their privileged positions in the political system to strengthen their hold over the state. The presidency, which in accordance with the National Pact was allocated to the Maronites, became the means for attaining these goals.[6]

The Presidency: Inherent Source of Instability

The presidency emerged as the symbol for Maronite hegemony in Lebanon; almost all the political crises in independent Lebanon were centered around this institution. Ambitious Maronite politicians divided their community and undermined the political system in their unremitting pursuit of the presidency. The Muslims, for their part, demanded that non-Maronites also be allowed to be elected for this position, or alternatively, that the power of the Muslim prime minister be increased at the expense of that of the president. But the first two presidents—Bishara al-Khoury (1943–1952) and Camille Chamoun (1952–1958)—did precisely the opposite. Under Khoury, Lebanon was transformed from a parliamentary democracy into a presidential republic, with the president wielding a strong influence over the government and Parliament. Although Khoury had professed himself defender of the constitution during the French Mandate, after independence he revised it to secure another term in office. He portrayed himself as the president of all the Lebanese, but under his reign his family, relatives, and friends, and the Maronite community as a whole, strengthened their hold over the administration, the judicial system, the army, and the intelligence services. He perfected what may be defined as a method of "control and share"—integrating the feudal bourgeois elites of the Sunnis, Shi'is, and other communities into the political and economic systems in return for their support of the status quo. This may have provided Lebanon with a more stable political system, as those who benefited from it had a vested interest in maintaining it, but it led to widespread corruption. This modus operandi functioned as long as Khoury was able to maintain the delicate balance between the politicians, sects, and regions. But in September 1952 he was overthrown by a coalition comprising Camille Chamoun, who sought the presidency for himself, Kamal Junblatt, who called for reform, and Muslim politicians who demanded a greater share in running the state.[7]

Although prior to his election Chamoun had undertaken to introduce political and social reforms, he, too, increased the power of the president, as well as Maronite influence over the state institutions, claiming this was necessary to counter the growing threat of the pan-Arabist Nasserism then sweeping through Lebanon. Yet his intervention in the 1957 parliamentary elections to assure the election of loyal deputies, and his apparent design to revise the constitution in order to secure a second term for himself, reinforced the suspicion that he, like his predecessor, was motivated primarily by a thirst for power. As he tightened the Maronite hold over the state, Chamoun also pursued a pro-Western policy manifested in his support of the Eisenhower doctrine. For the Muslims, this was further proof that, despite the demographic changes, the Maronites continued to regard Lebanon as their own state, linked more closely to the West than to the Arab world. Unable to revise the system through legitimate political channels, the Muslims took to the streets.[8]

The 1958 civil war reinforced Maronite belief that the Muslims were alien to the "Lebanese idea," and that radical Arab states, led by Egypt, which was then united with Syria in the United Arab Republic, would continue to undermine Lebanon and strive to transform it into a truly Arab country. This was borne out by the growing support of the Maronite masses for the Phalange Party and for Chamoun's newly established National Liberal Party. Their fears were undoubtedly genuine, but they were also fueled by cynical politicians who had their own political agendas.

Unlike the traditional Maronite politicians, the new president, Fu'ad Shihab (1958–1964), strove to defuse intersectarian tension by introducing limited social and economic reform, and pursued a foreign policy aimed at improving relations with Egyptian president Gamal Abd al-Nasser. He attempted to reform the political and economic systems shaped by the previous two presidents by bypassing the politicians, the government, and Parliament, and relying instead on the army, the intelligence services, and the technocrats. His reforms, however, were opposed by his community and its three prominent leaders—Camille Chamoun, Pierre Jumayyil, and Emile Eddé. They gave various explanations for their stand, such as the need to defend Lebanese democracy and the interests of the Maronite community, but, as before, personal political considerations prevailed.[9]

Shihab considerably raised the Muslims' expectations but accomplished only a part of his declared goals. Despite his achievements, intersectarian, political, and socioeconomic tension remained high. Many young Muslims, Shi'is in particular, were attracted by militant leftist organizations seeking to totally revolutionize the Lebanese state. Paradoxically, Shihabism also reinforced the Muslim belief that the Maronites would not relinquish their hold over the state; although Shihab delegated more authority to the Sunni prime minister, the real power shifted to the army and the intelligence services, which were controlled by the Maronites.[10]

Intersectarian, political, and socioeconomic grievances intensified under Charles Helou (1964–1970). He was a weak president who, while continuing to advocate the Shihabist reforms, lacked the resolve to implement them in the face of strong opposition from his own community. The Arab defeat in 1967 and the emergence of radical Palestinian organizations, which perpetrated acts of violence and terror against Israel from Lebanon, deepened the tension and division between the Christians and Muslims. It increased Maronite contempt for the Arab Muslim world and reinforced their fears that the radicalized Muslims and the leftist parties backed by the armed Palestinian organizations would force them out of their privileged positions and completely transform Lebanon's unique character. The establishment of the Hilf—a coalition of the three main Maronite parties (Chamoun's National Liberals, Jumayyil's Phalange Party, and Eddé's National Bloc)—on the eve of the 1968 parliamentary elections, was the product of those fears, as well as of the immediate political interests of their three leaders. The 1969 political crisis, precipitated by the Christian-Muslim disagreement over the armed Palestinian presence in Lebanon and the ensuing Cairo Agreement of November that year, reinforced the Maronites' concerns that they had not merely to contend with Muslim demands for political concessions and socioeconomic reforms, but also to fight for their very existence in an independent, sovereign Lebanese state. Newly emergent militant organizations warned that in the face of the rapid natural increase in the Muslim population, augmented by 600,000 Syrian workers and 400,000 Palestinians, the Christians had to protect their position or, within a decade, lose their dominance and become a disadvantaged minority in the state they had created.[11]

The Civil War:
The Demise of Maronite Hegemony

For the past twenty years Christians, Muslims, and Palestinians have disputed the role of the Palestine Liberation Organization (PLO) in instigating the 1975 civil war. Kamal Junblatt and the Palestinian leaders have argued that the war resulted from political and social change within Lebanon and that, at the most, the Palestinian presence served as a catalyst.[12] In contrast, the Maronites view the 1975 war as the Lebanese people's defense of their independence and sovereignty against foreigners who were attempting to create a state within a state. The PLO embodied everything that the Maronites feared and resented in the Arab Muslim world. Under the slogan of Arab solidarity and the sacred struggle against Israel, the Maronites believed, the PLO was jeopardizing Lebanon's very existence. They regarded the Palestinian organizations as the tools of the militant Arab states, particularly Syria, Libya, and Iraq, sent to undermine Lebanon's western, liberal, and Christian character. The Palestinians, they charged, were radicalizing the Muslims and the left and turning them against the Lebanese state. Furthermore, they legitimized the use of violence to achieve political and socioeconomic goals. Indeed, the revolutionary Marxist ideology pursued by some Palestinian organizations stood in sharp contrast to the capitalist laissez-faire system advocated by most Christians.[13]

The Maronites' mistake was not in overestimating the Palestinian threat to Lebanon, but in ignoring the effects of their confrontation with the Palestinians on their delicate relations with the Lebanese Muslims. Although the Maronites accused the Palestinians of disloyalty to Lebanon, the overwhelming majority of the Muslim politicians and citizenry upheld the principle of an independent sovereign Lebanese state. Indeed, many shared their Christian colleagues' criticism of the Palestinians' contempt for Lebanon's sovereignty, while the Shi'is in the south paid dearly for the Palestinians' armed struggle against Israel. Yet the Muslim leaders, facing the radicalization of their communities, were forced to take a more militant stand in support of the Palestinian cause. Instead of promoting the common goals of the Lebanese Christians and Muslims, the Maronites accentuated the differences in the attitudes of the two communities toward the Palestinians. Instead of accepting some of the Muslim demands for political and socioeconomic reform and thereby mitigating intersectarian tension, they insisted on retaining control of the state and its resources. It is therefore not surprising that the Muslims and the leftist parties began to regard the Palestinians as a means to change the status quo and extract political concessions from the Maronites.[14]

At the time of the presidential election of August 1970 the Maronites and Lebanon as a whole stood at a crossroads. Elias Sarkis, the Shihabist candidate, advocated caution and the continuation of the socioeconomic reforms to defuse the growing sectarian and social tension. Sulayman Faranjiyya, who had emerged as a last-minute compromise candidate backed by Camille Chamoun, Pierre Jumayyil, and Raymond Eddé, represented the militant and conservative Maronite stand. Faranjiyya's election by a majority of a single vote resulted from political maneuvering—an integral part of all presidential elections in Lebanon. Yet it also marked Maronite resolve to pursue an uncompromising stand against both the Palestinian armed presence in Lebanon and the Muslims' demands for reform.[15]

Faranjiyya's presidency proved to be disastrous for Lebanon. The country desperately needed a skillful and wise leader during the stormy period of the early 1970s, but Faranjiyya, a member of a feudal family from the Maronite stronghold of Zgharta, lacked the necessary political acumen in Arab and international foreign policy. His election led to a rise in nepotism, patronage, and clientelism, providing further confirmation for the Muslims' conviction that the Maronites were exploiting the state for their own ends. Instead of dealing with their political and socioeconomic grievances, he exacerbated them. He proclaimed that he would restore law and order, but instead he weakened the authority of the army and the intelligence services. He also failed to mobilize the support of the Arab world, which Lebanon needed to withstand the Palestinians. In April 1973 he was drawn into a costly confrontation with the PLO that, coupled with erroneous political decisions, antagonized the Muslim leadership even more. The country thus began its rapid descent into the civil war that erupted two years later.[16]

Many Lebanese have speculated whether a Sarkis victory in 1970 might have prevented the civil war. Perhaps, these people suggest, if Faranjiyya, Chamoun, and Jumayyil had made, a few years earlier, the political concessions they were eventually forced to make in February 1976, Junblatt and the PLO might not have been able to mobilize the Muslim masses against the Maronites' hegemony.

It was no mere coincidence that the Phalange Party, the most radical Maronite faction, was involved in the April 1975 incident with the Palestinians that sparked the war. Escalation into a full-blown civil conflict was rapid. Years of pent-up fear, animosity, and political and socioeconomic tension erupted violently. The clashes between the Maronites and the Palestinians soon expanded into a Muslim-Christian war, as each community upstaged its opponents with acts of terror. Innocent civilians were kidnapped and slaughtered merely because of their religion or sect. The Maronites' worst fears were realized: instead of ruling Lebanon, they were fighting for their very survival.

For more than three decades the Maronites had disregarded the declared goal of the National Pact: the creation of a pluralistic and tolerant Lebanese society with no sectarian or religious discrimination. It can be argued that in the unstable and divided Middle East this was a utopian and unattainable goal. But it was the Maronites who, during the Mandate, had rejected attempts to strengthen the Christian majority by reducing Lebanon's territory, or by adopting a decentralized system in which each region would maintain a large degree of autonomy. In fact, the efforts to create a pluralistic and just society under a parliamentary democracy were never really given a chance; the Maronites were determined to retain their hegemony at any cost, whether because of fears rooted in their past, or because of greedy and ambitious politicians who saw their own interests as synonymous with those of their community and of Lebanon as a whole.

The Price of Miscalculation

The same politicians who had played a key role in the escalation into the civil war were responsible, together with the new generation of militia leaders, for their community's demise. During the fifteen years of the war, the Maronites' freedom of action became increasingly limited, while the price they had to pay for making the wrong decisions rose sharply. In the early stages they were still able to mobilize their resources and defend the Christian regions to a degree that surprised even their opponents. Money was collected, weapons were purchased, and thousands of young Maronites left their jobs, schools, or universities to volunteer for the militias to protect their families and homes. As the war continued however, the shortsightedness and irresponsibility of their leaders became ever more apparent. Decisions were increasingly influenced by young militant militia commanders who advocated the use of force. Moderation was regarded as treason, and leaders who believed in accommodation and reconciliation were either ignored or forced to flee the country. The consequences for the community were dire. Under growing pressure, a small number of leaders and groups made a series of fateful decisions that precipitated the Maronites' downfall. These included: their acquiescence in Syria's intervention in the summer of 1976; Bashir Jumayyil's decision in 1978 to wage a war against the Syrians; the collaboration with Israel that resulted in its invasion in June 1982; and 'Awn's "war of liberation" against Syria in 1988–1990. At the same time, the community was demoralized by internal strife, which culminated in the violent clashes between the Jumayyil and Faranjiyya clans, between the Lebanese forces and Chamoun's Numur militia, and between Michel 'Awn and Samir Ja'ja'.

The request by Faranjiyya and Jumayyil in May 1976 for Syria to send its forces into Lebanon had far-reaching consequences: it changed the nature of the civil war, led to Israeli and U.S. involvement in Lebanon, and caused a deep rift within the Maronite community. The Maronites, who had always distrusted and feared that the Syrians would be well aware of their ambitions to dominate Lebanon, should have known that after inviting them into their country it would be extremely difficult to force them out. They should also have known that by acquiescing in Syrian military intervention, they were surrendering their freedom of action, granting the Syrians the role of arbitrator, and enabling them to dictate a political solution to the civil war. Moreover, they should have realized that Syria's policy in Lebanon would be determined not only by its desire to secure its interests there but also by broader considerations, including its rivalry with Israel, its position in the inter-Arab arena, and its relations with the superpowers.[17]

It can be argued that the Maronites' request to Syria for help was hasty and made in panic, as they feared that the Christian forces would be unable to withstand the combined offensive of Junblatt's National Front and the PLO. The conditions of the deal were clear, however: Asad would protect the Maronites against the Druze, the leftist organizations, and the PLO, and impose a political solution based on the Constitutional Declaration of February 1976; in return, the Maronites would agree to Syria's "special role" in Lebanon.

Despite strong domestic opposition, Asad largely kept his promise during the second half of 1976 and early 1977. The Druze, the leftists, and the Palestinian forces were defeated, and Kamal Junblatt, who had led the offensive against the Maronites, was assassinated in March 1977. The Maronites recovered their military and political power; Asad now expected them to fulfill their part of the deal.

At the beginning of 1978 the Maronite community faced three options. Faranjiyya, who had maintained close ties with the Syrians for many years, and who was grateful to Asad for preventing his ouster from the presidency, advocated close cooperation with Syria. Sarkis, who had been elected president in May 1976, proposed probably the most pragmatic solution under the circumstances: to seek a reconciliation between the Christians and Muslims, and rebuild the state, while limiting the Syrian presence in Lebanon with the help of other Arab countries and the United States. Chamoun and Jumayyil, who now led the Lebanese Front, a coalition of Christian parties and organizations, could have supported Sarkis, who represented the legitimacy of Lebanon and Maronite control of the presidency. Yet they ignored him and undermined his authority, regarding him as merely a Syrian tool. Pressured by Bashir Jumayyil, who had emerged from the first two years of the war as a charismatic and popular militia leader, they backed his armed struggle against the Syrian forces in Lebanon. The consequences proved costly. Support for Jumayyil by the Lebanese Front deeply divided the Maronite community, provoked Syria's rage, and undermined all efforts to end the civil war.[18]

Bashir Jumayyil had originally opposed collaborating with Syria and considered its armed presence in Lebanon as a foreign occupation. With the Maronites' political and military position improving, and with Asad facing increasing domestic opposition, in early 1978 he and his close advisers concluded that conditions were favorable for forcing the Syrian army out—initially from the Christian region and later from Lebanon as a whole. He confronted the Syrian

Army, hoping that this would galvanize the Maronite community and win its support for his stand and, at the same time, mobilize international pressure on Syria to withdraw. By the end of the year most of the leaders of the Lebanese Front, headed by Chamoun, backed his strategy. But this was a dangerous ploy, failing as it did to take into account Asad's ruthlessness and ability to exploit the personal and intersectarian rivalry within Lebanon.[19]

In the late 1970s and early 1980s the Syrian regime was indeed in deep trouble. At home Asad was opposed by the Muslim Brotherhood and criticized by his own party for supporting the Maronites against the Palestinians and the left—Syria's traditional allies in Lebanon. Sadat's peace initiative had left him with no credible military option against Israel. In the inter-Arab arena Syria was challenged by Iraq and, after the outbreak of the Iraq-Iran war, it became increasingly isolated. Relations with the United States also deteriorated following its opposition to the peace process. With his regime threatened both at home and abroad, the Syrian president could not sustain a defeat in Lebanon. Bashir presented him the opportunity to abandon his controversial cooperation with the Maronites and return to the traditional Syrian policy of supporting the Muslims and the left in Lebanon. It also allowed him to settle his differences with the PLO in the aftermath of Sadat's peace initiative. Syria thus escalated its attacks on Bashir's forces, supported the Maronites' opponents, and took every opportunity to sow discord in the Maronite camp.

The conflict with Syria deeply divided the Christians and reinforced Bashir's determination to impose his will on all the Christian militias by force. Yet Tony Faranjiyya's assassination in June 1978 and the ensuing feud between the Jumayyil family and the Lebanese Forces on the one hand, and Sulayman Faranjiyya and his followers in Zgharta on the other, considerably weakened the Maronite community and allowed the Syrians to maintain their hold over the Christian area in north Lebanon. With the submission of Danny Chamoun's Numur militia in July 1980, Bashir now had control over most of the Christian forces. The Maronites' fate now lay in the hands of one man—Bashir Jumayyil.[20]

Raising the Stakes: The Alliance with Israel

Bashir Jumayyil and the Lebanese Front compounded their mistake of confronting the Syrian Army with an even more dangerous decision—to seek a strategic alliance with Israel against Syria. The Maronites had established close ties with Israel back in 1976, when it supplied them with weapons and trained their militias. This cooperation had been limited, however, as Israel's Labor government had refused to intervene directly in the civil war. As the Lebanese forces escalated their armed struggle against the Syrian Army, and the West showed itself reluctant to come to their aid, Bashir came to believe that only Israel, the strongest military power in the region, could save the Maronites. He hoped that, under the rightist Likud government, Israel would invade Lebanon, defeat the PLO and the Syrian Army, ensure his election as president, and restore Maronite hegemony. For his policy to succeed, however, the Israeli leaders had to be persuaded to wage a war against not only the Palestinian forces in the south, but against the PLO and the Syrian Army in Beirut.[21]

Here again the Maronites chose a course of action without sufficiently weighing its chances of success or the price of failure. As in the spring of 1976, when they had appealed to Syria for help, they disregarded that Israel's intervention in Lebanon would be primarily determined by its own interests, as well as its domestic and international constraints. More significantly, Bashir ignored the consequences of such an alliance on Maronite relations with the Muslims in Lebanon, with Syria, and with other Arab countries. Convinced that only by cooperating closely with the Arab world could they ensure Lebanon's political stability and economic prosperity after independence, Maronite politicians had been anxious to dispel any accusations of disloyalty to the Arab cause. By collaborating with Israel, the Arabs' most vilified enemy, Bashir Jumayyil deligitimized the entire Maronite community in the eyes of the Lebanese Muslims, the Syrians, and the rest of the Arab world. He disregarded the fact that once Israel fulfilled the task expected of it by the Christians and withdrew from Lebanon, the Maronites would have to continue to coexist with the Muslims. Moreover, his policy transformed the Maronites and Lebanon into a direct strategic threat to Syria. The stakes for Asad were now high—he had to ensure Syrian control over a Lebanese state in which the Maronites could no longer endanger Syria's interests.

In the summer of 1982 Bashir's gamble appeared to have paid off; Israel invaded Lebanon, defeated the PLO and the Syrian Army, laid siege to west Beirut, and forced the Palestinians and Syrians out of the city. The United States and other Western powers, whose intervention the Christians had been seeking unsuccessfully since 1975, sent forces to supervise the PLO evacuation of Beirut. The euphoria in the Christian camp reached its peak after Bashir Jumayyil's election as president. But the basic faults in Bashir's policy were instantly apparent. He had been elected with Israel's backing but declared himself president of all the Lebanese. He also quarreled with Prime Minister Menachem Begin over his refusal to conclude an immediate peace treaty with Israel. His assassination in September 1982 by a Syrian agent was inevitable and marked the beginning of the Maronite community's demise. He left a weak and divided Christian camp, lacking leadership or a clear direction, to face a vengeful Syrian regime.[22]

With the rise of the militant Shi'i organizations, and with Syria determined to punish the Maronites and restore its hold over Lebanon, even a strong and charismatic president would have found it difficult to unite the

Maronite community, initiate a national conciliation, and bring an end to Lebanon's status as a battlefield for Syro-Israeli confrontation. Amin Jumayyil, the new president, possessed no such skill. He was a mediocre politician who lacked the charisma and self-confidence of his younger brother and was elected at this time of crisis only because he carried the Jumayyil name. During his six years in office (1982–1988) the Christian camp disintegrated rapidly and Lebanon descended into an even deeper quagmire.[23]

Facing the Syrian Rage

After the failure of their gamble on Syria in 1976 and on Israel in 1982, the Maronites turned to the United States, which had played a key role in solving Lebanon's civil war a quarter century earlier. The United States, they assumed, would persuade Israel, its close ally, to withdraw from Lebanon at minimal cost, pressure Syria into evacuating its forces, and rebuild Lebanon's government and army, in which the Maronites would continue to enjoy considerable influence. But again they miscalculated. They ignored the possibility that the U.S. administration, having resisted direct intervention in Lebanon since 1975, might back down in the face of strong domestic opposition; that the Israeli government, under pressure from its own public, would insist on a peace treaty to justify its war in Lebanon; and that Asad would react violently to what he saw as an American-Israeli-Maronite plot to isolate and humiliate Syria in the aftermath of the Camp David Accords and Ronald Reagan's peace initiative. After a series of suicide-bomb attacks by Shi'i fundamentalists on U.S. targets, the United States pulled out of Beirut in early 1984. It was soon followed by France, Britain, and Italy, whose troops were serving in the multinational forces. Israel followed suit in 1985 but retained its security zone in south Lebanon. Amin Jumayyil and the Maronite community were left to confront a vindictive and hostile Syrian regime.[24]

Syria was no longer willing, as it had been in 1976, to content itself with maintaining its influence in Lebanon by sponsoring a political solution. It insisted on a formal agreement that would subjugate Lebanon in order to safeguard Syria's long-term interests there. The Tripartite Militia Agreement it initiated in 1985 was intended to secure these goals by allowing it to station its forces permanently in Lebanon, supervise the rebuilding of the Lebanese Army and security services, and control Lebanon's foreign policy. When the Maronite leadership rejected the agreement, Syria boycotted Amin Jumayyil's administration, undermined all efforts to end the civil war, and encouraged its allies in Lebanon, including those in the Christian camp, to attack the regime.[25]

During his final year in office, Amin Jumayyil desperately sought to renew a dialog with Asad and persuade him to offer a less humiliating deal for the Christians, but to no avail. He was despised and ignored by the Syrian president and lacked any real influence over the Lebanese Forces or the army command, which were becoming increasingly intransigent toward the Syrian occupation. The final fiasco came in the summer of 1988 when Jumayyil failed to persuade his community to heed the U.S. administration's advice to accept the candidate whom Syria had proposed as the next Lebanese president. In a last-minute effort to prevent the prime minister, Salim al-Huss, from declaring himself acting president, Jumayyil appointed General Michel 'Awn, the commander of the army, as prime minister. Lebanon now had two prime ministers—one Maronite and the other a Sunni. Lebanon was thus left without an elected president—the last symbol of Maronite political hegemony.[26]

The crisis over the presidency and the threat of renewed large-scale intersectarian violence, in which the Syrians would be involved directly, prompted the United States and its ally, Saudi Arabia, to renew efforts to seek a political solution. This initiative, in which the Arab League was involved, ended in the Ta'if Agreement of October 1989. Isolated, weakened, and beset by internal strife, the Maronites were forced to make long-overdue political concessions. The agreement stipulated that power be transferred from the Maronite president to the Sunni prime minister and the Shi'i speaker of the house, and that Christians and Muslims be equally represented in the Parliament. Although Syria's unique position in Lebanon was recognized, its military presence was confined both in space and time. Indeed, Asad was far from pleased with the agreement.[27]

Michel 'Awn: The New Savior?

The Ta'if Agreement offered the best opportunity, after fourteen years of civil war, to begin a national reconciliation under Arab supervision and limit Syrian hegemony in Lebanon. The Maronites had again to make a fateful decision: either to pursue national reconciliation and rebuild their state, and only later—with Arab and international help—demand the withdrawal of the Syrian Army, or to continue the struggle to free Lebanon from Syrian domination before solving the internal crisis. Evidently they had learned nothing from their previous mistake of confronting the Syrians alone. Once more the militants gained the upper hand, and Michel 'Awn, who had emerged as the popular hero and "new savior" of the Maronites, declared a war of liberation against the Syrians.[28]

Throughout the following year 'Awn, supported by many young Maronites, conducted a self-defeating struggle against the Syrians and the Ta'if Agreement. Like Bashir Jumayyil before him, he sought first to impose his authority over the entire Christian camp. In violent clashes with the Lebanese Forces led by Samir Ja'ja', thousands of Maronites were killed or wounded, and the Christian strongholds in East Beirut and Mount Lebanon, which had sustained the attacks of leftist organizations, the Palestinians, and the Syrians, were largely destroyed. Hundreds of thousands of disillusioned Christians who had remained in Lebanon during the civil war now fled the country. Each faction had more than sufficient arms and ammunition to wreak havoc among its opponents. Saddam Husayn, who had ended his war with Iran in 1988, was happily supplying both sides with weapons in order to undermine his rival Hafiz Asad's position in Lebanon.[29]

The Maronite leaders' gamble had again backfired. Iraq's invasion of Kuwait in August 1990, and Syria's decision to join the Arab coalition led by the United States and Saudi Arabia, gave Asad a free hand in Lebanon. When the Syrian Army finally attacked 'Awn's headquarters in the presidential palace in Ba'abda in September 1990, his forces surrendered with little resistance and he himself sought refuge in the French Embassy and later in Paris. Determined to teach the Maronites a lesson, the Syrians massacred hundreds of 'Awn's supporters and imprisoned and tortured many more.

With its regional and international standing on the rise, and the Maronites defeated and isolated, Syria unilaterally revised the Ta'if Agreement. Elias Hirawi, the new president, began to rebuild the state institutions under close Syrian supervision. The sectarian militias were forced out of Beirut and were later disarmed and incorporated into the Lebanese Army, while Syrian officers helped organize the army and intelligence services. In May 1991 the Lebanese Parliament, many of whose members had been appointed by Syria, ratified the Treaty of Brotherhood and Cooperation between the two states. Lebanon thus became politically, militarily, and economically linked to Syria. No longer able to influence the political system, the Maronites boycotted the July 1992 parliamentary elections. Their boycott however, made little difference. Indeed it helped the Syrians ensure the election of their Christian candidates to the Parliament. The political marginalization of the Maronites in Lebanon was thereby complete.[30]

Coping with Marginalism

Writing in 1985 on the future of the Christians in Lebanon, Ghassan Tueni argued that they faced three options. The first could be defined as the "Maronite option"—a militant strategy of isolation and confrontation with the Arab Muslim world. This policy had already backfired, leaving the Maronites weakened in the face of a hostile Muslim majority. The second, the "Coptic approach," which he also rejected, was one of silence and submission, of a closed community content with religious freedom. Tueni proposed adopting the strategy of his own Greek Orthodox community, namely a synthesis of the first two options. The Christians, he argued, should unreservedly participate and contribute to the Lebanese society, in which they should enjoy equal rights.[31]

Now, more than a decade later, the Maronites still face similar options. Some, particularly in the diaspora, are still hoping that regional and international changes will enable them to restore their influence or introduce a decentralized system into Lebanon, one that would allow them to enjoy a certain degree of autonomy in Mount Lebanon. Others believe that in light of the rising tide of Islamic fundamentalism, particularly among the Shi'is, the Christians should strive to abolish sectarianism and turn Lebanon into a liberal, secular democratic country. Such hopes, however, are unrealistic in view of the demographic, political, social, and economic transformation that Lebanon has undergone in the past twenty years. The number of Christians is declining rapidly as the young, educated, and better-off continue to emigrate, leaving behind the older and weaker sectors of the community. Even the economy, particularly trade and finance, formerly dominated by the Christians, is being taken over by wealthy Sunnis and Shi'is. It is no mere coincidence that the reconstruction of Beirut as a major regional and international financial and commercial center is being carried out by a company controlled by Lebanon's prime minister, Rafiq Hariri.[32]

In recent years, Maronite leaders, including those in the church, have been calling for the community to adjust to the new reality, claiming that accommodation, compromise, and cooperation with the Muslims is the only way to secure their rights. They argue that the Maronites should end their historical conflict with Syria and the Arab Muslim world, and stress their Arabism and their community's contribution to the emergence of Arab nationalism. Paradoxically, some have even gone so far as to endorse Syria's presence in Lebanon both to prevent it from becoming an Iranian-style Islamic republic and to ensure their community's influence in the political system, through their hold on the presidency. Many Maronite leaders who had supported Israeli intervention in Lebanon are either denying or trying to justify their involvement with Israel.[33]

In 1920 the Maronites, helped by France, had established Greater Lebanon as a homeland and refuge for persecuted Christians in the Arab Muslim world. Whatever the future holds for the Maronites, Christian Lebanon under the Maronite hegemony, which had existed until 1975, is a thing of the past. The Maronites now share the fate of other Christian minorities in the Middle East, whose rights and very survival depend on the goodwill of the Muslim majority.

Notes

1. See a series of articles: "The Christians in Lebanon in the Second Republic," in *al-Hayat* (London), February 1994; *al-Shira'* (Beirut), 15, 22, and 29 August, and 5 September 1994.

2. Edward E. Azar and Renée E. Marlin, "The Cost of Protracted Social Conflict in the Middle East: The Case of Lebanon," in Gabriel Ben-Dor and David B. DeWitt (eds.), *Conflict Management in the Middle East* (Lexington, Mass.: Lexington Books, 1987), pp. 29–44; Kamal Salibi, "The Maronite Experiment," *Middle East Insight* 5, no. 1 (January–February 1987), pp. 21–30.

3. K. S. Salibi, *A House of Many Mansions: The History of Lebanon Reconsidered* (Berkeley: University of California Press, 1988); Amin Jumayyil, *Al-Rihan al-kabir* (Beirut: Dar al-Nahar, 1988); Joseph Abu-Khalil, *Qissat al-Mawarina fi al-harb* (Beirut: Sharikat al-Matbu'at lil-Tawzi' wal-Nashr, 1990). Abu-Khalil was editor of the Phalange newspaper *al-Amal* and a close aide of Bashir Jumayyil.

4. Raymond G. Helmick, "Internal Lebanese Politics: The Lebanese Front and Forces" in Halim Barakat (ed.), *Toward a Viable Lebanon* (London: Croom Helm, 1988), pp. 306–323; Michael Hudson, "The Problem of Authoritative Power," in Nadim Shehadi and Dana Haffar Mills (eds.), *Lebanon: A History of Conflict and Consensus* (London: The Centre for Lebanese Studies, 1988), pp. 229–230; Tewfik Khalaf, "The Phalange and the Maronite Community: From Lebanonism to Maronitism" in Roger Owen (ed.), *Essays on the Crisis in Lebanon* (London: Ithaca Press, 1976), pp. 43–57.

5. *Al-Shira'*, 29 August 1994; Ghassan Tueni, *Une Guérre pour les Autres* (Paris: Jean-Claude Lattes, 1985), pp. 99–100; Helmick, "Internal Lebanese Politics"; Paul Salem, *Bitter Legacy: Ideology and Politics in the Arab World* (Syracuse, N.Y.: Syracuse University Press, 1994), pp. 237–239. For a critical and even hostile view of the Maronite role in Lebanon, see Kamal Joumblatt, *I Speak for Lebanon* (London: Zed Press, 1982).

6. Farid Khazin, "The Communal Pact of National Identities: The Making and Politics of the 1943 National Pact," *Papers on Lebanon,* no. 12 (1992), and N. Shehadi, "The Idea of Lebanon," *Papers on Lebanon* no. 5 (1987); Salem, *Bitter Legacy,* pp. 232–233.

7. Michael Hudson, *The Precarious Republic: Political Modernization in Lebanon* (New York: Random House, 1968); Nawaf Salam, "The Institution of the Presidency in Elections in Lebanon" in Nadim Shehadi and Bridget Harney (eds.), *Politics and the Economy in Lebanon* (Oxford: The Centre for Lebanese Studies, 1989), pp. 69–74.

8. Hudson, *The Precarious Republic,* pp. 108, 273–290; Tueni, *Une Guérre,* pp. 74–75.

9. K. S. Salibi, *Crossroads to Civil War: Lebanon 1958–1976* (London: Ithaca Press, 1976), pp. 3–20.

10. Michael Hudson, "The Problem of Authoritative Power" in Shehadi and Mills, *Lebanon,* pp. 238, 263.

11. Charles Helou, *Hayat fi dhikrayat* (Beirut: Dar al-Nahar, 1995); Abu-Khalil, *Qissat al-Mawarina,* pp. 17–20.

12. Joumblatt, *I Speak,* p. 64; Rashid Khalidi, "The Palestinians and Lebanon," in Barakat, *Toward a Viable Lebanon,* pp. 133–144.

13. Abu-Khalil, *Qissat al-Mawarina,* pp. 25–28; Theodor Hanf, *Coexistence in Wartime Lebanon: Decline of a State and Rise of a Nation* (London: The Centre for Lebanese Studies and I. B. Tauris, 1993), pp. 373–393.

14. Hanf, *Coexistence,* pp. 402–403; Fouad Ajami, *The Vanished Imam: Musa al-Sadr and the Shi'a of Lebanon* (Ithaca, N.Y.: Cornell University Press, 1986), pp. 150–161; Owen, *Essays on the Crisis,* pp. 48–50.

15. Meir Zamir, "The Lebanese Presidential Elections of 1970 and Their Impact on the Civil War of 1975–1976," *Middle Eastern Studies* 16, no. 1 (January 1980), pp. 49–70.

16. Ibid.; Tueni, *Une Guérre,* pp. 87–90.

17. Abu-Khalil, *Qissat al-Mawarina,* pp. 57–64; Karim Pakradouni, *La Paix Manquée* (Hebrew translation) (Tel Aviv: Ma'arachot, Israel Ministry of Defense, 1986), pp. 21–25, 35–40; Itamar Rabinovich, *The War for Lebanon, 1970–1985* (Ithaca, N.Y.: Cornell University Press, 1985), pp. 51, 60–67.

18. Pakradouni, *La Paix Manquée,* pp. 96–102; Meir Zamir, "Politics and Violence in Lebanon," *The Jerusalem Quarterly,* no. 25 (fall 1982), pp. 3–26; Salim Al-Huss, *Zaman al-amal wal-khayba* (Beirut: Dar al-'Ilm lil-Malayin, 1992). Al-Huss served as prime minister under Elias Sarkis.

19. Abu-Khalil, *Qissat al-Mawarina,* pp. 209–217; Pakradouni, *La Paix Manquée,* pp. 131–137; Hanf, *Coexistence,* pp. 231–234.

20. Abu-Khalil, *Qissat al-Mawarina,* pp. 77–81; Pakradouni, *La Paix Manquée,* pp. 133–134.

21. Abu-Khalil, *Qissat al-Mawarina,* pp. 41–55, 103–105. The author took part in the negotiations with Israel from 1976. See also Ehud Ya'ari and Zeev Schiff, *Israel's Lebanon War* (New York: Simon and Schuster, 1984).

22. Abu-Khalil, *Qissat al-Mawarina,* pp. 225–238.

23. Jumayyil, *al-Rihan al-kabir,* pp. 27–47; Tueni, *Une Guérre,* pp. 84–85.

24. Jumayyil, *al-Rihan al-kabir,* pp. 194, 208–213; Tueni, *Une Guérre,* pp. 261–279. Tueni served as Lebanon's ambassador to the United Nations in 1977–1982. See also George W. Ball, *Error and Betrayal in Lebanon: An Analysis of Israel's Invasion of Lebanon and the Implications for US-Israeli Relations* (Washington, D.C.: USA Foundation for Middle East Peace, 1984).

25. Jumayyil, *al-Rihan al-kabir,* pp. 133–251; Abu-Khalil, *Qissat al-Mawarina,* pp. 365–379.

26. Abu-Khalil, *Qissat al-Mawarina,* pp. 433–436; Hanf, *Coexistence,* pp. 567–572.

27. Josef Maila, "The Document of National Understanding: A Commentary," *Prospects for Lebanon,* no. 4 (Oxford: The Centre for Lebanese Studies, 1992).

28. George Nader, "Interview with General Michel 'Awn, Prime Minister of Lebanon," *Middle East Insight* 6, no. 3 (fall 1988), pp. 24–27.

29. Hanf, *Coexistence,* pp. 598–601.

30. Deirdre Collings (ed.), *Peace for Lebanon? From War to Reconstruction* (Boulder, Colo.: Lynne Rienner, 1994), pp. 52–60.

31. Tueni, *Une Guérre,* pp. 125–127.

32. See interviews in *al-Shira'* with Michel 'Awn, 27 June 1994, and Amin Jumayyil, 4 July 1994. See also 22 August 1994.

33. Helou, *Hayat fi dhikrayat,* pp. 229–253, Ghassan Tueni's interview with Charles Helou, broadcast on Lebanese television, 4 June 1993. See also an interview with Nasrallah Sfayr, the Maronite patriarch, in *Middle East Insight* 10, no. 3 (March–April 1994), pp. 12–19.

7

The 'Alawis, Lords of Syria: From Ethnic Minority to Ruling Sect

Eyal Zisser

On 15 June 1936, six 'Alawi notables signed a petition addressed to French prime minister Leon Blum. The petition declared that the 'Alawi people were different from the Sunni Muslims and that the 'Alawis refused to be annexed to Muslim Syria because the official religion of the Syrian state is Islam, and according to Islam, the 'Alawis are considered infidels.[1]

Among the 'Alawi notables who signed this petition was 'Ali Sulayman, a member of the Kalbiyya tribe from the small town of Qardaha.[2] Four decades later, on 16 November 1970, his son, Hafiz al-Asad, seized power in Syria and since 22 February 1971 has served as president. There could be no clearer evidence of the 'Alawi community's departure from its separatist path in favor of integration into the Syrian state and society. Moreover, this once isolated minority group has been transformed into the ruling community of Syria. Under 'Alawi rule, Syria has evolved from a feeble and unsettled state, whose very viability was in doubt, into a regional power with aspirations to hegemony in the Middle East.

The story of the 'Alawi sect is unprecedented and to a great extent unique in the history of the Middle East. Whereas most minority sects in the region have, indeed, managed to integrate into the modern Middle Eastern state, in most cases they have not been able to entirely overcome the sectarian barriers, certainly not to the extent of attaining veritable positions of power.

The case of the 'Alawis is unique not only because this sect ascended to a position of power, but also because of its humble origins. For many years, the 'Alawis were a separatist minority sect, socially and economically deprived, geographically isolated, and, moreover, considered heretical. Throughout its history, this sect lacked a tradition of a self-rule (even on its own territory) and had always been governed by others.

The history of the 'Alawi sect gives rise to a host of questions concerning their climb to the top. Why, for example, did the 'Alawis choose to coalesce with the Syrian state? How did they become its overseers and the guarantors of its stability? Most crucially, is their merger with the Syrian state irreversible, or is 'Alawi status in Syria, and by implication the future of the Syrian state, still uncertain?

The 'Alawis in Syria: Square One

The 'Alawi community is Syria's largest minority group. It constitutes approximately 12 percent of the state's population—more than two million people. Most—more than 70 percent—are concentrated in the 'Alawi Mountains, also referred to as Jabal al-Nusayriyya. 'Alawi concentrations can also be found along the Syrian coast, in the interior lowlands east of the 'Alawi Mountains, and in rural areas around the cities of Hama and Homs. About a quarter of a million or more 'Alawis now reside in Damascus and Aleppo.[3]

For many years, the 'Alawi community was regarded as contemptible and inferior by the surrounding Sunni society.[4] The 'Alawi Mountain region, where most members of the community dwelled, was a remote area lacking economic or political significance. The main difficulties that faced the 'Alawi community stemmed from religious friction. In the eyes of the Sunni majority, the 'Alawis (Nusayris), who broke away from the Shi'is some thousand years ago, were (and remain) non-Muslim, heretical, and idolatrous. A formal ruling handed down by Shaykh al-Islam Ibn Taymiyya (1263–1328) determined that spilling 'Alawi blood is permissible if the 'Alawis fail to repent and return to Islam.[5]

One salient feature in the life of the 'Alawi community through the years was a lack of internal cohesion, manifested by factionalism and individualistic orientations. The 'Alawis were and remain organized as a four-part tribal confederation of the Kalbiyya, Haddadin, Khayyatin, and Matawira/Numilatiyya. However, this tribal configuration was loose and unstable and in some regions, such as the coastal plain, there was no tribal framework whatsoever.[6]

The community also lacked any recognized, legitimate religious establishment. Clerics operated within an individual tribe or clan, and only rarely was an individual cleric's authority recognized by more than one tribe. The community was also divided into a number of religious groups: the Qamariyya, Shamsiyya, Ghaybiyya, and, in this century, the Murshidiyya.

The 'Alawis Under the French Mandate:
From Isolationism to Integration

A change in the status of the 'Alawi community came about only in the early 1920s with the collapse of the Ottoman Empire and the French entry into Syria. French divide-and-conquer policy encouraged separatist tendencies in Syrian society in order to weaken the Sunni majority and cripple its capacity to actualize nationalist aspirations to an independent Arab or Syrian state.[7] In 1920, France established "the Autonomous District of the 'Alawis" in the 'Alawi region along the Syrian coast. In 1922, they made the district into "the State of the 'Alawis," also known as "The Territory of the 'Alawis" (Territoire des Alaouites in the French documents, or Dawlat al-'Alawiyyin in the Arabic). Since 1930 the French used the less provocative name, "Government of Ladhiqiyya." An 'Alawi entity existed until 1936 and then was re-established upon the outbreak of World War II, lasting from 1939 to 1942. The French also sought to reinforce 'Alawi communal identity. They recognized the 'Alawis as a discrete religious group and installed a separate court system as they had done for the other religious communities in the state.[8]

'Alawi response to French policy was not uniform. Many took issue with the French authorities and feared for the integrity and preservation of 'Alawi autonomy. Thus, from the end of 1918 until mid-1921, Shaykh Salih al-'Ali led a rebellion against the French in the region. The rebels used Arab nationalist slogans in their appeals to the population and were in contact with Ibrahim Hanunu, who led the anti-French revolt in northern Syria, and with Faysal's regime in Damascus.[9] Once the al-'Ali revolt had been quelled, many 'Alawi notables changed their allegiances and joined the ranks of the supporters of France. The 'Alawis seem to have felt no sense of obligation to a pan-Arabist or pan-Syrian ideology, but they were grateful to the French for having elevated their economic and political status.[10]

Toward Integration Within Syria

How, then, did the 'Alawis make their way into the Syrian state? The accepted assumption is that the French themselves were responsible for this by abolishing the 'Alawi state in 1936 and coercively incorporating it into Syria, as part of the agreement they had reached with the Syrian "national bloc" leaders.[11] The Syrian-French Agreement was not ratified by the French legislature in Paris, but it was enough to strike a death blow to the separatist tendencies of the 'Alawi leaders and notables.

It would nevertheless appear that despite the decisive role of the French and of the Syrian national bloc leaders in transforming the political status of the 'Alawi community, the 'Alawi "decision" to unite with the Syrian state involved a number of additional factors.

There were, to begin with, geopolitical reasons for unification. In the framework of the Mediterranean new order that emerged in the 1930s, and especially after World War II, the geopolitical status of the 'Alawi district actually fostered Alawi integration into Syria and not the other way around. There were at least four reasons for this. First, the 'Alawi district lacked an economic infrastructure capable of supporting an independent state. Its sole prospect for economic development was its conversion into Syria's commercial gateway to Europe. Second, because of the region's negligible political and economic import, few European powers were interested in its lot, especially when their attention was focused in the south, on events in Lebanon and Palestine. Third, the 'Alawi majority in the 'Alawi district was not absolute, unlike the Druze majority in the Druze Mountains. Moreover, in some of the coastal towns that made up the political and economic center of the 'Alawi region, they were actually a minority.[12] Fourth, in 1939, the Turks annexed the Alexandretta District as stipulated in an agreement they had struck with France. Thousands of 'Alawis vacated the area, resulting in hostility against Turkey among the Syrian 'Alawis, who feared that Turkish expansionism would reach southward along the Syrian coast.[13]

Another factor behind 'Alawi unification with the Syrian state was the absence of Western support: in contrast to other minorities in the Middle East during the Ottoman period, primarily Christian communities and even the Druzes, the 'Alawis did not forge any special relationship with a Western power. The French, who were the first to demonstrate interest and become actively involved in the community's affairs, were motivated mainly by political interest. Thus, after signing the agreement with the national bloc in 1936, France informed the 'Alawis that it could not guarantee the preservation of an independent 'Alawi entity. The British, who ruled the Levant in tandem with the French from 1941 to 1945, endeavored diligently to merge the 'Alawis into Syria. It seems that the British and Americans regarded the area as possessing marginal strategic significance. In the 1930s the British established Haifa as the port for their Iraqi pipeline, whereas in the mid-1940s, the Americans chose the Lebanese port of Tripoli for receiving the Tapline pipe from Saudi Arabia.

'Alawi social structure was not conducive to autonomy. As already noted, the community lacked internal cohesion and even exhibited individualistic tendencies. In addition, the 'Alawis had no organized religious establishment and thus lacked both religious and educational institutions. Because they were a remote community with scant contact with the West, they were not exposed to the influence of Western ideologies. These seem to be some of the reasons why the 'Alawis, like the Druzes and unlike the Maronites, did not turn their tribal and communal identification into a separatist nationalism.[14]

Finally, it seems that the "Syrian option," that is, entry into the framework of the Syrian state, was the only way not to miss out on the fruits of modernity that were being harvested in the Levant: cultural enrichment, material wealth, social betterment, political emancipation, and ideological sophistication. For example, in the sphere of education, the 'Alawi areas suffered from a dearth of schools capable of providing professional training. Thus 'Alawi youth interested in upward mobility had no choice but to attend the Syrian public schools. As a result, they encountered and adopted Arab and Syrian nationalist views. Hafiz al-Asad's own background typifies this. He left the home of his birth, Qardaha, at age fourteen and moved to Ladhiqiyya, where he received his high school education. There he began to participate in anti-French demonstrations and by age sixteen had already joined the Ba'th Party.[15]

Onward and Upward

With Syrian independence, some members of the 'Alawi community began the process of meshing their co-religionists with the Syrian state. The two most practical paths to this end (which eventually brought 'Alawis to the summit of power in Syria) were the army and the radical political parties, especially the Ba'th and the Parti Populaire Syrien (PPS).

The army was already a means of upward mobility for the 'Alawis, other minority communities, and rural Sunnis at the time of the French Mandate. The 'Alawis found a common language with these similarly underprivileged groups and sometimes a basis for collaboration in the struggle against social and economic discrimination. Following the decline of the Sunni officer class, which had dominated the army as a result of their intensive involvement in politics that generated personal, regional, and ideological struggles, the 'Alawi officers formed a more cohesive and coordinated group than officers from other backgrounds.[16]

The young 'Alawis who were exposed to the radical worldviews circulating in Syria in schools or in the army were eventually swept up by them. These views apparently reflected the latent wishes and aspirations of that generation of 'Alawis, enabling them to envision their role in the emerging political, social, and economic order in Syria and in the region at large. They found in the radical ideologies (especially in their socioeconomic aspect) an answer to their feelings of alienation and deprivation. The nationalist dimension of these ideologies (whether Arab nationalist as in Ba'thist doctrine, or Syrian nationalist as in the creed of the PPS) held out the promise of a full merger as equals with the surrounding Syrian or Arab nation.

The 'Alawis' role in the "struggle for Syria" in the 1950s was marginal. They did not oppose the efforts made by successive Syrian governments to restrict 'Alawi representation in the Parliament and amalgamate the community into the Syrian state. The 'Alawis were scattered among various political forces, most of them radical, which were controlled at that time by non-'Alawis.[17]

After the Ba'th Revolution of 8 March 1963

On 8 March 1963, the Ba'th revolution overturned the political establishment and, in fact, terminated an entire political system, which was the only one Syria had known until that time. The main force behind the coup was "the Military Committee," a group of army officers who were close to the Ba'th Party but not formal members. The leadership of the Military Committee comprised five officers, all of minority stock: three 'Alawis (Salah Jadid, Muhammad 'Umran, and Hafiz al-Asad) and two Isma'ilis ('Abd al-Karim al-Jundi and Ahmad al-Mirr).[18]

Despite 'Alawi dominance of the Military Committee, the 'Alawi officers needed additional partners to pull off the coup, both within the Military Committee itself and among the army ranks. Moreover, after the coup, the Military Committee appealed to the veteran leaders of the Ba'th Party, Michel 'Aflaq and Salah al-Baytar, requesting their sponsorship. Thus between 1963 and 1966, they, alongside senior Sunni officers such as Amin al-Hafiz, served as window dressing for the Ba'th regime.

One must ask why the 'Alawi officers balked at revealing the extent of their role to the Syrian public. First, they were quite young, inexperienced, and lacking in self-confidence. Second, the officers seem to have feared that the Syrian public was not prepared to accept 'Alawi hegemony. Third, in light of the challenges facing the Ba'th regime from the outset, it was imperative that the officers muster as broad support as was possible, even if this meant sharing power. Fourth, the 'Alawi cabal was insufficiently crystalized and had no leader acceptable to all members in the group. Finally, the 'Alawi officers regarded themselves as Arab-Syrian nationalists, and not representatives of the 'Alawi community, and therefore attempted to avoid the appearance of operating qua 'Alawis and in pursuit of 'Alawi interests.

Between 1966 and 1970 as well, once the 'Alawis indisputably held the Syrian reigns of power, Salah Jadid, the man in control and an 'Alawi, declined to serve as president. He preferred to remain behind the scenes, as assistant to the secretary-general of the regional command of the Ba'th Party, and left the titular offices of power to a Sunni president, Nur al-Din al-Atasi. Only with Hafiz al-Asad's ascent to power, on 16 November 1970, following the corrective revolution he conducted against Salah Jadid and his supporters, was the veil lifted. On 22 February 1971, Asad was elected president of Syria, thereby revealing unambiguously the 'Alawi hegemony over the army and the Syrian state.

It is appropriate to note three central elements in the process of 'Alawi mastery over Syria, which became more salient with Asad's triumph, and which preserve the regime he has continued to lead through the late 1990s. They are the consolidation of the 'Alawi community, especially within the army and the Ba'th Party, behind the universally accepted leadership of Hafiz al-Asad; the metamorphosis of the 'Alawi community into the main support of the regime; and the arranging of a covenant between the 'Alawis on the one hand and other minorities and rural Sunnis on the other.

The need to unify the 'Alawi community behind Asad's leadership became apparent soon after the Ba'th coup of 1963, when an acute conflict erupted among the three ringleaders of the Military Committee, Salah Jadid, Muhammad 'Umran, and Hafiz al-Asad, over control of the 'Alawi community and over that of Syria. The struggle was conducted along ideological lines, such as over differences between Salah Jadid's radical domestic and foreign policies and Hafiz al-Asad's more moderate and pragmatic policies. Yet there were also personal, family, and even tribal dimensions to the dispute. Asad hailed from the Kalbiyya tribe, 'Umran from the Khayyatin, and Jadid from the Haddadin.

In 1965, Hafiz al-Asad and Salah Jadid joined forces to depose Muhammad 'Umran. He was exiled from Syria and eventually assassinated by agents sent by Asad on 4 March 1972, in Tripoli, Lebanon. Between 1966 and 1970, Asad and Jadid constantly vied for advantage. Asad won this protracted feud, and after his corrective revolution on 16 November 1970, Jadid and his circle were imprisoned. Even in jail, Jadid was considered a threat to the regime, and for this reason he remained incarcerated until his death on 18 July 1993.[19]

After Asad seized power in Syria and became the de facto leading figure in the 'Alawi community, he turned his attention to strengthening his grip on this community. His first step was to bolster his position within his family and tribe. It is as a result of this effort that the core of Asad's regime has been composed of members of the Kalbiyya tribe, headed by members of the Asad family: his brothers Rif'at and Jamil (until the mid-1980s), his son Basil, and, since his death, Bashshar and Mahir. Alongside them in the highest echelons of the regime are members of the Makhluf family, the largest and most prominent in the area of Asad's birth. Asad is married to Anisa Makhluf, whose cousin, 'Adnan Makhluf, was the commander for many years of the Republican Guard, the elite force responsible for the regime's security.[20]

Asad's second step in consolidating his hold on the 'Alawi community was to arrange a system of alliances among its families, tribes, and clans by means of marriage and the appointment of family and tribal representatives to important posts in the regime. For instance, Asad appointed members of leading families from other tribes to key positions: 'Ali Duba, whose family comes from the Matawira/Numilatiyya tribe, was appointed head of the Military Security Department; and 'Ali Haydar, from the Haddadin tribe, was appointed commander of the Special Forces. There are also strategic marriages between the Asads and those prominent families of the 'Alawi community whose members command crucial posts in the army, including the match of Rif'at Asad's daughter with the son of the then Third Division commander Shafiq Fayyad (now commander of the Third Corps), in an attempt to cool passions aroused in the 1983–1984 struggle over government succession.[21]

Once he secured the allegiance of the 'Alawi community, or at least the recognition by most of its members of his leadership, Asad turned it into the main prop of the regime. The 'Alawis gradually gained sway over the army and internal security forces. Today, they fill most of the commanding positions in the elite units of the Syrian Army and supervise most organs of state security. Three out of the four bodies of internal security are in the hands of 'Alawis: 'Adnan Badr Hasan heads Political Security, Ibrahim Huwayji heads Air Force Security, and 'Ali Duba heads the Military Security Department.[22] In the government and party, 'Alawis such as Minister of the Interior Muhammad Hirba, Minister of Information Muhammad Salman, and Ahmad Dighram, a member of the regional command, hold many of the vital offices. 'Alawi domination of high political posts, however, is not as absolute as that of the army and internal security.[23]

With the 'Alawi community firmly behind him and its members serving as the engine of his regime, Asad directed his efforts to building bridges between 'Alawis and others. The 'Alawis are cognizant of their weaknesses; therefore, 'Alawi officers have always sought partners along their road to power and today endeavor to broaden the base of support for their policies and ideology as much as possible. Other minority groups, principally the Druzes and Isma'ilis, are longtime confederates. Thus, the leadership of the Military Committee comprised two Isma'ilis and later a Druze in addition to 'Alawis. The 'Alawis, however, did not require Druzes and Isma'ilis as ruling partners, but rather as supporters and assistants, and when the non-'Alawi members of the Military Committee attempted to preserve and fortify their standing in the mid-1960s, a power struggle ensued in which the non-'Alawis were toppled.[24]

No less important was the coalition between 'Alawis and rural Sunnis. Their understanding was originally based on a common interest in extirpating the old regime, in effect the entire old order in Syria, and in implementing a just distribution of power and resources. Provincial Sunni officers and politicians proved to be convenient and loyal confederates, as they rallied around the regime without reservation in its most trying hours. The present configuration of Syria's political leadership reflects this relationship. The vice president, 'Abd al-Halim Khaddam, is a Sunni from the town of Banyas. Prime Minister Mahmud al-Zu'bi and Foreign Minister Faruq al-Shar' are Sunnis from Dar'a, and the minister of defense, Mustafa Talas, is a Sunni from the village of Rustan near Homs.[25]

Since the early 1990s, a new pact has been in effect—this time between the 'Alawi officers and the urbanized Sunni economic elite, prompted by the "economic openness" policy recently adopted by the regime. This is a symbiotic covenant between Sunnis, whose priority is political stability as a means of achieving economic stability, and 'Alawis, who deliver political stability in exchange for recognition of the regime's political legitimacy from the erstwhile foes of Ba'th hegemony and 'Alawi power.[26] One manifestation of this covenant was the expansion of the representation of the Sunni economic elite in the Syrian People's assembly following the elections to the Assembly that took place in May 1990 and in August 1994 and, consequently, the expansion of the authorities of this assembly, especially in the social and economic spheres.[27]

Is 'Alawi Integration Irreversible?

Many observers claim that the 'Alawis are so firmly meshed into the fabric of Syrian state and society as to be permanent. This opinion is founded on two main arguments: at present, there is no real threat to the 'Alawis' sway over Syria, and as a result, they continue to regard their integration with the rest of Syria as their best option, perhaps their only one. So far, the sect has managed to preserve stability in Syria. For the time being, the community is successful as well in preserving its internal unity, and the regime acts to reinforce it as much as possible.[28]

Furthermore, the large migration of 'Alawis into Syria's large urban centers, which followed the community's ascent to power, would seem to strike a demographic coup de grace to notions of 'Alawi separatism. Many settled in Aleppo, and a larger number settled in Damascus, where more than a quarter of a million reside today. They constitute in great measure the political and economic elite of the 'Alawi community, although the 'Alawi Mountains remain their center of gravity and source of communal power.[29]

The 'Alawis and the Syrian State: "The Other Option"

Nevertheless, one cannot overlook the fact that the 'Alawis' integration into the Syrian state and their rise to the status of its dominant community paradoxically carry the seeds of their own destruction and a reversion to the separatist option. To begin with, the success of the 'Alawis aggravated tensions between them and other segments of the Syrian population, chiefly the urban Sunnis. What is more, this success changed the face of the 'Alawi community and of its territorial base in ways that could expedite adoption of the separatist option in the future, in the event that the Sunnis move to dismantle 'Alawi hegemony.

Such a move is by no means inconceivable. For one thing, the Sunni majority still regards the 'Alawis as socially inferior. While recognizing the 'Alawis' political and military puissance and appreciating the economic strides they have made, the average Sunni still harbors feelings of condescension and contempt toward them. There is much evidence of an abiding Sunni unwillingness to accept 'Alawi integration into Syrian society. Intermarriage between the two communities, for example, is rare.[30]

Furthermore, the Sunnis still see the 'Alawis as heretics and illegitimate as Muslims, as the Muslim Brotherhood stressed in the revolt that began in 1976.[31] The regime's efforts to win religious legitimacy for the 'Alawi community have failed. The Syrian regime also encouraged relations between 'Alawis and Shi'is throughout the Muslim world, with emphasis on Iran, and even arranged for Iranian religious activity in Damascus. However, despite their political alliance with the ruling Ba'th Party in Syria, the Iranians refused to give religious accreditation to the 'Alawi community.[32]

Because the 'Alawis became fully identified with the Ba'th regime, the entire community has been further stigmatized by Ba'thist secularism and its putative anti-Islamic ideology. The community was also tainted by the regime's harsh suppression of its opponents and seen as guilty by association of the Ba'th's radical social and economic policies that hurt the middle and upper classes of urban Sunni society.

During the Muslim Brotherhood Revolt of 1976–1982, the fury against both the regime and the 'Alawi community was plainly evinced as the rebels attacked 'Alawis who had no connection to the regime, and made efforts to frustrate the integration of 'Alawis into the Syrian state and society. These deeds provoked the 'Alawis to respond in kind, for example at Ladhiqiyya in mid-1981, because they perceived the regime's reaction as inadequate. According to a number of reports, the revolt prompted population transfers of 'Alawis from Sunni areas and vice versa.[33] Indeed, following the suppression of the rebellion, the Islamic movement in Syria was effectively crushed and suspended all organized activity. It would, nevertheless, seem that Islamic sentiments in Syria have remained as they were, although they are now submerged.[34]

Additionally, the 'Alawis' climb to the apex of Syrian government induced fundamental changes in their community and heartland that cannot but help shape the 'Alawi future in Syria.

First of all, ever since Asad took power, the regime has channeled a substantial portion of the state's resources to the 'Alawi region for its development. Its transportation and communication systems have been retooled, and its ports—Ladhiqiyya, Banyas, and Tartus—enlarged. A comprehensive economic infrastructure, including factories, refineries, and power plants, was installed. Education and health care systems were significantly improved.[35]

The newfound prosperity of the 'Alawi region in itself will not necessarily reawaken separatism, but if such a tendency resurfaces in the future for whatever reason, the region might well be capable of supporting a viable independent entity, whereas earlier in the century isolationist plans had to be abandoned, in part, because of the region's economic helplessness.

Second, the integration of the 'Alawis with Syria did not erase or weaken the 'Alawis' sense of ethnic identity, that is, the internal communal cohesion cemented by notions of duty and loyalty, but rather revitalized it. The advantages of this sense of unity were evident during the struggle for control of the country. The banding together of the community was accompanied by the emergence of a legitimate leadership over it: that of Hafiz al-Asad and his family. Such features as communal unity under a common leadership stand in sharp contrast to the conditions of 'Alawi society of the 1930s and 1940s. A prominent symbol of 'Alawi communal coordination was the founding, in 1980, of a political-military organization for the 'Alawi region to support the government's efforts in combating the Muslim Brotherhood. Called 'Ali al-Murtada, at one point it numbered tens of thousands of members and was headed by Asad's brother, Jamil al-Asad. The association crumbled in the mid-1980s, however, during the conflict over the succession between Asad and his brother, Rif'at.[36] Another example of communal cohesion was the rallying of 'Alawi officers who opposed the coalition of the president's Sunni protégés around Rif'at al-Asad during the president's illness and before he recovered in November 1983.[37]

It is worth mentioning in this context the argument made by Alain Chouet in his article "'Alawi Tribal Space Tested by Power: Disintegration by Politics." According to Chouet, with the second generation of 'Alawi power, the internal forms and external contours of the community have already lost their traditional structure. The transformation appears irreversible, whatever happens in the future to the dominance of the ruling family and community. Among the 'Alawis, the notion of tribe, still of primordial importance to Hafiz al-Asad's strategies when he was establishing his authority, is disappearing in favor of two vaguer concepts, the extended family (at the more immediate level) and the nation (in a higher sense). Nevertheless, Chouet continued by arguing:

> In fact, what we have witnessed is a social transition from a defensive organization centered on a geographically anchored tribal affiliation, to a conquering and aggressive organization based on the tactical capacity of skillful "godfathers" to manage their relations with the rest of the country, even the region, and to instrumentalize their clients. The notion of "'Ashira", exclusionist clan solidarity founded on family proximity and blood ties in a closed isolated economy, is thus giving way, without losing the operating models, to that of "'Asabiyya", an inclusive solidarity founded on the func-

tional benefits that members can bring to the "band" ("*jama'a*") in an urban context open to the larger world.[38]

Thus, it seems that the arguments made by Chouet support our assumption that the sense of ethnic identity among the 'Alawis ('Asabiyya) was strengthened, although as Chouet remarked, not any more on a familial or a tribal basis, but on a different one.

There is no doubt that President Asad's leadership and the convergence of the 'Alawi sect around it are the true keys to 'Alawi control of Syria. This being the case, one must question the future of the Syrian regime when Asad departs the scene. Indeed, the re-eruption of the struggle over succession since the mid-1990s has already generated cracks in the stability of 'Alawi rule and especially in the cohesion of the 'Alawi top leadership. As this stability and cohesion constitute the major source of power for the sect, the continuation of 'Alawi rule over Syria depends, to a large extent, on their preservation.

Since 1990, President Asad has clearly been making efforts to ensure the continuation of his dynasty, especially in view of his increasing awareness of his age and state of health.[39] Asad had tried to promote his elder son Basil as an heir, but after Basil's death in a road accident in January 1994, he transferred this goal to his second son, Bashshar. These efforts were accompanied by Asad's attempt to revitalize Syria's military and security ranks in order to boost his son's chances.[40]

Asad's measures led to the re-emergence of the succession issue and to the continuation (albeit moderate, at this stage) of the struggle over the succession, whose roots extend back to the previously mentioned conflict of 1983–1984, when Asad suffered a heart attack and his brother Rif'at tried unsuccessfully to exploit his brother's convalescence to promote his own chances to be heir.[41] Furthermore, it seems that high-ranking 'Alawi officers felt threatened by Asad's effort to revitalize the top ranks, as well as by his desire to promote his son, who is both young (in his thirties) and inexperienced. Asad's response to this dissatisfaction was typified by the arrest of 'Ali Haydar (the former commander of the Special Forces and one of the props of the Syrian regime) in July 1994, after he spoke against Asad.[42]

Although in 1998 the regime seems to have contained the crisis, it is clear that its stability and the appearance of cohesion that it has projected for many years have been eroded. Moreover, there are doubts as to whether members of the sect would be able to maintain cohesion once Asad departs the scene and a struggle over the succession ensues (e.g., between his son Bashshar; his brother Rif'at, who returned from exile in 1992 and is now in Syria; and other 'Alawi officers). A brothers' war, or perhaps one between Asad's family and other families and tribes, might lead to the disintegration of the regime and, subsequently, to the end of 'Alawi dominance.[43]

Conclusion

In the late 1930s, the 'Alawis decided to throw in their lot with that of Syria. The attractions of such a move, such as the prospects of social and economic mobility for 'Alawi youth, were irresistible for several reasons: the nonfeasibility at the time of the separatist option due to the lack of Western sponsorship, the absence of a common ideology and an economic infrastructure to support an independent 'Alawi entity, and the debilitating infighting among rival circles.

The 'Alawis did well in the path they chose for themselves. They succeeded in becoming a vital part of the Syrian state, ultimately mastering it and contributing in return the blessing of a stable central government. Under Asad, the 'Alawis managed to consolidate a coalition of forces that represent wide sectors of Syrian society, among them other minorities, rural Sunnis, and some parts of the Sunni urban elite. These forces support the regime because it is worthwhile for them to do so or because they have no better alternative. As a result, Syria has been able to develop from its unsteady and feeble origins into a regional power.

In view of the aforementioned, one may ask whether the rise to power of the 'Alawis in Syria heralded a new era in sect-state relations and intersectarian relations in Syria. This, indeed, seems to be the case, as Syria, since the 1970s, appears to have undergone a novel experience in which minority sects endeavored to integrate into the state (or the state manages to impose its control over the various sects) and cooperated among themselves within the framework of the state, if only on a provisional basis.

Thus, the possibility that the 'Alawis would once more embrace, willingly or otherwise, the separatist option, seems remote and purely speculative. However, as has already been demonstrated here, the integration of the sects into the state did not abolish the sectarian frameworks or the sectarian identity and affiliation of Syrian citizens; nor did it do away with the psychological and other barriers standing between the sects. It would thus seem that the fortunes of the 'Alawi sect in Syria since this country gained its independence constitute a separate and independent chapter in the history of this sect, but by no means the concluding one. Indeed, the 'Alawi road to integration with the Syrian state was littered with the resentments created by friction with other communities. Moreover, changes in the 'Alawi community and region make the separatist option workable if the desire or need for it were to arise. Moreover, as previously noted, 'Alawi communal loyalty remains as strong as ever. When Patrick Seale interviewed the mayor of Qardaha about 'Alawi identity during his research for his biography of Asad, the mayor was quick to wave the flag of Arab nationalism: "We have neither tribes nor families, for we are all members of the Ba'th family under the direction of Hafiz al-Asad." When Seale pressed him on the point, however, the mayor confessed to his city's links to Kalbiyya, Asad's tribe and the leading 'Alawi tribe, which constitutes the basic and perhaps strongest affiliation for 'Alawis.[44]

From this it follows that the process of 'Alawi integration with Syria and the rise to hegemony produced the potential for its own collapse. Indeed, certain indications and even outright threats issued by Sunnis about the fate awaiting the 'Alawis if the Sunnis depose them—threats that were partly realized during the revolt of the Muslim Brotherhood—prompted 'Alawi counterthreats that, in such an event, the 'Alawis would secede from Syria and withdraw to the 'Alawi region where they constitute the majority, and which they have turned into a formidable economic and political base during their rule of Syria.[45]

Moreover, despite the stability of the Syrian regime, there have recently been signs that may attest to a danger to its cohesiveness in the event of Asad's departure and to a possible eruption of a struggle over the succession. In such a case, the shackles binding the coalition led by Asad may disintegrate. Sunni sectors, such as the rural Sunnis and Sunni businessmen, who now support the regime (and implicitly 'Alawi hegemony in Syria), regarding it as the key to stability in the country, might change their mind. This could lead to the deterioration of the 'Alawi regime or encourage opposition groups that have so far been submerged. As in the past, Sunni pressure against the 'Alawis might induce 'Alawi counterpressure. It may be reasonable to assume that all sides would wish to avoid escalation, but in time of crisis, such as the scenario described previously, all boundaries might be crossed.

It would therefore seem that although the 'Alawis have crossed the Rubicon in merging with Syria, they left some bridges intact. If, for one reason or another, the 'Alawis lose their position of supremacy in Syria, or if separatist aspirations reassert themselves, the 'Alawis will have come full circle, completing a long journey that brought them out of their isolation in the 'Alawi district into the thick of Syrian affairs, only to lead them back again. One cannot predict what Syria would be like were this to occur, but it is safe to assume that it would be profoundly different than it is at present, under the 'Alawis.

Notes

1. For the full text of the petition, see Matti Moosa, *Extremist Shi'ites: The Ghulat Sects* (Syracuse, N.Y.: Syracuse University Press, 1987), pp. 287–288.

2. 'Ali Sulayman was appointed in 1926 by the French Mandate authorities to the committee for drafting a constitution for the 'Alawi state. See Patrick Seale, *Asad of Syria: The Struggle for the Middle East* (London: I. B. Tauris, 1988), p. 20. It should be noted that according to some sources, Asad is of the Matawira tribe and not the Kalbiyya. See Moshe Ma'oz, *Asad—The Sphinx of Damascus* (in Hebrew) (Tel Aviv: Dvir, 1988), pp. 33–34. See also Bassam Tibi, "The Simultaneity of the Unsimultane-

ous: Old Tribes and Imposed Nation State in the Modern Middle East," in Philip S. Khoury and Joseph Kostiner (eds.), *Tribes and State Formation in the Middle East* (London: I. B. Tauris, 1991), pp. 138–140.

3. For more on the 'Alawi community, see Mahmud A. Faksh, "The Alawi Community of Syria: A New Dominant Political Force," *Middle Eastern Studies* 20, no. 2 (April 1984), pp. 133–135; Peter Gubser, "Minorities in Power—The Alawites of Syria," in R. D. McLaurin (ed.), *Political Role of Minority Groups in the Middle East* (New York: Praeger, 1979), pp. 17–48; Daniel Pipes, "The Alawi Capture of Power in Syria," *Middle Eastern Studies* 25, no. 4 (October 1989), pp. 429–450.

4. Until the beginning of the twentieth century, the 'Alawis were known eponymously as Nusayris, after Muhammad bin al-Nusayr, who was among the founders of the 'Alawi faith. It was only after the establishment of the French Mandate that the Nusayris began to call themselves and be referred to by others as "'Alawis," although this appellation was already used by Shi'i Muslims to denote the followers of 'Ali. See Moosa, *Extremist Shi'ites*, pp. 255–256.

5. Moosa, *Extremist Shi'ites*, p. 414; Martin Kramer, "Syria's Alawis and the Shi'ism," in Martin Kramer (ed.), *Shi'ism: Resistance and Revolution* (Boulder, Colo.: Westview, 1982), p. 238.

6. Gubser, "Minorities in Power," pp. 22–23, 26.

7. In this context, see Philip Khoury, *Syria and the French Mandate: The Politics of Arab Nationalism* (Princeton, N.J.: Princeton University Press, 1987), pp. 59–61; Faksh, "The Alawi Community," pp. 136–138.

8. For French policy toward the 'Alawis, see Itamar Rabinovich, "The Compact Minorities and the Syrian State, 1918–45," *Journal of Contemporary History* 14, no. 4 (October 1979), pp. 693–712.

9. For more, see Khoury, *Syria and the French Mandate*, pp. 99–102; Moosa, *Extremist Shi'ites*, pp. 282–284; and Pipes, "The 'Alawi Capture of Power," p. 438.

10. The case of Sulayman al-Murshid (1900–1946) is a conspicuous instance of this type of collaboration with the French; al-Murshid established and led a social-religious movement to promote 'Alawi separatism. Al-Murshid became an ardent advocate of an independent 'Alawi state under French auspices. After the 'Alawi district was annexed to Syria, al-Murshid succeeded in being elected to the Syrian Parliament in 1943 but was hanged in 1946 by the central government in Damascus on charges of subversion. After his death, his son Mujib took up his cause, inciting a failed uprising against the central government in 1952. The Murshidiyya movement exists to this day as a religious sect and perhaps as a sociopolitical association as well, focused on Murshid's sons, Saji and Mujib. See Gitta Yaffe, "Suleiman al-Murshid: Beginning of the Alawi Leader," *Middle Eastern Studies* 29, no. 4 (October 1993), pp. 624–640; Khoury, *Syria and the French Mandate*, pp. 478, 524–525; Moosa, *Extremist Shi'ites*, p. 418.

11. See Khoury, *Syria and the French Mandate*, pp. 485–493.

12. Gubser, "Minorities in Power," p. 19.

13. See Seale, *Asad*, pp. 27–30. On the question of Alexandretta, see also Khoury, *Syria and the French Mandate*, pp. 494–514; Robert B. Satloff, "Prelude to Conflict: Communal Independence in the Sanjak of Alexandretta, 1920–38," *Middle Eastern Studies* 22, no. 2 (April 1986), pp. 147–180; Yosef Olmert, "Britain, Turkey and the Levant Question During the Second World War," *Middle Eastern Studies* 23, no. 4 (October 1987), pp. 437–452.

14. Bassam Tibi goes even further, claiming that the "national ideology of Arabism serves as a legitimizing formula in the tribal set-up in Syria." Tibi, "The Simultaneity of the Unsimultaneous," p. 142.

15. Seale, *Asad,* pp. 11–13; *Tishrin,* 9 March 1988.

16. See Michael van Dusen Hillegas, *Intra- and Inter-Generational Conflict in the Syrian Army,* Ph.D. dissertation, the Johns Hopkins University (Ann Arbor, Mich.: University Microfilms, 1991).

17. For example, following the 22 April 1955 assassination of the army's second in command, 'Adnan al-Maliki, by an 'Alawi sergeant and PPS member, Yusuf 'Abd al-Karim, forces throughout the spectrum of Syrian politics united to eliminate that party. Salah Jadid, for instance, belonged to the Ba'th Party, whereas his brother, Major Ghassan Jadid, was the senior representative of the PPS Party in the Syrian Army. Ghassan Jadid fled to Lebanon where he was murdered in 1957. For more see Gubser, "Minorities in Power," p. 40; Patrick Seale, *The Struggle for Syria: A Study of Post-War Arab Politics* (New York: Oxford University Press, 1965), pp. 183–184, 268–273.

18. See Itamar Rabinovich, *Syria Under the Ba'th 1963–66: The Army-Party Symbiosis* (Jerusalem: Israeli University Press, 1972).

19. *Le Monde* (Paris), 24 August 1993; Gubser, "Minorities in Power," p. 41. See also Seale, *Asad,* pp. 183–184.

20. *Al-Muharrir,* 30 March 1992; *al-Majalla,* 20 March 1994. See also Eyal Zisser, "The Renewed Struggle over the Succession," *The World Today* 50, no. 7 (July 1994), pp. 136–139.

21. See Seale, *Asad,* pp. 428–430; Eyal Zisser, "The Succession Struggle in Damascus," *Middle East Quarterly* 2, no. 3 (September 1995), pp. 57–64; see also Alain Chouet, "Alawi Tribal Space Tested by Power: Disintegration by Politics," *Maghreb-Machrek,* no. 147 (January–March 1995), pp. 93–119—Foreign Broadcast Information Service: Middle East and North Africa, Daily Report (DR), 3 October 1995, pp. 13–14.

22. *Al-Muharrir,* 26 September 1994; Middle East Watch, *Syria Unmasked: The Suppression of Human Rights by the Asad Regime* (New Haven, Conn.: Yale University Press, 1991), pp. 38–53.

23. Tishrin, 30 June 1992; see also Eyal Zisser, "Syria," *Middle East Contemporary Survey (MECS),* vol. 16 (1992), pp. 727–728.

24. Nikolas van Dam, *The Struggle for Power in Syria: Sectarianism, Religion and Tribalism in Politics, 1961–1978* (London: Croom Helm, 1979), pp. 71–82.

25. For more on Syria's political leadership, see *al-Watan al-'Arabi,* 26 August 1988; *al-Sharq al Awsat,* 18 January 1993.

26. Raymond Hinnebusch, "State and Civil Society in Syria," *Middle East Journal* 47, no. 2 (spring 1993), pp. 243–257.

27. *Al-Hayat* (London), 25 August, 3 September; *Tishrin,* 24, 25 August 1994. See also Eyal Zisser, "Syria," *MECS,* vol. 15 (1990), pp. 654–655.

28. See Raymond A. Hinnebusch, *Authoritarian Power and State Formation in Ba'thist Syria: Army, Party and Peasant* (Boulder, Colo.: Westview, 1990).

29. See Seale, *Asad,* pp. 492–495, 441–460.

30. Interviews with Syrian academics, Paris, 20 August 1989; Geneva, 24 April 1995.

31. For more on this, see Umar F. Abdallah, *The Islamic Struggle in Syria* (Berkeley, Calif.: Mizan Press, 1982), pp. 42–47; Thomas Mayer, "The Islamic Opposition in Syria, 1961–1982," *Orient* 24, no. 4 (December 1983), pp. 588–609.

32. Kramer, *Shi'ism,* pp. 250–252. Additionally, see Yair Hirshfeld, "The Odd Couple: Ba'thist Syria and Khomeini's Iran," in Avner Yaniv, Moshe Ma'oz, and Avi Kuver (eds.), *Syria and Israeli Security* (in Hebrew) (Tel Aviv: Ma'arachot Press, 1991), pp. 187–198.

33. Seale, *Asad,* pp. 421–440; Middle East Watch, *Syria Unmasked,* pp. 8–21. See as well, Eli Fridman, *The Muslim Brothers and Their Struggle with the Regime of Hafiz al-Asad, 1976–1982* (in Hebrew), Master's Thesis, Tel Aviv University, 1989, p. 57; Samuel J. Pickering, "Pedagogia Deserta: Memoirs of a Fulbright Year in Syria," *American Scholar* 50, no. 2 (spring 1981), pp. 179–196.

34. See *al-Hayat,* 28 September 1994; interview with Syrian academics, Paris, 24 March 1995.

35. *Middle East Economic Digest* 38, no. 20, pp. 2–3; The Economist Intelligence Unit, *Country Profile—Syria 93–94* (London, 1993). See also Faksh, "The 'Alawi Community," p. 140.

36. Seale, *Asad,* p. 427.

37. Ibid., pp. 423–425.

38. Chouet, "Alawi Tribal Space," p. 14.

39. *Al-Wasat* (London), 10 May 1995.

40. *Al-Sharq al-Awsat,* 7 March 1994; *al-Dustur,* 12 September 1994. See also Zisser, "The Renewed Struggle over the Succession"; "The Succession Struggle in Damascus."

41. Seale, *Asad,* pp. 421–440.

42. *Al-Muharrir,* 9 September 1994; *Yedi'ot Aharonot,* 25 November 1994.

43. See Zisser, "The Succession Struggle in Damascus," pp. 63–64.

44. Seale, *Asad,* p. 9. For more on the interrelationship between the 'Alawis and the Syrian state, see Tibi, "The Simultaneity of the Unsimultaneous," in Khoury and Kostiner, pp. 125–152.

45. Interviews with Syrian academics, Paris, 20 August 1989, Oxford, 25 February 1990.

PART THREE

The Gulf

8

Nation Building in Multiethnic Societies: The Case of Iraq

Ofra Bengio

At the turn of the twentieth century the fate of Iraq seems dubious. Will it survive into the next century as one unified state, or will it break up into three separate entities? Fear of the latter eventuality, or what has been termed the "Balkanization" or "Lebanonization" of Iraq, mounted significantly in the aftermath of the Shi'i and Kurdish uprisings (intifadas), which broke out almost simultaneously in March 1991. The two spontaneous uprisings rocked Iraq for nearly a month, pitting the Shi'is and the Kurds—the majority of Iraq's population[1]—against the central government in Baghdad.

The intifadas appeared to be extremely dangerous because they took place at one of the most difficult moments of the country's history (immediately after the Gulf War); because they seemed to have united the Kurdish north and the Shi'i south against the Sunni center; and because they had all the ingredients of a civil war never before witnessed on such a scale in modern Iraq. Yet as surprising and as traumatic as the intifadas were, they illuminated Iraq's most endemic problem, namely, that to all intents and purposes it remained a country of three minorities acting with cross purposes: the Arab Sunnis, the dominant minority; the Kurds, the assertive ethnic minority; and the Shi'is, the politically marginalized minority.

This chapter will examine the status of each of the three from a historical perspective after seventy-five years of statehood; the relationships and interaction among the three; their respective role in strengthening or weakening the state; and the extent to which they have attained their own particular goals. The conclusion will attempt to assess to what extent the ideology of nation building, disseminated from the center, has succeeded in galvanizing Iraqis into a single Iraqi nation and to what extent it has remained a fig leaf for extending the Sunnis' role as a dominant minority over the other two.

The Sunnis: Perpetuating the
Anomaly of the Dominant Minority

The Sunni-led Ba'thi regime that came to power in 1968 was more dedicated than any of its predecessors to the ideal of Iraqi nation building and state building. Its long tenure in power could have been an important contributing factor to the success of such an endeavor. Yet three decades of rule produced the opposite results: Iraq is further than ever from the ideal of a nation-state. Indeed, it is suspected of being on the verge of social and political disintegration and even of breakup into three separate parts: Sunni, Shi'i, and Kurdish.

Two sets of problems account for this development: the first is systemic, having to do with the very makeup of the Iraqi state itself; the second is occasional, related to Ba'thi ideology and policies. As for the former it should be recalled that Iraq lacks what political scientists identify as the cornerstones for the formation of a nation, such as common territory, religion, language, and race. Concerning the territorial framework, it is ironic that both the Sunni Arabs and the Kurds have been challenging it since the framework took shape in 1926: the Sunnis because they sought to include Kuwait in it, and the Kurds because they sought to exclude themselves from Iraq. In this regard it is noteworthy that the Shi'is appear to be the only element not to have challenged the territorial boundaries of Iraq, presenting themselves as the real Iraqi patriots. However, the Shi'is do present a problem on another score. Because of the Sunni-Shi'i cleavage, religion has not served to promote common identity and feelings in Iraq; in fact, it has played the opposite role.

As far as language, race, and common history are concerned, the Kurds differ from the Iraqi Arabs on all these scores. Thus, from the very start a conflict developed in Iraq between two nationalisms in the making, an all-Iraqi one and a Kurdish one, or, in other words, between territorial nationalism disseminated from the center and ethnonationalism disseminated in the north of the country.

Sandwiched between the Kurdish minority and the Shi'i numerical majority, the Sunnis attempted to promote the ideal of a state that would function as a melting pot for forging a new identity and consciousness for all Iraqis. This ideal, however, was marred by the Sunni concept that the new identity should embody Arab Sunni desires, interests, and ideals, and not necessarily those of the other two groups. In other words, the new "Iraqism" would not be the sum or amalgamation of the three components of the society but would reflect only one of them. Thus, Iraqi nationalism turned out to be but a thin cover for promoting the rule of the dominant minority over the other two. Finally, Iraq was kept together not through the voluntary will of all of its partners but mainly by the force of arms of an external power, namely, Britain—between 1920 and 1932 (the end of the British Mandate) by direct means, and between 1932 and 1958 by indirect ones.

Inheriting all these problems, the Ba'thi regime adopted policies that further complicated their solution. Ba'thi efforts at nation building were exclusive, contradictory, extremist, and violent. For one thing, by its very nature the Ba'thi pan-Arab ideology excluded from its vision the separate identities of both the Kurds and the Shi'is. For another, Ba'thi practice realized this ideological tenet to the full, at least as far as the Shi'is were concerned. Ba'thi attempts to blur Shi'i identity were manifested, inter alia, by making the term *Shi'i* or *Shi'a* almost a taboo in Iraqi discourse.[2]

The Ba'thi treatment of the Kurds was much more complicated but equally detrimental to the creation of an Iraqi nation. Although at the beginning of its rule the Ba'th recognized the unique national identity of the Kurds within the Iraqi state, it ended up unleashing a genocidal war against them some fifteen years later.[3] Such contradictory and extremist attitudes only served to alienate the Kurds from the Iraqi nation and to encourage them to separate themselves from it. The Ba'thi policy of excluding the Shi'is and the Kurds from the mainstream of national identity was accompanied by efforts to discourage contacts and cooperation between these two political minorities. The geographical location of the Sunni Arabs in the center of the country only facilitated their role as a buffer between the Kurdish north and the Shi'i south. Needless to say, this divide-and-rule policy could hardly contribute to the creation of one united Iraqi nation. As it happened, it was only after the Gulf War that the Shi'is and the Kurds began to cooperate against the Ba'th, although so far with no great success.

Another characteristic of the Ba'thi policies was the use of force and violent means to accelerate the nation-building process, instead of letting natural and gradual processes achieve this goal. Thus, the building of a strong army, the strongest in the country's history, was to compensate for the weak social, political, and national bonds between the different partners in the state and provide the glue for keeping them together. In a way this was a continuation of the monarchical era, when the country was kept together by force of arms.

Similarly, the wars that Iraq initiated, first against Iran and then against Kuwait, might have been designed to evoke patriotic nationalist feelings among Iraqis of different ethnic groups and religious denominations. In his book on the Second Gulf War, Sa'd al-Bazzaz, in fact, hinted at this aim, saying that Iraqi politicians and social scientists have regarded the role of war as one of rejuvenating society and promoting solidarity and unity among its different members.[4]

Even if we accept the argument of political scientists that conflict is one of the most important elements in the final crystallization of a nation, this truism does not necessarily apply to Iraq. Simultaneously with the war against an external enemy, Iran, the Ba'th also unleashed "wars" against the internal one, the Kurds, with the result that the latter conflict served to enhance Kurdish national identity instead of the desired all-Iraqi national one. Furthermore, it united Iran and the Kurds against Iraq. However, the war with Iran, which the Ba'th hoped to use to evoke patriotic feelings among the Arab Shi'is, was problematic for the latter in that it placed them on the horn of a dilemma: choosing between loyalty to their state and loyalty to their religion. The persecutions meted out to them at the hands of the Ba'th did not make their dilemma any easier.

Mindful of the possibility that Sunni-Shi'i cleavages could be a major stumbling block before the creation of a single Iraqi nation, the Ba'th emphasized from the start the secular tendency of its regime. Similarly, perceiving tribal loyalties as militating against an all-Iraqi national one, the Ba'th sought from the start to break the tribes' power and to erode tribal loyalties. Yet, as we shall see, due to different internal and external developments, the Ba'th was forced to abandon its earlier course and revert to both "political Islam" and "political tribalism."

In dealing with its "minorities," the Ba'th experimented with all the methods available to the dominant minority, from pluralism to assimilation, oppression, and annihilation. Needless to say, such fluctuations and contradictions in Ba'thi policies could hardly contribute to the development of a clear-cut Iraqi national identity.[5] Indeed, Ba'thi policies increased the awareness and self-identity of both the Kurds and the Shi'is, pushing the Kurds to seek self-determination and the Shi'is to demand a greater share of power. The following sections will discuss the Kurdish and Shi'i minority problem from their own perspective and in relation to the state, and will evaluate the balance of power in this triangle of Sunnis, Shi'is, and Kurds.

The Kurds: Between Annihilation and Self-Determination

The Golden Opportunity

As the end of the twentieth century approaches, the Kurds of Iraq appear at first glance to have attained an outstanding achievement: autonomy under international auspices, something that neither the Iraqi Kurds themselves nor Kurds and ethnic groups in the other Middle Eastern countries have achieved since the late 1940s. A closer analysis of the situation, however, might cast doubts on the importance and durability of this achievement. To evaluate its real importance, one should examine the Kurdish autonomous entity against the backdrop of developments in the domestic, regional, and international arenas.

The idea of autonomy for the Kurds of Iraq is as old as the Iraqi state itself. Only in 1970, however, some fifty years after British-mandated Iraq was first established, was the idea put into practice, when the Ba'thi government agreed to grant the Kurds autonomy. The maturation of the idea in 1970 was the result of two important coinciding factors: a high degree of politicization among the Kurds, resulting in the crystallization of ethnonationalism among them, and the relative weakness of a new regime that sought to consolidate its grip on power and buy much-needed time via a tactical solution to the endemic Kurdish problem.

Once the Ba'th managed to alter the balance of power in its favor, it moved to crush the autonomy through a combination of military force and political overtures toward the Kurds' main backer at the time, Iran. As the Kurds lacked any international recognition, let alone support, the government could crack down on them harshly without any protest from the international community, because the matter, the government argued, was an internal Iraqi affair.

Although the first experiment with Kurdish autonomy was short-lived, lasting only four years, it was nonetheless an important one for a number of reasons: it gave the Kurds a model to which to aspire in the future; it forced the regime into a commitment that it found difficult to negate altogether; and, most important, it further enhanced the separate identity of the Kurds. The contradiction inherent in the Iraqi government's policy of alternating political concessions with physical annihilation reached its height during the infamous *anfal* campaigns in 1988, in which approximately 50,000 Kurds were reportedly killed.[6] This, in turn, added another dimension to Kurdish ethnonationalism, which was by now in open conflict with an Iraqi Arab nationalism disseminated from the center of the state, Baghdad.

The second experiment in Kurdish autonomy came some twenty years after the first one against the backdrop of entirely different domestic, regional, and international conditions. For the Kurds, their autonomous entity was established, quite paradoxically, at one of the weakest points in their history, namely, in the wake of Saddam Husayn's crushing of their uprising in April 1991 and the panicked temporary flight of some two million Kurds to Turkey and Iran. For the regime, too, this development marked one of the lowest points in its twenty-five years of rule and reflected its state of paralysis in the aftermath of the Gulf War. This time, autonomy was imposed on Baghdad, leaving it with a very narrow margin of maneuverability and little ability to undermine it.

Thus, the Gulf crisis initiated by Saddam Husayn, which seemed for a time to be an entirely external affair, had very serious repercussions on the future of Iraqi Kurds and the Iraqi state itself in a number of ways. First, the invasion of Kuwait blatantly challenged international norms regarding the inviolability and "sacredness" of the territorial states formed in the Middle East after World War I. Ironically, it gave the Kurds the opportunity to use this precedent to forward their own political goals at Iraq's expense. Second, the UN became directly involved in the Kurdish question, as exemplified by the dispatch of a small UN force to northern Iraq. Third, one of Iraq's neighbors, Turkey, which was its erstwhile ally on the Kurdish issue, openly turned itself into the lifeline for the Kurdish autonomous entity. Most important of all was the fact that the Western countries, in marked departure from past policies, were the ones that initiated and "protected" the Kurdish autonomous entity.

Although caused primarily by the Gulf crisis, the changing attitude of the West seems to have coincided with the thinking regarding the prospective "new world order" in the wake of the end of the Cold War. Part of the new reality was the rise of what has been termed the "third wave of ethnonationalism,"[7] marked by the establishment of no fewer than fifteen new states.[8]

Internal Constraints

The Kurdish administration that was set up in 1992 appeared to mark a turning point in the Kurds' long, turbulent struggle for self-determination. Three points stood out: (1) The modus vivendi and modus operandi reached between the two rival parties, the Kurdistan Democratic Party (al-hizb al-dimuqrati al-Kurdistani; KDP) and the Patriotic Union of Kurdistan (al-ittihad al-watani al-Kurdistani; PUK), held out the promise of a long-elusive unity among the Kurds; (2) the conduct of more or less democratic elections made it possible to set up an authentic, legitimate Kurdish parliament not imposed by the Iraqi regime; and (3) the Kurds' political goal changed from autonomy to a federated state with Iraq.[9] But as high as the hopes were, so were the depths after the fall into disillusionment. Barely a year and a half had elapsed since the establishment of the Kurdish autonomous entity when all the underlying latent and deep-seated problems sprang up to militate against the chances of ultimate success.

Most serious by far was the flare-up of internal fighting on a scale not witnessed for thirty years. The fighting started in October 1993 on a local level between the Islamic movement in Iraqi Kurdistan—al-haraka al-Islamiyya fi Kurdistan (IMK)—and the PUK, but after a few months, in May 1994, it deteriorated into full-fledged warfare between the two main groupings, with smaller parties and groups siding with each camp. According to one source, the fighting, which has been going on intermittently since 1994, pitted 25,000 *peshmergas* from the KDP against 15,000 from the PUK.[10] It resulted in the crumbling of the Kurdish administration, the death of about 3,000 Kurds, and the division of Kurdistan into three zones of influence: Irbil and Sulaymaniyya under the control of the PUK; Dhok and the districts around Irbil under the control of the KDP; and Halabja and the bordering areas under the IMK.[11] Accordingly, the KDP came to control the oil route in the north—the region's main source of income—while the PUK controlled the more populous southern provinces.[12] But even this "division of power" did not last long, because in August 1996 the Irbil region became the site of internecine fighting, with the region changing hands between Mas'ud Barzani and Jalal Talabani three times over. As of 1998, Irbil is in Barzani's hands.

Analyzing the developments in Iraqi Kurdistan since the Gulf War highlights the intricacies, weaknesses, and constraints at play, most of them legacies of past policies and behavior either of the Kurds themselves or of regional and international players. Most debilitating of all were the Kurds' internal problems and constraints. The first of these had to do with the failure of the Kurdish community to crystallize into a strong national movement. Although the Kurds had all the ingredients of a separate ethnonational group, including a common history, language, and identity, they lagged far behind the rival Arab national movement in the cultural, socioeconomic, and political domains. Unlike Arabic, the Kurdish language was slow to develop into a symbol of identity and a unifying force for three main reasons: the language became orthographically standardized only in the twentieth century; there were many Kurdish dialects and two alphabets, Latin and Arabic; and the Kurdish language became the victim of the central government's assimilation policies, or what was termed "linguicide."[13]

Even more divisive were tribal loyalties and ties that continued to dominate Kurdish society, much more than among Sunni Arabs or even among the Shi'is. Although Kurdish tribal leaders from Shaykh 'Ubaydallah to Mulla Mustafa Barzani had played key roles in galvanizing and leading the Kurdish movement, tribal loyalties also put brakes on the development of a more general and all-encompassing Kurdish nationalism.[14] During the early 1970s, rivalry and enmity between the tribes led some of the tribes opposed to Mulla Mustafa Barzani to cooperate with the Ba'th against the KDP, which he led. Worse still, during the *anfal* campaign, Kurdish tribal leaders acted as accomplices of the army, thus helping to send "thousands of Kurds to their death."[15] However, tribal leaders played an important role in the uprising of March 1991 because they "defected" from the regime camp and participated in the uprising.[16] Another twist took place during the latest fighting between the KDP and PUK. Aware of the power that tribal leaders wielded among the Kurds, both Mas'ud Barzani and Jalal Talabani attempted to mobilize the support of particular tribal leaders against each other. It was not surprising, then, that the trigger to the May fighting among the Kurds was a conflict between rival chiefs over land rights.[17]

Part and parcel of this social-structural constraint has been the political constraint, namely, the Iraqi Kurds' lack of unity and common sense of purpose. To a great extent there has even been a decline in their likemindedness since Mulla Mustafa Barzani's first Kurdish autonomy experiment in 1970–1975: instead of one charismatic leader, Mulla Mustafa Barzani, there were now, in the 1990s, two weak ones, Jalal Talabani and Mas'ud Barzani, and instead of one dominant party, the KDP, there were two main ones, the KDP and PUK, as well as (according to one source) fifteen smaller parties.[18]

The political picture was further complicated by two relatively new developments. The first was the establishment in 1988 of a new group under

Iranian auspices—the aforementioned IMK—a new phenomenon on the Kurdish scene.[19] The other development was the vacuum left in Iraqi Kurdistan by the Iraqi army's withdrawal, which made possible the establishment there of different elements—both non-Kurdish Iraqi opposition forces, such as Shi'is, Communists, and other opposition groups, and Kurdish groups from other countries, namely, the Turkish radical leftist Kurdistan Workers' Party (Parti Karkaren Kurdistan; PKK) and the Iranian KDP, which increased their respective footholds in the area.[20] These two developments had near-fatal implications for the viability of the Kurdish autonomous entity, for they added a new dimension to the Kurds' deep-seated tendency toward factionalism and internal strife. The worst of these was the "war of attrition" between the Iraqi KDP and the PKK.[21] In December 1995 the two parties announced a cease fire, but it was broken again in summer 1997.

Another debilitating factor was that the Kurds still lacked a well-defined vision and clear-cut political goals for the future, mixing together at times such various programs as autonomy, federalism, and independence.[22] Several factors may account for this lack of clarity. The fact that the Kurds have never in their long history established an independent state of their own, except for autonomous principalities, means that they did not have a model of statehood to imitate, as the Arabs, for example, had. The Kurds themselves were undecided with respect to their ultimate political goal, altering it depending on changing political circumstances. Thus, when they perceived that the fortunes of Baghdad had declined following the Gulf War, they were quick to raise the more assertive slogan of federation, instead of the previously advocated autonomy. Yet the fear of antagonizing surrounding countries, which had extended varying degrees of support to the Kurds at different periods, played an important part in the Kurds' reluctance to adopt an overly audacious political stance.

Another very serious constraint is the economic one. Ironic as it might appear, Kurdistan is one of the richest regions in Iraq, with an abundance of water, oil, and minerals. But the Kurds themselves were not able to reap the fruits of these riches. Although Western powers allowed them to build an autonomous administration, they never let them exploit the oil in their soil so as to enable the autonomous entity to achieve economic self-sufficiency.[23] Worse still, the area suffered the impact of a double embargo, both the Iraqi regime's embargo against it and international sanctions against Iraq as a whole. In addition to further impoverishing the region, this situation turned the control of what little income there was in the area into the main bone of contention between the two warring parties, the KDP and the PUK.[24] Another severe consequence of the embargo was that Iraqi Kurdistan became a regional center for illegal trade in alcohol, drugs, and other goods. Furthermore, the surrounding countries used this economic crisis to increase their infiltration into the area and establish a political foothold there.

The Impact of the Regionalization and
Internationalization of the Kurdish Issue

Turning to regional factors, it should be said that the geostrategic constraints facing the Kurds now became more manifest than ever. Baghdad's loss of control of Kurdistan for the first time in its modern history left a power vacuum that the surrounding countries sought to fill. In fact, these countries perceived in this vacuum both an opportunity and a danger: an opportunity for each to extend its hold in the area but a danger that another country would fill the vacuum first or that the Kurds themselves would become sufficiently independent to have a major impact on their own territories.

As a result of the changing circumstances after the Gulf War, the roles played by the surrounding countries vis-à-vis the Kurdish issue also changed. From the 1960s to the late 1980s Iran had been the major player of the Iraqi Kurdish "card," in an effort to destabilize its rival and enemy, Iraq. After the second Gulf War, Turkey emerged as the main player.[25] Turkey granted qualified support to the Iraqi Kurds, but for different reasons. Its aim was not to destabilize Baghdad but to prevent a permanent influx of Iraqi Kurds to its territory, to build a Turkish stronghold in Iraqi Kurdistan, and to fight the PKK.

The conflict between Turkey and the PKK had spillover effects on Iraqi Kurdistan, causing the flight of Turkish Kurdish refugees into Iraqi Kurdistan, but worse still triggering Turkish attacks on Iraqi Kurdistan. The largest of these was the invasion of spring 1995—code-named "Operation Steel"—which lasted thirty-six days and involved some 35,000 Turkish soldiers, and the operation of spring 1997, code-named "Sledge-Hammer," which lasted for more than a month and involved between 25,000 and 50,000 soldiers. Far from uprooting the PKK, however, the invasion exacerbated the plight of the Iraqi Kurds, increased the conflicts between the PKK and KDP, and raised fears (both among the Iraqi Kurds and in Baghdad) of Turkey's intention to adjust the Iraqi border southward.[26] The ambiguity of the Turkish stance regarding the Kurds of Iraq was also manifested in the tripartite meetings held regularly with Iran and Syria with a view to containing the Kurds.

To the Iraqi Kurds' chagrin, the struggle for Iraqi Kurdistan now involved not two countries—Iraq and Iran—as had been the case between the 1960s and the 1990s, but all of the surrounding countries as well. Instead of facing one foe, Iraq, the Kurds therefore had to contend with four countries—Iraq, Iran, Turkey, and Syria—each of which opposed the Kurdish struggle for self-determination, while using different approaches and methods to combat the nascent entity. But for the first time in their modern history, the Kurds began to use others in their internal fighting. A case in point was the flare-up of internecine fighting at the end of August 1996, when the KDP used the Iraqi Army against the PUK. Nevertheless, whether this will help the Kurdish national cause is more than doubtful.

Nor was the changing role of the international community more encouraging for the Kurds. Although Western countries, particularly Britain, France, and the United States, were instrumental in setting up the Kurdish "safe haven" in 1991, which later developed into an autonomous entity, their motives and ultimate goals were completely different from those of the Kurds. The three immediate motives of the Western countries were contending with world public opinion on the Kurdish plight; solving Turkey's severe problem caused by the flight of the Kurds to its territory; and, last but not least, weakening Saddam Husayn's regime. Having achieved these short-term goals, the brokers of Iraqi Kurdish autonomy were now motivated by different considerations, none of which put the Kurdish cause in the forefront.

First of all, France began early on to seek accommodation with Saddam Husayn's regime, putting an end to whatever commitment it might have had to the Kurds. As for Britain and the United States, despite all their attempts to weaken Saddam Husayn, they still adhered to the principle of the territorial integrity of Iraq and opposed the emergence of a full-fledged Kurdish autonomous entity in Iraq. Their fear was threefold: that the regional balance of power would tip in Iran's favor; that a Yugoslav-like syndrome would develop in Iraq, dragging them into the Iraqi quagmire; and that the West's ally, Turkey, would be hurt by developments in Iraq. Alongside the fears of the new wave of ethnonationalism and its repercussions in the region, the West was also motivated by long-term considerations such as the desire to renew economic and business ties with Iraq sometime in the future. Here, too, France played the leading role. These ambiguities, which characterized all the players on the Kurdish scene, helped complicate the issue even more and render it more intractable than ever.

Assessing the Kurds' situation in historical perspective, one can say that their role as a card to be played by others has become more manifest than ever. Had they been more assertive and more united, the picture might have been different. For now, however, they can only destabilize the host country, but they cannot reap the fruit of the resulting instability. One can perceive that the Iraqi Kurds have not one, but two, Achilles' heels. The first was that they did not present a clear-cut political goal around which all Iraqi Kurds could mobilize. The second was that their entity did not serve as a center of gravity for the Kurds outside Iraq's borders. Consequently, the situation somewhat resembled that of preceding centuries, when Kurdistan was a border area possessing no strong political center of its own, and its fate depended largely on the balance of power between the Ottoman and Persian Empires.

Paradoxically, the very success of establishing the autonomous entity was also the main enemy, as it unleashed all the surrounding countries against the Iraqi Kurds. Meanwhile, the international community was either unwilling or unable to endow the Kurds with what it lacked itself—cohesiveness and unity. In fact, both the countries of the region and Western countries played the Kurdish card against Iraq and not for the Kurds' sake. The late Mulla Mustafa Barzani once described such cynical treatment by the Shah, saying that he had held the Kurds as if holding a drowning man by his hair above the water, letting him neither drown nor live.[27] It seems that as long as they do not learn to swim by themselves, the Kurds are doomed to such treatment by all and sundry.

The Shi'is:
In Search of Identity or Real Representation?

In contrast to the Kurds, the Shi'is have been, by and large, quite passive. Thus, in the seventy-five years of modern Iraqi history there have been only two serious initiatives by the Shi'is aimed at effecting political change in their favor: the "Great Iraqi Revolution" of 1920 and the intifada of 1991.[28] Both attempts failed dismally, and rather than improve the Shi'is' political status they weakened it even more. For all the differences between the two uprisings in terms of political goals, leadership, and modes of action, there were certain common denominators at the root of the Shi'i community's failure to assert itself as the political majority. In tracing the line of historical continuity between the two events, one can find certain recurring factors that account for the inherent weakness of this community. Surprising as it might seem, the 1920 revolt was far more coherent and effective than that of 1991; this suggests that the Shi'i community has suffered a continuous decline as a political power.

By far the Shi'is' most serious drawback has been their inability to articulate a common political goal that would unify and guide them as a group. This lack of a common goal was inherent already in the 1920 experience. The Shi'is shared with the Sunnis and others the goal of frustrating the British Mandate, but they did not have a clear-cut goal of their own for the post-uprising period, such as wresting power from the Sunnis. The Shi'i intifada of 1991 highlighted to an even greater extent the lack of unity in goals and methods: the intifada was an act of sheer vengeance against a regime that was seen to be crumbling, but it lacked any positive goal or vision for the future.[29] In this sense the Shi'i intifada contrasted sharply with the Kurdish one. True, the Kurdish intifada, too, had a negative aspect, namely, avenging the past sufferings of the Kurds at the hands of the Ba'th, but it also had a positive one, the achievement of self-rule. Thus, the Shi'i intifada was directed against the regime, whereas that of the Kurds was against the state. This point highlighted the great difference between the struggle of ethnic and religious groups in modern Iraq. Although the Kurds could proclaim themselves Kurds and demand Kurdish rights, the Shi'is could not play the same game.

Inherent Causes of Political Weakness

From the very beginning the Shi'is were caught in an ideological and political dilemma. They were unwilling to identify themselves as Shi'is because in modern terminology it would have the immediate connotation of *ta'ifiyya* (sectarianism).[30] Politically they could not articulate their demands in strictly Shi'i terms because this might be interpreted as an attempt to jeopardize the unity of the state to which they were committed no less than the Sunnis. In religious terms, they could not act along strict confessional lines, because this would undermine the ecumenical approach that they professed. The only way left for the more politically oriented religious leaders was to articulate their ideology in general Islamic terms and not specifically Shi'i ones.[31] This constraint was extremely harmful to the Shi'i cause, as it diluted any central goal they might have had and rendered it amorphous. As a result, the Shi'i political groupings that did emerge failed to attract the support of either the secular or the religious Shi'is, who felt that their specific problems were not addressed by these groups.

Another problem accentuated by this lack of clear vision and a unified goal was the extreme weakness and the fragmentation of the Shi'i political groupings. Analyzing the real causes of this weakness, Muhammad Taqi al-Mudarrisi, a Shi'i opposition leader, ascribed it to a lack of self-confidence, extreme dependence on outside forces, disunity and fragmentation, weak or nonexistent contacts with the Iraqi masses, and helplessness vis-à-vis the government machinery that sought to crush the opposition.[32] Thus, there was neither a strong leading Shi'i personality, nor a unified leadership, nor a well-knit organization with followings inside Iraq.[33] This again compared negatively with the 1920 uprising. In the 1920 experience religious leaders had a prominent role;[34] in 1991, their role was marginal. As a result the intifada was leaderless and haphazard.[35]

Another point that should be emphasized is that in 1920, despite the differences between the religious and the political tribal leaderships, the former succeeded in mobilizing the tribes for the common cause of fighting the British.[36] In 1991 the two were alienated from each other. Moreover, if one is to believe Ba'thi testimony, not only did the tribal leaders not join in the intifada, but they proved staunch supporters of the regime, at times even more than Ba'thi members themselves.[37]

Another aspect of the Shi'is' weakness in both cases was their inability to sustain their struggle for a long time. For all their tenacity and steadfastness, the Shi'i religious leaders in 1920 could not carry on their struggle much beyond the revolution itself. Similarly, the 1991 intifada remained a mere episode with no serious follow-up. Notwithstanding their inherent weakness, the Shi'is appeared extremely threatening to the outside world, mainly because of their supposed radicalism or their link with Iran. Hence, the approach of outside powers toward them ranged from active participation in suppressing them as in the 1920s and 1930s to inaction or indifference to their fate as in the aftermath of the Gulf War. Even the no-fly zone set up in August 1992 to protect the Shi'is turned out to be a farce, certainly when compared with the safe haven in the Kurdish north.

The causes of Western inaction was a combination of fear of fragmentation of the Iraqi state; the strengthening of Shi'i fundamentalism in Iraq and its alliance with Iran; and, paradoxically, a lack of confidence in the Shi'i leadership and its ability to generate a change in the center. Thus, on the face of it, in the 1990s the West appeared to play an opposite role to the one played in the 1930s vis-à-vis the Shi'is, using the air force against the Iraqi government to protect the Shi'is and not vice versa. In practice, however, the West used its "umbrella" over the Shi'is as a pretext for punishing the Iraqi government and protecting Kuwait, but by no means for protecting or supporting the Shi'is.

Consequently, the combination of objective weakness and an image of strength made the Shi'is unreliable allies, thereby decreasing support to them from the outside world. It was ironic that during the Iran-Iraq War the Islamic Republic of Iran chose the Kurds as its allies against Iraq and not its co-religionists, the Shi'is. Similarly, when attempting to destabilize Saddam Husayn's regime after the Gulf War, Iran once again turned mainly to the Kurds and not to the Shi'is.[38]

The Ba'thi Onslaught

The Shi'i intifada prompted the government to act quickly to quell the rebellion and to take additional steps to break the Shi'is as a political force.[39] The government's success was due to three main factors: the Shi'is were a less formidable enemy than the Kurds; the Ba'th had learned the lessons of its mistaken policies in the northern safe haven, which boomeranged against it there; and, most important, the Ba'th has kept the initiative in its hands ever since.

In tackling the Shi'i problem, the regime acted on five levels simultaneously: military, geographic-demographic, political, religious, and ideological. In contrast to the north, where the regime withdrew its forces of its own will, thus enhancing the detachment of the Kurdish area from the Iraqi body, in the south it did the reverse. Despite the no-fly zone of August 1992 that Western forces imposed on Iraq, which prohibited the Iraqi army from flying planes from the 32° parallel southward, the Iraqi army intensified its presence and its activities even in the marshes, where it had never set foot before.

Since the intifada, the marshes have become the stronghold of the Shi'i opposition, including army deserters, pro-Iranian Shi'i opposition groups, and ordinary outlaws. As the topography rendered the activity of land forces almost impossible, the Iraqi regime embarked on an ambitious program of draining the marshes. Explaining the strategic motives behind such a policy,

President Saddam Husayn's son 'Udayy said they were threefold: (1) using the drained marshes to develop agriculture in the area, so as to balance greedy cultivators; (2) "ensuring total security in the area"; and (3) preventing tribal conflicts.[40]

The drastic measures taken by the regime to drain the marshes brought them under Ba'thi control by the end of 1994. According to a study by an international team of scientists, between 1985 and 1992 43 percent of 15,000 square kilometers of permanent lake and marshes "had been transformed into dry land and more has been drained since." The work was concentrated in the 'Amara marshes, which, according to one report coordinator, no longer existed as an ecosystem, as 230,000 hectares had been drained in the area. Furthermore, water that had previously fed the area was diverted into a canal that flowed into the Gulf.[41] Even if one were to accept the Ba'th's claim that the project was necessary for agricultural reasons, there was no doubt that the strategic by-products were tremendous, for it allowed the regime to pacify an area that had been the main base for the Shi'i opposition.

Non-Iraqi sources reported that these draining operations dramatically improved the government's access to the area, making it possible to continue clamping down on the rebels. Thus, a 15,000-strong army division was reportedly operating in the 'Amara region in early 1994, and about 58,000 Shi'i Iraqis had reportedly fled to Iran by that time. The Shi'i opposition, for its part, reported sporadic operations against government troops and personalities.[42] It also tried its hand at psychological warfare, appealing to the army to topple the regime and distributing antigovernment leaflets.[43] On the whole, however, the Shi'i opposition in the south was on the defensive, with the initiative remaining firmly in the government's hands. Significantly, the UN and Western powers were well aware of Ba'thi activities, but they never took any action to stop the draining that caused the destruction of an entire civilization, to ensure food supplies to the population, or to set up a safety zone as in the Kurdish north.

The Ba'th Plays with Tribalism, Nationalism, and Islam

One of the regime's most important means of controlling the Shi'i south in general, and particularly the marshes, was through alliances with Shi'i tribal chiefs. The Ba'th's renewed interest in the tribes, or what one may call the revival of tribal politics, dates back to the beginning of the intifada. It is impossible to prove Saddam Husayn's claim that the tribal chiefs stood at the forefront of stopping the Shi'i rebels. However, the uprising did convince him of the need to approach the tribes either to mobilize the more friendly ones to support the regime or to break the reluctant ones. Either way, the regime reached the conclusion that it could not afford to disregard the tribes any longer.[44]

In a reversal of policy, which had regarded the tribes as reactionaries and tribal loyalties as a divisive element to be opposed, the Ba'th now portrayed them as a symbol of patriotism meriting the government's support and encouragement. Whereas in the 1970s the Ba'th made anything related to tribes—even the use of names of tribal origin—taboo, in the aftermath of the intifada the tribes and their chieftains gained such wide publicity that they became the media's heroes.[45] Husayn's changing approach toward the tribes was manifest in his policy of arming the more loyal tribes, dividing the power in the south between the Ba'th Party and the tribal leaders to such an extent that one can speak of a kind of dual leadership.

The government's growing awareness of the important role of the tribal leadership was manifested in an article in *Babil* that called for re-establishing tribal councils (*majalis*). The councils, it maintained, would deal with various security, economic, and social issues. These would include supervising various agricultural activities; resolving conflicts among tribes; organizing the mobilization of the tribal youth for the army; and, finally, supervising security affairs in their areas and on local highways to prevent actions by gangs of thieves that the "official authorities alone could not check or control."[46]

Mobilizing the support of the tribes turned them once again into the tools of others. In the nineteenth century and early 1920s they were the tools of the religious leaders,[47] in the 1930s those of various politicians in Baghdad,[48] and in the 1990s those of the Ba'th regime. However, strengthening certain tribal leaders as a means of controlling the Shi'i south could boomerang. Thus, one of the results was the renewal of the intra-tribal conflicts that were so rampant in the 1930s. Though not to be compared in their scale and intensity with the older ones, these conflicts had the potential of becoming intractable and seriously destabilizing for the regime. In one such case reported by *Babil,* the conflict became so severe that the commander of the 7th Army Corps had to intervene to put an end to it.[49] Moreover, by early 1997 the clash between tribal and state interests became so strong that the government had to call on tribes to give national interest first priority.[50]

Husayn's appeal to and appeasement of the tribal leaders was motivated by yet another important consideration: driving a wedge between the Shi'i masses and Iran on the one hand, and between them and the Iraqi 'ulama on the other. One way to do this was to break the power of Shi'i religious leaders systematically through surveillance, arrest, and even physical liquidation. In a report to the UN on human-rights violations in Iraq, UN investigator Max van der Stoel expressed concern about the disappearance of Shi'i religious leaders after the March 1991 uprising: "There were 10,000 clerics last spring before the uprising in Iraq," he wrote, "barely 700 after; and now hardly any can be seen anywhere."[51]

A gentler way to divest the Shi'i clergy of their powers was to "confiscate" the conduct of religious affairs from them and to bring about the nationalization of religion in Iraq. Among the Ba'th's steps in the last few years was the appointment of Muhammad al-Sadr as the *al-marja' al-a'la* (supreme religious authority) of the Shi'is instead of Abu Qasim al-Kho'i, who died in August 1992. The appointment of the young and inexperienced al-Sadr was not only a breach of all Shi'i religious norms but also a blatant interference by the Sunni government in a purely Shi'i internal affair. To further increase the state's monopoly over religious affairs, Saddam Husayn made the Ministry of Religious Affairs and *awqaf* directly connected to the president, and the only ministry with a separate budget of its own.

Another move was the June 1994 decision to establish the Authority for Management and Investment of Awqaf Properties. The authority, which intended to open up branches in the governorates "in light of the size of religious trusts in each governorate," was to manage all *awqaf* properties with the exception of those under private management.[52] Divesting Shi'i clergy of the *awqaf* they had managed for centuries could deal a death blow to their religious, economic, and political influence among the Shi'i rank and file.

The other side of the coin was the regime's attempt to don the mantle of Islam, in a reversal of the policies of the 1970s, when strict secularism was the order of the day. Thus, Saddam Husayn now ordered the establishment of two Islamic universities, as well as colleges and schools for teaching Islamic subjects. The graduates of these universities and colleges were later to be employed in various government-sponsored religious posts.

The largest and the most publicized project to disseminate the government "religion" was the "national campaign of faith" (*hamla wataniyya imaniyya*), embarked upon in the summer of 1993 and carried on throughout 1994–1997. The aims of the campaign were to teach selected parts of the Qur'an, with a view to propagating "the correct (*sahih*) religious preaching and guidance" among the people so as "to immunize them against the deviant trends and to expose some sick social phenomena."[53] By the end of 1995 some 20,000 teachers and five million students of various ages were said to have participated. Moreover, the campaign came to include judges, prisoners, and women, as well as Ba'thi members, a "revolutionary" phenomenon in itself, considering the secular character of the Ba'th. Moreover, in September 1997 a new radio station, "The Holy Qur'an Radio," was inaugurated.[54] Meanwhile, the general public, too, was allowed a greater dose of Islam, through televised Friday *khutbas* and other religious programs.

All these activities were to have the effect of severing the traditional link between the Shi'i masses and their religious leadership, as well as disseminating a more "neutral" brand of Islam. As the regime came to control all religious issues from Islamic curricula to religious posts to public sermons, it is not improbable that it had in mind an attempt to "Sunnize" the Shi'is. As confessional issues remained the dividing force between Sunnis and Shi'is and as previous attempts to secularize the state had failed, it was hoped that propagating the "Ba'thi brand of Islam" might ultimately turn it into a unifying factor between Sunnis and Shi'is.

To counter the propaganda emanating from Tehran and various Iraqi Shi'i opposition groups, the Ba'th sought to appeal to the Shi'i sense of Iraqi patriotism and to invoke their pride in their Arabism. Saddam Husayn repeatedly lauded the Arabs for their "leading role in conveying religion and its meaning to all mankind," including to Iran. Yet he warned that "Iranian Shi'ism" has always been "alien to the Arab mentality," seeking "to tarnish the Arabs and their history."[55] Similarly, the Iraqi media put growing emphasis on such ideals as Arab honor, valor, and loyalty. They also portrayed the 1920 revolution as the most important event in modern Iraqi history and the symbol of Iraqi patriotism and unity.[56] Invoking that revolution as a counterweight to the intifada was to have the effect of strengthening the Shi'is' sense of patriotism, their affinity with the state, and their commitment to its unity and survival. Raising the specter of the partitioning of Iraq was yet another device for emphasizing the common fate of the Arabs (Sunnis and Shi'is) as well as driving a wedge between the Shi'is and the Kurds, who stood to jeopardize Iraqi unity.[57]

In assessing the status of the Shi'is in Iraq the following points should be highlighted: so far the Shi'is have failed to change their status from a numerical majority to a political one. If anything, since the establishment of the Iraqi state, their power as a political community has been on a steady decline. Conventional wisdom puts the blame for such an anomaly on the British and foreign forces. Although these certainly played a role, the main factor may have been the historical balance of power dating back to Ottoman times, if not earlier, between the Sunnis and the Shi'is, and the latter's inability to change it in their favor. The Shi'is' feebleness stemmed not only from their inability to seize the centers of power in the state, such as the army and the security services but more important from a lack of esprit de corps; the absence of a clear and common goal for the community as a whole; and the virtual disappearance of their leadership, both religious and secular. The Shi'is have never challenged the Iraqi state. Moreover, secession from the state is not an option for them at all. As they form the majority in the country and in Baghdad itself, they might endanger the regime but they will not jeopardize the unity of the Iraqi state.

Conclusion

Like many other countries in the Middle East (and in the rest of the world), the Iraqi state was born with a built-in minority problem. However, the Iraqi case is much more complicated than the Egyptian or even the Algerian one, for example, for two main reasons. First, Iraqi society is extremely heterogeneous and fragmented. In addition to the three minorities discussed in this chapter, there are smaller religious and ethnic minorities, including the Turkmens, the Assyrians, and the Yezidis. Second, a minority has ruled the state since its inception. The combination of the two factors has had far-reaching implications for the Iraqi polity as well as for Iraqi state building and nation building.[58]

The urge of the Arab Sunni minority to retain its monopoly on power has unleashed a process whereby the regime has become even more totalitarian. Any democratization or opening up of the system was bound to loosen the Sunni hold on power and hence to put an end to Sunni hegemony. Accordingly, force and coercion were needed to keep the Kurds and Shi'is under control, and these, in turn, increased the separate identity of each of the two groups.

The process of nation building and state making was also affected by the two aforementioned inherent problems. If in the 1990s the idea of an Iraqi federation composed of the Sunnis, Shi'is, and Kurds began to gain currency among Ba'thi opponents, this was not a sign of the strength of the Iraqi state.[59] On the contrary, it reflected the identity crisis that Iraqi society as a whole was undergoing and that found its expression in the rising trends of tribalism and Islamism. At the same time, it reflected the failure of the ideology of nation building disseminated from the Sunni center and the concurrent increasing forces of fragmentation among the Shi'is but mainly among the Kurds. In fact, the general picture emerging from the earlier discussion is, paradoxically, one of weakness of all three components simultaneously. Still, it must be emphasized that in this "triangle of weakness" the Sunni government remained the strongest of the three minorities as it continued to hold all the centers of power (army, bureaucracy, etc.). The net result of this mutual weakening, however, was a further fragmentation of Iraqi society.

One question still remains: What are the chances of the formation of such a federation or its viability? First, the Shi'is do not appear to be natural candidates for such a plan, because they are the majority even in Baghdad itself and because they are intermingled with the Sunnis, with no "natural" boundaries between them. Second, the Kurds might have been suitable candidates for a federation, but they have three main enemies: themselves, the other partners in the state (both Sunnis and Shi'is), and, most important, all the surrounding countries. Finally, the lack of democracy in Iraq and the intense opposition of the Sunni center to such an idea is bound to nip it in the bud.

To conclude, without generalizing about the correlation between multiethnic societies and the process of nation building, in the Iraqi case the correlation was negative. Iraq is as far as ever from the Sunni-Ba'thi ideal of a cohesive nation-state.

Notes

1. In the early 1990s the Shi'is were estimated at about 55 percent and the Kurds 22 percent of Iraq's total population. Richard Tapper (ed.), *Some Minorities in the Middle East* (London: Centre of Near and Middle Eastern Studies, 1992), p. 87.

2. When reference to the Shi'is could not be avoided, the government preferred the more neutral term *Ja'fari madhhab*. As President Husayn said, "Our people are one, not two, peoples. They incorporate . . . Sunni Muslims, Ja'farites and others" (Radio Baghdad, 8 September—Foreign Broadcasting Information Service: Near East and South Asia, Daily Report [DR], 9 September 1992).

3. See Middle East Watch, *Genocide in Iraq: The Anfal Campaign Against the Kurds* (New York: Human Rights Watch, 1993).

4. Sa'd al-Bazzaz, *Harb talid ukhra: Al-ta'rikh al-sirri li-harb al-khalij* (Amman: Al-ahliyya lil-nashr wal-tawzi', 1992), p. 14.

5. For such an effect on the Shi'is see Hasan al-'Alawi, *Al-Shi'a wal-dawla al-qawmiyya fil-'Iraq, 1914–1990* (n.p., 1990), p. 39.

6. Middle East Watch, *Genocide*, p. 13. See also Kan'an Makiya, *Cruelty and Silence: War, Tyranny, Uprising and the Arab World* (London: Penguin Books, 1994).

7. Fred W. Riggs, "Ethnonationalism, Industrialism and the Modern State," *Third World Quarterly* 15, no. 4 (December 1994), pp. 583–611.

8. John Hutchinson and Anthony Smith (eds.), *Nationalism* (New York: Oxford University Press, 1994), p. 11.

9. Voice of the People of Kurdistan, 5 October—DR, 7 October 1992; *al-Manar al-Kurdi*, November 1992.

10. *Turkish Daily News*, 8 March—DR, 13 March 1995.

11. *Economist*, 10 August 1996; *Mideast Mirror*, 29 August 1996.

12. *New York Times*, 26 August 1994; *Milliyet*, 24 February—DR, 1 March 1995; *Turkish Daily News*, 8 March—DR, 13 March 1995.

13. Amin Hassanpour, *Nationalism and Language in Kurdistan, 1918–1985* (San Francisco: Mellen Research University Press, 1992.) See particularly chapter 5, pp. 102–148.

14. Martin van Bruinessen, *Agha, Shaikh and State: On the Social and Political Organizations of Kurdistan* (Rijswijk, Netherlands: Europrint, 1978), p. 10.

15. For their role, see Middle East Watch, *Genocide*, pp. 161–166.

16. Sixty thousand pro-government Kurdish auxiliaries who acted on behalf of the government reputedly took part in the intifada; Agence France Press (AFP), 12 March—DR, 18 March 1990.

17. *Al-Sharq al-Awsat*, 5 May 1994. In 1994 Baghdad attempted once again to reactivate Kurdish tribal forces against the antigovernment Kurdish Peshmerga. *Al-Sharq al-Awsat*, 11 April 1994.

18. Voice of the people of Kurdistan, 5 January—DR, 10 January 1995.

19. *Watha'iq al-idana* (Damascus: PUK publications, 1994), p. 9.

20. The best known of these groups was the Unified Iraqi National Congress (INC), which was established in 1992 with the aim of unifying the different Iraqi opposition forces and ousting the Ba'th from power. Internal conflicts both within the INC and among the Kurdish groups themselves proved fatal for the success of such a plan.

21. For the causes of the conflict, see *The Middle East*, no. 250 (November 1995).

22. The Kurds are not the only group whose movement pursued different goals; the same has occurred among national movements in Africa, for example. Benyamin

Neuberger, *National Self-determination in Postcolonial Africa* (Boulder, Colo.: Lynne Rienner, 1986) p. 63.

23. Kurdish attempts to produce their own oil by establishing the "Kurdoil" company were nipped in the bud.

24. The KDP controlled the main source of hard currency as it collected fees on goods crossing the border point in Zakho. Its income was estimated at $100,000 daily. *Al-Safir,* 2, 3 August—DR, 10 August 1994; *al-Hayat,* 1 October 1994; *International Herald Tribune,* 8 April 1995; *The Middle East,* no. 250 (November 1995).

25. For the Turkish role, see Kemal Kirisci, "Provide Comfort or Trouble: Operation Provide Comfort and Its Impact on Turkish Foreign Policy," *Turkish Review of Middle Eastern Studies* 8 (1994–1995), pp. 43–67.

26. *Middle East International,* 12 May 1995; *The Middle East,* no. 250 (November 1995).

27. Relayed to the author by a person who wants to remain anonymous.

28. On the 1920 revolution, see Pierre-Jean Luizard, *La Formation de L'Irak Contemporain: Le Role Politique des Ulemas Chiites a la Fin de la Domination Ottomane et au Moment de la Construction de l'État Irakien* (Paris: Centre National de la Recherche Scientifique, 1991), pp. 381–414.

29. See, for example, *Alif Ba,* 27 March 1991; *Financial Times,* 15 April 1991. For Shi'is' own description of these acts, see *al-Wasat,* 3 January 1994.

30. For a discussion on *ta'ifiyya,* see Ofra Bengio, *Saddam's Word: Political Discourse in Iraq* (New York: Oxford University Press, 1998), pp. 100–103. In his book, 'Alawi blamed the Sunnis of being sectarian, *al-Shi'a wal-dawla,* pp. 257–285.

31. Muhammad Baqir al-Hakim, a leader of one of the Shi'i groups, repeatedly declared the intention of establishing "a greater Islamic republic" in post-Saddam Iraq but never mentioned specific Shi'i demands. Quoted, for example, in *Frankfurter Allgemeine,* 29 July—DR, 31 July 1992.

32. Muhammad Taqi al-Mudarrisi, *Al-'Iraq wal-haraka al-Islamiyya* (London: Al-Sifa lil-Nashr wa-al-Tawzi', 1988), pp. 32, 41–42, 77, 81–83.

33. For Shi'i self-criticism on this issue, see *al-'Iraq al-Hurr,* 19 February 1992. The proliferation of splinter groups reached its height in 1993 when there were reportedly eighty-eight opposition groups of both Shi'i, Kurds, and other Sunni groups. *Al-Hayat* (London), 15 February 1993.

34. Yitzhak Nakash, *The Shi'is of Iraq* (Princeton, N.J.: Princeton University Press, 1994), pp. 66–72; Luizard, *La Formation de l'Irak,* pp. 403–413.

35. There are contradictory reports regarding the role played by the Shi'i Grand Ayatollah Abu al-Qasim al-Kho'i. Even if he did lead the intifada, however, as claimed by a Shi'i opposition leader in exile, or give it his blessings, as *al-Wasat* claimed, by mid-March he was in the regime's "custody," denouncing the intifada on television. Iraqi News Agency, 20 March—DR, 23 March 1991; *al-Wasat,* 3 January 1994; *al-Majalla,* 25 January 1995.

36. Nakash, *The Shi'is of Iraq,* pp. 66–72.

37. President Saddam Husayn in Radio Baghdad, 7 October—DR, 8 October 1992.

38. The KDP blamed the alliance between PUK and Iran as the trigger for the fighting between the two factions. *Al-Wasat, International Herald Tribune,* 14 October 1996; *Mideast Mirror,* 18 October 1996.

39. On the campaign unleashed by the Ba'th against the Shi'i 'ulama, mosques, and institutions in the aftermath of the intifada, see *Al-Milal wal-nihal, wal-a'raq,* 1995 report (Cairo: Ibn Khaldun Center, 1995), pp. 47–52.

40. *Babil,* 17 February 1993.

41. *Middle East International,* 10 June 1994. Satellite photographs later showed that about 90 percent of the marsh region has disappeared. *Wireless File,* 14 June 1995.

42. Voice of Iraqi Islamic Revolution, 15, 22, 26 January—DR, 18, 24, 26 January 1994; *Middle East International* 4 February 1994; *Wireless File,* 22 March; *al-Hayat,* 2 April 1994; Rahim Francke, "Race to the Finish Line," *Middle East Insight* (May–August 1994), p. 40.

43. Voice of Iraqi Islamic Revolution, 29 January—DR, 1 February 1994; *Babil,* 2 February 1994.

44. Although political tribalism became manifest mainly after the Gulf War, many argued that it never disappeared. The Moroccan intellectual al-Jabiri suggests that tribalism has been part and parcel of Arab political history since time immemorial and that it was the main cause for their inability to develop a civil society. Muhammad 'Abid al-Jabiri, *Al-'Aql al-siyasi al-'Arabi* (Beirut: Al-markaz al-thaqafi al-'Arabi, 1991), pp. 373–374.

45. President Husayn granted hundreds of these people medals of valor and published their names in the media, for example, *al-Thawra,* 28, 30 June 1995; *al-Jumhuriyya,* 2, 4 July 1995.

46. *Babil,* 4 June 1994.

47. During the 1920 revolution the tribes received their orders from the 'ulama. Luizard, *La Formation de l'Irak,* pp. 406–409.

48. Hanna Batatu, *The Old Social Classes and the Revolutionary Movements of Iraq* (Princeton, N.J.: Princeton University Press, 1978), pp. 118–119.

49. *Babil,* 10 October 1993. For earlier reports on such clashes see, *Babil,* 17 May, 21 October 1992; *al-Jumhuriyya,* 1 November 1992. In the summer of 1995, the mainly Sunni tribe of al-Dulaymi in the al-Anbar governorate, northwest of Baghdad, staged open riots against the regime. Ofra Bengio, "Iraq," *Middle East Contemporary Survey (MECS),* vol. 19, 1995, pp. 312–315.

50. *Al-Thawra,* 2 April 1997.

51. *Wireless File,* 26 March 1992.

52. *Al-Qadisiyya,* 11 June—DR, 12 June 1994.

53. *Al-Jumhuriyya,* 22 January 1994.

54. *Al-Jumhuriyya,* 8 March, 8 October 1994, 10 July, 2 August 1995, 7, 21 May, 8 June 1997; *Babil,* 23, 24 April, 16 June, 9 July 1994; *al-Qadisiyya,* 1 September 1994, 8 May 1995; *al-Thawra,* 9, 11 November 1994, 26 July 1996, 25 September 1997.

55. For example INA, 12 May—DR, 14 May 1987; *Alif Ba,* 13 May 1987; *al-Jumhuriyya,* 28 January—DR, 5 February 1988.

56. Thirty-seven Iraqi books were written about the 1920 revolt. *Al-Thawra,* 27 June 1989.

57. For example, *Babil,* 7 March, 25, 26 August 1992; *al-Thawra,* 4, 10, 25 October 1992; *al-Jumhuriyya,* 2 September 1992.

58. For a recent study on the subject see Khaled Salih, *State-Making, Nation-Building and the Military: Iraq, 1941–1958* (Goteborg, Sweden: Goteborg University, 1996).

59. *Al-Sharq al-Awsat,* 7 September 1995; Jordan television, 26 September—DR, 27 September 1995; *Newsweek,* 30 October 1995. See also Pierre-Jean Luizard, "The Iraqi Question from the Inside," *Middle East Report* 25, no. 2 (March–April 1995), pp. 18–22; Ofra Bengio, "Iraq," *MECS,* vol. 19, 1995, pp. 330–332.

9

The Shi'is in Bahrain: Class and Religious Protest

Uzi Rabi and Joseph Kostiner

The fall of the Shah of Iran in 1979 and the establishment of a revolutionary Islamic government have had far-reaching implications for the Arab countries of the Gulf, from Kuwait in the north to the Sultanate of Oman in the south. In particular, these events marked the opening of a new era for the traditionally passive and cautious Shi'is of the Gulf and signaled a drastic change in their political behavior. For the first time, Shi'i groups began to raise their own deep-rooted grievances, conveying a strong message of Islamic fervor and antigovernment sentiment.

Shi'is everywhere have traditionally considered themselves socially and economically deprived (*mahrumin*) and generally treated as second-class citizens. Indeed, there are many examples of discriminatory measures against Shi'is in the Arab Gulf states. In Saudi Arabia and Kuwait, for example, they were not allowed to openly perform their ceremonial flagellations during the *'Ashura* observances. And the maintenance of Shi'i prayer houses has often been neglected by the authorities to such a degree that many have fallen into ruin.

Oil revenues were often not shared fairly with Shi'i communities. While major Saudi, Kuwaiti, and Bahraini towns grew into flourishing industrial centers, the Shi'i-populated neighboring settlements lagged behind. Shi'i participation in political life has also been severely limited. The Shi'is were excluded from any role in the formulation of policy, including major positions in the armies, security forces, and foreign and defense establishments of all the Arab Gulf states until the 1980s.[1] The fact that they were underprivileged and politically underrepresented made them a potentially combustible element.

Until 1979, Islam in the Gulf had not triumphed over political and socioeconomic interests and did not constitute a major component in the local ethos. The establishment of a revolutionary Islamic government in Iran changed all that. From its inception, the Khomeini regime posed a threat to

171

the Arab Gulf countries through its direct approach to their Shiʻi communities, many of whose leaders were old acquaintances of the new government in Iran. The Iranians cultivated a network of politically conscious Shiʻa as the potential spearhead for future revolutions. They provided sanctuary, training, and other assistance to a variety of liberation fronts and opposition forces operating in the Gulf. By the fall of 1979, Shiʻa demonstrations had begun in Saudi Arabia. A particularly violent upheaval occurred in the oil-producing eastern province of al-Ahsa, where the population was predominantly Shiʻi. Encouraged by their militant co-religionists in Iran, Shiʻi leaders decided they would march in public during 'Ashura, in open defiance of a longstanding law banning any public demonstration on that day.[2] Kuwait was subject to an increasing number of acts of sabotage on a different level, the Shiʻi bombings on 12 December 1983 being the most vivid example. This was followed in May 1985 by an unsuccessful attempt on the life of the Kuwaiti ruler, Jabir al-Sabah. In June 1986, saboteurs attacked oil installations, almost paralyzing Kuwait's oil industry.[3]

The Shiʻis of Bahrain

This chapter focuses on the political behavior of the Shiʻis of Bahrain and its development under the rule of the Al Khalifa Sunni dynasty. It will consider the various factors in this development: the socioeconomic status of the Shiʻis, their religious behavior, the political climate prevailing among the Sunnis, and Iran's postrevolutionary policies. From these factors, two major motivations emerge for Shiʻi political behavior, the first related to class affiliation, the second to religious fervor.

The Shiʻis of Bahrain cannot easily be defined as either rebellious or quietist; the picture is far more complex, particularly against the background of Iran's revolutionary regime. In the first place, unlike other states in the region, Bahrain carries the burden of an ancient Iranian claim to its territory. The Bahraini-Iranian dispute seemed to have been settled in 1971, when the Shah relinquished the claim of sovereignty over Bahrain and recognized its independence. But the Iranian revolution revived the issue, albeit in a new form.

Second, the religious structure of Bahrain, marked by a high proportion of Shiʻis, is unique in the Gulf. According to the best available estimates, Shiʻis make up 65 percent of the citizen population of 370,000, although no census has ever verified this figure.[4] Political sensitivities make any census unlikely, for the ruling Al Khalifa family is Sunni. Moreover, the majority of Bahraini Shiʻis follow the principles of the twelver sect (Ithna 'Ashariyya) of Shiʻi Islam. They originate mainly from Iran and southern Iraq and have a history of close ties with their fellow Shiʻis in those states. Many of them were naturally sympathetic to the Iranian revolution of 1979. Shaykh 'Ali Salman, for example, who came to head the Shi'i opposition in the 1990s, had been a noted student leader during his university days in Saudi Arabia. Like many other Shi'i clerics in Bahrain and elsewhere in the Gulf, he completed his religious education in the Iranian holy city of Qom before returning to Bahrain in 1992.[5]

Most Shi'is belong to the middle and lower classes of Bahraini society; they predominate in the distressed rural areas. No wonder that recent unrest has been centered in Shi'i communities like Jidd Hafs, a poor and mainly Shi'i area to the west of Manama, the capital.[6] By contrast, Sunni Muslims—notably the ruling Al Khalifa family and other leading clans—are mainly urban.[7] Sunnis dominate Bahrain's government as well as its military and security establishments.

Originating from Najd, the Al Khalifa family arrived in Bahrain in the eighteenth century. They found a quite prosperous population of Shi'i farmers, who owed their well-being to the abundant sources of fresh water on the island. The Al Khalifas proceeded to take control through appropriation of much of the islands' fertile land and an alliance, formed in the nineteenth century, with Britain.[8] One may assume that many of the Shi'is—descendants of the original inhabitants—have not, even after two centuries, completely accepted rule by a Sunni dynasty, which they still regard as usurpers.

The Al Khalifa regime inflicted discrimination and hardship on the Shi'is, including sporadic physical attacks by Sunnis. Sunni groups sometimes attempted to prevent Shi'is from practicing their religious ceremonies, particularly the *'Ashura* festivities. Shi'is were barred from land ownership, were not employed by state security bodies, and could not hold supreme ministerial offices. The Sunni-dominated security forces persecuted them continually as prime suspects of subversion.[9]

However, socioeconomic, judicial, and political developments in Bahrain mitigated the discrimination. Between the mid-1920s and the mid-1960s, the Shi'is were given legal protection for their personal security and property, their separate religious and judicial practices were recognized, and in principle, they were permitted to run their lives without interference.[10]

To maintain sociopolitical support and stability, Bahrain's rulers have utilized the island's small oil income to develop business opportunities for the elite families and a welfare system for the lower classes. They have also followed a policy of appointing Shi'is, particularly from notable families, to secondary ministries, while excluding them from paramount positions. Members of the Al Khalifa clan occupy the most prominent (foreign and defense) portfolios, whereas representatives of other elite families, including Shi'is, can be found in other ministerial and high-ranking administrative posts. For example, in the mid-1970s, Shi'is held five ministerial portfolios: health; legal affairs; commerce and agriculture; public works, power, and water; and transport and communication.[11]

In a similar fashion, the Shi'is were given opportunities in public administration, the private sector, and the Bahrain Petroleum Company (BAPCO),
primarily in middle-ranking posts. Apparently, as Fuad Khuri remarks, the
public sector and business became major outlets for the Shi'is: although
largely barred from owning land, Shi'is constituted about 70 percent of man-
agers and employees of private companies.[12] The Shi'is were thereby able to
compensate themselves somewhat for their lower status.

Although deprivation tended to unite them emotionally, the Shi'is of
Bahrain are divided along geographic and ethnic lines, by living conditions and
even praying styles—all of which have given rise to varied types of political behavior. Ethnically, Shi'is of Persian origin, collectively known as *al-Baharna*
(the indigenous inhabitants) make up the largest portion of the island's original
population. Among them are several prominent families that form an integral
part of the political establishment. In addition, there is a sizable community of
Arab Shi'is, originating from Saudi Arabia's eastern province, al-Ahsa. Mainly
small traders and manual and service workers, they have developed a degree of
self-sufficiency. They manage the most important mourning house (*ma'tam*),
where Imam Husayn's martyrdom is commemorated in a totally different style
to that of the processions staged by the *Baharna*.[13]

Socioeconomically, relatively few Shi'is are part of the elite. They form a
considerable proportion of the bureaucracy, as middle-ranking state and pri-
vate-sector administrators (though not in the Bahraini Defense Forces), and
many are small traders, artisans, and craftsmen.[14] Albeit economically dependent on the Al Khalifa rulers, the Shi'i middle class has developed its own
mode of political bargaining and has occasionally supported opposition
movements. Shi'is predominate in Bahrain's lower class, including indigenous agricultural workers, peasants, and fishermen. They are mostly *Baharna*,
and have suffered more than the upper classes from the Al Khalifas' land ex-
propriations, which transformed them into tenants. Much weakened by the
country's rapid urbanization, this group has become marginalized and relatively impoverished in shantytowns such as Jidd Haffs.

It is thus clear that the Shi'is of Bahrain do not form a compact minority
with a cohesive sociopolitical character and a uniform political outlook. Deprivation and compensation had tended to balance each other among the Shi'is,
preventing the emergence of an angry, rebellion-seeking community. Socioeconomic, ethnic, and cultural divisions also worked against a united Shi'i political response.

What then motivated Shi'i groups (rather than the entire Shi'i population)
to adopt opposition stands and even turn to violence? The motive was not to
topple the government and revolutionize the ruling system: most Shi'is
viewed themselves as patriots. Moreover, the divisions and balances within
the Shi'i population usually prevented majority adoption of extremist positions. The groups involved in opposition activities arose mainly from the mid-

dle and lower classes, namely, from among the administrators, students, and town-based manual workers. Their motivations grew out of socioeconomic and political change as well as ideology.

First sparked by British initiatives and later by a relatively small, but significant, oil income, Bahrain went through successive stages of development. Shi'i groups were involved in all the accompanying processes: occasional labor unrest, the evolution of trade unionism, demands for increased pay, and greater political freedom, notably through the activity of the National Assembly. Adding to the effects of these developments were regional ideologies that either infiltrated Bahrain from the outside or were brought in by foreign (mainly Palestinian) workers. Shi'is who occasionally took opposition stands over the socioeconomic grievances of the middle and lower classes hardened their positions under the impact of a second factor—regional ideological and socialist-radical influences—and developed a strong class identity. Even if expressed in an antigovernment form, this class identity was not purely Shi'i separatist or sectarian, which many Shi'is would have opposed. Rather, it was more inclusive and nationalistic. Indeed, Shi'is of the middle and lower classes often cooperated with Sunnis on broad issues of reform.[15] For middle and lower class Shi'is, who formed the majority of Bahrain's citizens, religious and class identities were interrelated; their struggle for an improved sociopolitical position was combined with preservation of their Shi'i identity.

Some Shi'i activists however, despite their participation in broad opposition movements, did not relate to Shi'i tradition as merely a ritual and communal experience but as their major motivation. Mainly young, relatively well educated, sometimes of a clerical bent, they held opposition views that went beyond class identity and cooperation with the Sunnis against the government. These activists saw themselves as the guardians of Shi'i values and communal interests, which, they felt, had to be maintained in the face of an assimilating class framework.

Shi'i opposition activity was thus characterized by contrary sociopolitical tendencies: most of them tended to channel their interests into classlike formations and cooperate with the Sunnis. A small minority, while active in such frameworks, also promoted more purist Shi'i interests and values. Over the years both tendencies interacted in various opposition groups.

The Shi'i Role in Bahraini Opposition Movements

In the 1930s, Sunni and Shi'i leaders launched parallel efforts to persuade Bahrain's rulers to create a representative assembly, in the face of a centralizing administration that had contributed to the growing gap between the ruler and his people. Whereas up to the 1920s, most Bahrainis had been able to approach their ruler personally, they were now forced to go through the mechanism of a government bureaucracy. In addition, both Sunnis and Shi'is of the middle class complained about the ineffective educational system, which was not producing adequate manpower for either the government or the oil indus-try—both heavily dependent on foreign labor. They also attacked the Bahrain Petroleum Company's (BAPCO) employment conditions, which discrimi-nated against nationals.[16]

A more serious challenge to the rulers was posed by radical Arab nation-alism in the 1950s. Inspired by Nasserist agitation, a general strike took place in 1954. As a result, nationalist activists, including both Sunni and Shi'i stu-dents, administrators, and manual workers formed a Higher Executive Com-mittee (HEC), one of whose goals was to secure a peaceful modus vivendi be-tween followers of both denominations.[17] As a majority of the workers, the Shi'is stimulated class identity, calling for the formation of a legislative as-sembly and the right to establish trade unions. Sunnis and Shi'is alike were careful not to allow the situation to get out of hand and tried to reach a negoti-ated settlement with the government. At the same time, radical demands for political change were being heard from working-class activists grouped in the National Front for the Liberation of Bahrain (NFLB). This persuaded the HEC leaders to rally around the rulers in order to stave off the NFLB threat. A group of Shi'i zealots based in prayer houses and clubs remained active, how-ever, rioting and demonstrating for several more weeks, until they were ar-rested and their groups disintegrated.[18]

The late 1960s and early 1970s were marked by an upsurge of labor un-rest, led by the NFLB and the Popular Front for the Liberation of Oman and the Arab Gulf (PFLOAG). Bahrain's ruler, Shaykh 'Isa bin Salman, sought to preempt the radical threat in 1972 by establishing a Constituent Assembly and drafting a provisional constitution, which was boycotted by the NFLB and the PFLOAG. Nonetheless, a thirty-member National Assembly (*al-majlis al-watani*) was elected in 1973, and permission granted to form trade unions.[19] Bahrain was the second state in the Gulf (after Kuwait) to create an elected parliament, but the first to suspend it. By May 1975, the experiment had ended. 'Isa dismissed the assembly and has ruled by decree since then. By the mid-1970s, the government had managed to weaken the radical leftist move-ments. For the next two decades, Islamist, predominantly Shi'i groups domi-nated opposition activity. In the earliest clerical bid for export of the Islamic revolution to other Gulf states, a leading Iranian clergyman, Ayatollah Hasan Ruhani, declared in 1979—even before the fall of Mehdi Bazargan's govern-ment—that Bahrain should be annexed to Iran, unless its rulers agreed to adopt "an Islamic form of government similar to the one established in Iran."[20] Ruhani's words were a portent of things to come. Since the summer of 1979, revolutionary Iran had attacked the Bahraini regime with inflamma-tory rhetoric and hostile actions, fomenting a new wave of demonstrations in-volving hundreds of people, mainly Shi'is demanding treatment befitting their majority status. They could now rely on an aggressive regional power with an explicitly antimonarchic and antiexploitative ideology.

Among the more radical groups propagating Islamic resurgence in the Gulf was the Islamic Front for the Liberation of Bahrain (IFLB—al-Jabha al-Islamiyya li-tahrir al-Bahrayn), which was collaborating with the Iraqi-based Shi'i underground, the Islamic Call (al-Da'wa al-Islamiyya).[21] Led by the Shi'i cleric Hadi al-Mudarrisi, an Iranian who had fled his country during the reign of the Shah, the IFLB organized public demonstrations that were broken up by police in August 1979.[22] Although their ideas sprang from socioeconomic grievances, such Shi'i clerics were also receptive to Iranian ideology. They upheld Shi'i religious symbols and ideas that were more radical than those of class-related opposition movements, and engaged in revolutionary activities.[23] With Iranian support and a new Iranian-inspired ideology that combined universal as well as Shi'i ideas, the activists of the IFLB did not simply fade away as others had in earlier years. They prevailed and continued to act against the government.

During the 1980s, opposition activity mainly comprised large-scale acts of sabotage committed by small, well-trained underground groups. Obviously, this reflected Iran's interest in causing harm to the pro-Iraqi Gulf states. The perpetrators themselves had been frustrated over the failure of the first popular wave of Shi'i demonstrations and believed that a more violent response was called for. On 13 December 1981, the Bahraini security forces announced the arrest of a seventy-five-member group bent on toppling the Al Khalifa regime and announcing the establishment of an Islamic republic. The plot had been organized by the IFLB, with Mudarrisi designated to head the new regime. IFLB members trained in Iran were infiltrated into Bahrain, where they were to take over strategic locations and gain control over the state.[24] Additional attempts to subvert the Bahraini government were made over the next decade. The most notable was another coup attempt in December 1987, again bearing the hallmarks of Iranian support for its proxy, the Tehran-based IFLB, led by Hojjat al-Islam Hadi al-Mudarrisi.[25] However, this strategy, focusing on sabotage and terror directed against the Al Khalifa family, did not enjoy broad support and failed to attract the majority of the Shi'i population.

Against the backdrop of the second (Iraqi-Kuwaiti) Gulf War, a new phase of Shi'i-dominated opposition activity began. There were two major causes: the eroding image of the Gulf rulers and economic recession. As in earlier cases, the spark of uprising came from foreign influences that rocked the entire Arab Gulf region. Bahrain's rulers, along with those of the other Gulf nations, had lost their credibility: they had failed to foresee the Iraqi invasion and succeeded in defending their states only with the help of 500,000 foreign troops. This resulted in a growing demand for the rulers' accountability to their people and wider political participation. Oman, Qatar, Kuwait, and Saudi Arabia began to take cautious steps in this direction soon after the war.

But the Al Khalifa family in Bahrain tenaciously resisted the trend, fearing that a more open political process would increase, rather than contain, pressure on the ruling family.[26]

During the postwar era, the continuing frustration of a new generation of young Bahrainis has been exacerbated by economic conditions.[27] Bahrain has virtually exhausted its small oil reserves and become dependent upon richer neighbors for help in building up its industrial and financial base. With its oil position eroded, the government has made an enormous effort to diversify into a service and, to a lesser extent, industrial center for the Gulf region. But this service-oriented economy has slumped as a result of the Gulf's economic problems. Gross domestic product (GDP) fell by about 2.5 percent in 1994; the government responded by raising tariffs and indirect taxes, and slashing expenditures by a planned 4.9 percent in 1995. The traditional Kuwaiti aid had dried up during the war and Saudi Arabia's assistance was also on the wane.[28] The large and growing population of young people (an estimated three quarters of Bahrain's 370,000 nationals are under twenty-five) meant that new jobs should be created rapidly.[29] But because foreigners make up some 65 percent of the workforce, there has been little room for labor market growth. According to opposition sources, unemployment was as high as 30 percent.[30] Particular criticism was directed against Shaykh 'Isa for continuing to allow an influx of cheap foreign labor rather than provide jobs for Bahrain's citizens. In July 1994, a petition was signed by 1,200 unemployed youth requesting the government to deal with their problem; the response was to crack down on protesters.

Politics by Petition: The New Wave

The July 1994 protest recalled a case in late 1991, when a Sunni theologian, Shaykh 'Abd al-Latif al-Mahmud, was arrested after delivering a speech critical of the autocratic Gulf regimes. Shaykh al-Mahmud argued that progress among the Gulf Cooperation Council's (GCC) states would evolve only through domestic political reform, leading to the establishment of elected parliaments, implementation of the rule of law, and freedom of expression. He also demanded a clearer distinction between public finance and allocation of wealth to the ruling families. Shaykh al-Mahmud's ideas were summed up in a petition calling for restoration of an elected National Assembly. The petition also cast doubt on the Al Khalifas' nation-building principles: the personal, patronizing contacts of the Al Khalifa family with elite families, their absolute rule, and the exclusion of the majority of the population from the political process. Signed by over 150 public figures representing most of Bahrain's Sunni and Shi'i ideological and political movements, and described as "the first joint political action of its kind in Bahrain," the petition was submitted to Shaykh 'Isa.[31] Subsequently, nineteen political activists, all Shi'is, were arrested on charges of belonging to the banned IFLB and distributing antigovernment literature. The accused pleaded not guilty, claiming they were campaigning for democratic rights in Bahrain.[32] In this instance Shi'is and Sunnis worked together to press for change, in an action that once more demonstrated Shi'i tendencies to cooperate with Sunnis on broad issues.

The ruling family resisted the demands for reform. After the short-lived experiment of the National Assembly (1973–1975), the government feared reestablishment of an organ that might be used to launch attacks on the ruling family. By the end of 1992, however, the winds of change were sweeping Bahrain, and the political struggle intensified. In November, 300 intellectuals, professionals, and clergymen signed a second petition presented to Shaykh 'Isa, calling for greater political freedom within the framework of the constitution. The emir's response was to threaten those involved with imprisonment or exile, effectively suppressing the movement. Not surprisingly, Bahrain then became a focus of attention by human rights organizations, including Amnesty International, which reported that all political organizations had been formally banned, trade union rights severely circumscribed, and all but the most important Shi'i religious festivities prohibited under the country's Sunni minority rule. Amnesty called upon the Bahraini regime to improve the country's "dismal human rights record."[33]

The government did attempt to dissipate political tension and appease the opposition.[34] In December 1992, Shaykh 'Isa announced formation of a thirty-seat consultative council.[35] Appointed rather than elected, however, this council was limited to an advisory role, and its deliberations were not open to the public.[36] In addition, the regime announced new social welfare benefits to "alleviate hardships faced by the poorer people," reducing utility and housing costs and subsidizing socially deprived groups.[37]

Growing Radicalism

The opposition movement hitherto described has been superseded since late 1994 by a more radical struggle, which brought leading Shi'i figures to the fore. The arrest on 5 December 1994 of a popular young Shi'i clergyman, Shaykh 'Ali Salman, resulted in riots instigated by the actions of several Shi'i clerics. Shaykh 'Ali and two other clerics, Hamza al-Dayri and Haydar al-Sitri, had been the leading figures in a campaign to gather signatures for a new petition demanding restoration of the elected National Assembly that had been suspended by the regime almost two decades before.[38] Thousands of Bahrainis, mostly Shi'is, signed the petition and thereby became the target of government persecution. With strict press censorship in force, they were unable to initiate a political discourse.[39]

The clerics' campaign and its aftermath reflect a new kind of Shi'i opposition activity. Still motivated to address broad constitutional and economic concerns, Shi'is continued to cooperate with Sunnis. However, the leaders of the new movement were Shi'is, and the tone and the pace of events were set by a Shi'i-led organization. The group of Shi'i activists that had been marginal to opposition movements in the 1930s and 1950s, and a more important but still marginal part of the terrorist-oriented groups in the 1980s, became the leaders of the opposition in the 1990s. There are two probable reasons for this development. First, younger clerics like 'Ali Salman, exposed to Iranian indoctrination, had internalized its propaganda, leading them to associate universal ideas of justice and equality with Shi'i values and motives. Since his return to Bahrain in 1992, Shaykh 'Ali took a strong line against the Al Khalifa regime, spicing his rhetoric with a heady dose of Shi'i revolutionary fervor and depicting Shi'is killed by the security forces during the latest riots as martyrs on behalf of God.[40] Second, the younger clerics' growing acquaintance with lower-class Shi'is had bridged the traditional gaps between different ethnic and denominational groups and established a common antigovernment denominator among them. To be sure, most Shi'is still advocated cooperation with the Sunnis, under the banner of universal ideas. But a group among them, led by more radical, pro-Iranian clerics, had evolved and was building support among the lower classes, stressing clearly identifiable Shi'i communal interests and grievances.

According to opposition accounts, demonstrations in 1995 constituted an expression of popular anger at growing unemployment and misrule.[41] During the week preceding Shaykh 'Ali's arrest in December 1994, protests spread from mosques in Manama to Shi'i villages surrounding the capital, triggering further police raids and arrests.[42] These villages were at the center of an uprising that climaxed in March 1995, with nightly explosions and arson attacks on targets ranging from petrol stations to banks.[43] The perpetrators called it "the Bahraini Intifada," and it reflected the strengthening of the more radical activist camp. There was growing cooperation between intellectuals who demanded the return of constitutional rule and unemployed, village-based rioters, led by a group of Shi'i preachers inspired by 'Ali Salman and his colleagues. Although 'Ali and other leaders were deported in January 1995, unrest continued, even after the government had announced the release from prison of 200 detainees. Bahraini security forces responded harshly, sealing off entire districts, raiding many homes, and using tear gas and live ammunition to quell the unrest. Toward the end of May 1995, after fourteen civilians and three policemen had been killed, scores injured, and between 700 and 1,600 imprisoned, the revolt seemed to have lost some of its momentum.[44] The imprint of a more extremist trend was evident in the prominence of Shi'i leaders in the riots, the slogans stressing discrimination and suppression, and the participation of lower-class members in the actions.

However, the time-honored form of broad, intercommunal operations was not abandoned. To gain more support, the leaders of the radical stream tried to frame their views in a universal language that would convince the more moderate, less partisan groups while also reflecting their concepts of justice and participation. Shi'i opposition publications stressed that their movement was not religiously exclusive, pointing out that it included both Sunnis and Shi'is and reflected a broad range of political views, notably Islamist, liberal, leftist, and nationalist.[45] There were reports that a national dialogue was underway among elements representing these trends.[46] They all focused on a common goal: to reinstate the *majlis* and limit absolute rule. Moreover, they openly claimed that the state intelligence services—headed since 1966 by a British officer, Ian Henderson[47]—were deliberately trying to provoke Sunni-Shi'i antagonism[48] through the distribution of leaflets attempting "to create fear among the communities and hence justify their repressive campaign."[49] The Shi'i hard-liners seemed to be trying to distance themselves from a sectarian profile. The image they now tried to project was that of patriotism. "The confrontation in Bahrain," lamented a spokesman on behalf of the IFLB, "is between the people of all sorts and the regime."[50]

A most unusual attempt at broad cooperation among opposition groups came in early May 1995, when a group of twenty prominent Bahraini women, in an unprecedented move, sent an open letter to the ruler, Shaykh 'Isa.[51] They expressed deep concern over the deteriorating situation in the country, in particular the heightening tension and the increasing levels of violence. The signatories were all highly placed professionals from most walks of life in Bahrain. They included lawyers, university professors, and civil servants.[52] By reminding both the regime and its opponents of the rights of women to equality in all spheres of life and their right to obtain full participation in the political process, they underscored the broad character of the opposition movement.[53]

The following months saw a number of tentative attempts to heal the breach. In May, the government expressed its determination to find jobs for 4,000 Bahrainis every year in order to reduce unemployment, one of the underlying causes of the unrest. Some of the positions would be created by "Bahrainization," a strict scheme to replace foreign workers with nationals, of which the Shi'is were a majority, and forcing many of the country's 250,000 expatriates to leave, especially low-skilled workers from the Indian subcontinent. Talks between the government and opposition leaders were resumed.

As in the past, however, the government pointed to outside instigation as the source of internal trouble.[54] It accused "extremist organizations" supported by an unidentified "foreign party"—apparently an allusion to Iran.[55] Although it was seldom stated publicly, Bahrain held Iran primarily responsible for the riots. Indeed, statements by Iranian leaders and media suggested that Tehran would prefer a different regime in Manama. Maintaining an official posture of impartiality, senior Iranian officials have refrained from direct public comment on unrest in Bahrain, claiming that "the crisis [there] was a domestic issue."[56] Instead, they emphasize Tehran's desire for the victory of an indigenous Islamic opposition, referred to as the "Muslims" who were "clashing with the police" in "some Arab countries" (i.e., Bahrain), adding that "[they] are much closer to victory than we were in the mid-1970s in Iran."[57] The Iranian media, more keenly supportive of the Muslim reformists of Bahrain, regarded a change of regime as ideologically and strategically advantageous for Tehran. No wonder then that the Bahraini government claimed the upheaval was not related to jobs or internal politics but fomented by a group of young Shiʻi clerics recently returned from Iran.[58] Dismissing opposition activists as a minority of troublemakers, the Bahraini government downplayed all outbreaks of unrest.

Since 1991 both trends within the Shiʻi opposition have also been active in London. The leading groups are the Bahrain Freedom Movement (BFM) and the IFLB.[59] The BFM, originally set up in 1982, represented constitutionalist views and had its roots in the parliamentary experiment of the 1970s but was barely active for many years. Inspired by the 1994 petition, it began a struggle for restoration of the National Assembly and the suspended key articles of the constitution. Its leaders struck a balance between liberal and religious views, encouraging Sunni-Shiʻi cooperation. Their propaganda material did not mince words, calling the Al Khalifa clan tyrants and attacking the British government for supporting the Bahraini ruler. When interviewed, UK-based leaders like Mansur al-Jamri and ʻAla al-Yusuf claimed to respect the popular will.[60] They offered to come to terms with the Al Khalifas if they would ease their iron grip over society and hold elections.[61] A statement issued by the BFM listed the demands of the organization as follows:

1. Release Shaykh ʻAli Salman and all those arrested in the uprising.
2. Implement Bahrain's constitutional order and set a date for elections.[62]
3. Allow exiled politicians to return to the island without any restrictions.[63]
4. Revoke the ill-reputed state security law.
5. Deport the British commander of the intelligence apparatus, Ian Henderson, and the foreign team operating with him.[64]

But the BFM has been superseded by the more radical IFLB. Western observers and the Bahraini authorities have long regarded the Front as an Iranian proxy, operating from Tehran and bent on toppling the Al Khalifa regime. Shaykh ʻAbd al-Hamid al-Radi, a member of the Front's General Congress, who echoed the BFM in terming the riots an "intifada," argued that the "nature of the system is intrinsically anti-democratic" and that events had gone too far to merely restore the 1973 National Assembly.[65] The shaykh had clarified that the Al Khalifa clan had to be overthrown. Furthermore, in contrast to the BFM's claims,[66] the IFLB stated that the latest wave of demonstrations had nothing to do with the constitutional petition campaign.[67]

These differences were, however, not manifested on the ground. In Bahrain itself, the Shi'i opposition movement paraded universal principles but in fact had clerical Shi'i leaders, some of them inspired and others supported by Iran, and altogether dominated by Shi'i identity and interests.

The Shi'i character of the movement was evident in the response of Sunni intellectuals. Caught between a Sunni regime and a protest movement that was mostly Shi'i, Sunni intellectuals and administrators, mostly from the middle class, were left in an acute dilemma. Excluded from any real political role by the Al Khalifa family's dissolution of the National Assembly in 1975, they had been sponsoring petition campaigns (in 1991 and 1992) calling for restoration of constitutional government. Sunni opposition sources nevertheless regarded leaders of the Shi'i community, like the exiled Shaykh 'Ali Salman, as having been too heavily influenced by Iranian radicalism. Some Shi'i leaders were therefore viewed as seeking to emulate Khomeini's mass protest tactics, thereby alienating their erstwhile Sunni allies. A Sunni human rights' activist complained of what he called the Shi'i dedication to martyrdom, which undermined the developing reform movement.[68]

In November 1995, after a six-month hiatus, disturbances flared up again, with a spate of bombings, arson attacks, and other acts of sabotage. Two homemade bombs exploded at two luxury hotels, injuring three people and causing property damage. A third bomb exploded at a commercial complex on New Year's Eve, causing panic but no injuries. Another went off, apparently prematurely, in a car parked at a commercial market. Scores of people, mainly from the majority Shi'i community, were arrested in a huge government crackdown. Bahraini newspapers and other Arab media adhering to the official Bahraini line emphasized that some of those detained in connection with the bombings had confessed that they had been trained to prepare explosives in the Iranian city of Qom or in Hizballah camps in Lebanon.

The Shi'i leaders now issued more extremist propaganda and at the same time tried to associate themselves with other groups—liberals and Sunnis alike—as signatories of a statement declaring that the "Bahraini people will not surrender, no matter how severe the repression and terrorism."[69] Shi'i leaders also were pressing the government to release the detainees. A deal was struck, and several hundred individuals detained during the unrest were freed beginning mid-August. But the opposition leaders were demanding the immediate release of hundreds more who, under the deal, were to be freed by the end of September. They also called for a halt to the trials of detainees, the return of deportees, and the launching of talks on political reforms—in particular, restoration of the constitution suspended in 1975 and reinstatement of Parliament.

Shi'i religious institutions—privately funded religious centers or mourning houses—had long provided a political hub for Bahraini Shi'i preachers,
who continued to foment unrest. Addressing his worshipers at Friday prayers
in the village of al-Diraz, Shaykh 'Abd al-Amir al-Jamri, a member of the dissolved Parliament who emerged as the de facto leader of the opposition,
warned that the dangerous situation would get more complicated if the
Supreme Court of Appeals upheld a death sentence against one of the protesters, Ahmad Hasan Kambar. Al-Jamri declared that any solution to the crisis in
Bahrain should be comprehensive, depicting attempts by some businessmen
to improve the living conditions of the Shi'i community as a shortsighted initiative. Detained following the first wave of unrest and released in September,
al-Jamri also stressed that any solution lacking constitutional legitimacy
would be incomplete.

As for government plans to bolster the Shura council, a consultative assembly appointed by the ruler in December 1992 after he had rejected calls to
reinstate the disbanded Parliament, al-Jamri said that in order to receive popular support "such a body must be elected by secret ballot and it must have the
power of an independent legislature."[70] The Shi'i opposition therefore seemed
to have a wider resonance also with the Sunni middle and lower classes.

In response to al-Jamri's activities, the Bahraini security forces raided
mosques, and the government banned Friday prayers altogether at several
mosques. The re-arrest in January 1996 of the established leaders of the opposition movement—from Shi'i cleric 'Abd al-Amir al-Jamri to Sunni lawyer
Ahmad Shamlan—served to indicate the government's resolve.

But the Bahraini regime found itself in a dilemma, for its policy appeared
only to be provoking more resistance. In March 1996, an arson attack at a
restaurant left seven Bangladeshis dead and struck fear into the large expatri-
ate community.[71] In another development, the execution of a Shi'i convicted
of killing a policeman sparked a fresh round of violent protests in Manama's
Shi'i suburbs. The Bahraini security forces then sealed off the Shi'i districts
of al-Diraz and Sanabis.[72] As events escalated, the number of participants in
the riots rose to hundreds. The conflict was now between Shi'i youths—
mostly in the villages but also in some urban areas—and government forces.
The Bahraini regime found the disturbances difficult to quell precisely because they were loosely organized and involved the increasingly radicalized
younger generation.

Conclusion

The point of departure of this chapter was that Bahraini Shi'is do not constitute a separatist group easily prompted to rebel. To be sure, they harbored
feelings of political and socioeconomic deprivation, inflicted on them by the

Al Khalifa-led Sunni regime. But these grievances were counterbalanced by government policies aimed at protecting Shi'i lives and property, and helping them earn reasonable livelihoods in the private and public sectors. In addition, their own internal ethnic, socioeconomic, and even religiously based divisions prevented their appearance as a uniform grouping in Bahraini politics. In fact, Shi'is form a majority of Bahrain's population and regard themselves as being among the founders of the state. Consequently, despite their severe criticism of the government, they developed feelings of patriotism and loyalty to the state.

They therefore tended to cooperate with Sunnis in support of all-embracing, universal ideas, including economic improvement and constitutional government. The Shi'is were active primarily in class-based opposition activities. Class provided intercommunal cooperation, an arena in which to pursue universal goals, and a framework for organizing political action where they could also uphold their religious identity. However, not all the Shi'is were satisfied with this framework. The successive waves of opposition in Bahrain since the 1930s gave rise to small groups of zealous Shi'is, made up or led by clerics, who rallied around Shi'i interests, religious values, and identity. For them, the "Shi'i cause" had a higher priority than adherence to more universal, class-based or nationalist ideas. They were part of the broader opposition movements but took their cue from specific Shi'i grievances and religious perceptions. These groups, however, remained marginal, isolated from most of the Shi'i population, which regarded them as fanatical and unprepared for compromise.

The Iranian revolution of 1979 brought about a change in Shi'i political activity. Iran's new regime provided organizational support and an ideological package that wedded universal ideas of justice and equality to the Shi'i focus on martyrdom and the fight against oppression. Moreover, the Iranian government prepared a continuous flow of Bahraini clerics who had been cultivated in Shi'i schools. From 1979 to 1985, fervent Shi'i groups emerged to lead Shi'i activities with Iranian support. But their use of terrorism, which most Shi'is opposed, subjected them to government persecution (or exile) and isolated them from the Shi'i majority.

In the 1990s, against the background of growing economic difficulties, demands to restore constitutional practice all over the Gulf, and the declining image of the Gulf monarchs, the role of Bahrain's zealous Shi'i groups became more evident. Most Shi'is were again organized in a broad, class-based movement that upheld constitutional ideas. But this time, Iranian-inspired clerics and zealous Shi'is did not settle for a marginal role but took over leadership of the opposition movement as a whole. They used universal terms, spoke on behalf of all Bahrainis, and encouraged cooperation with Sunnis in fighting the government. The role of Shi'i clerics was dominant in activating and setting the pace and the breadth of the movement, and members of the

Shi'i lower class made up the rank and file. Their goals were comprehensive, focusing on major changes in the regime, and even its overthrow. The Shi'i activists were thus leading Bahraini society, alongside Kuwait and Saudi Arabia, into a vehement struggle for power and constitutional rights, which may well determine the nature of future regimes in the Gulf.

Their struggle attests to the fact that the present mode of state building in the Gulf—underpinned by social change, urbanization, education, and welfare, along with a prevalence of tribal and Islamic values in society—has exhausted itself. State funds are insufficient to provide for social services and mass employment, and the political arrangements can no longer satisfy a growing drive for democratization. Gulf states will need to reform their regimes, and, as part of this process, the role and position of the Shi'is will have to be altered.

Notes

1. *The Middle East,* July 1980; *Financial Times,* 5 May 1981, 24 April 1984.

2. *International Herald Tribune,* 4 December 1979; *Financial Times,* 4 December 1979.

3. See, for example, *al-Qabas,* 11 June 1986.

4. These figures were provided by the Agence France Press (AFP) and should be regarded as estimates. See AFP, 19 December—Foreign Broadcasting Information Service: Near East and South Asia: Daily Report (DR), 19 December 1994. According to another estimate, Shi'is were said to constitute more than 70 percent of the citizen population of 240,000 during the mid-1980s.

5. Andrew Rathmell, "Opposition in the Gulf—Further Insights," *Jane's Intelligence Review* 7, no. 7 (July 1995), p. 309.

6. *Financial Times,* 24 December 1994.

7. The homonym *Al* attests to the Arabic term for extended family.

8. See, for example, Andrew Wheatcroft, *The Life and Times of Shaykh Salman Bin Hamad Al-Khalifa, Ruler of Bahrain, 1942–1961* (London: Kegan Paul, 1995), pp. 39–77.

9. Fred Haley Lawson, *Bahrain: The Modernization of Autocracy* (Boulder, Colo.: Westview, 1989), pp. 27–31.

10. Ibid., pp. 9–11.

11. Fuad I. Khuri, *Tribe and State in Bahrain: The Transformation of Social and Political Authority in an Arab State* (Chicago: University of Chicago Press, 1980), pp. 154–173.

12. Ibid., pp. 128–131.

13. Ibid., pp. 167–168.

14. The rapid social change among the Shi'i community is best understood by reading accounts of Shi'i village life as it was but a few decades ago. For such an account, see Henry Herald Hansen, *Investigations in a Shi'i Village in Bahrain* (Copenhagen: National Museum of Denmark, 1968).

15. Donald L. Horowitz, *Ethnic Groups in Conflict* (Berkeley: University of California Press, 1985), pp. 95–140; Milton G. Esman and Itamar Rabinovich (eds.), "The Study of Ethnopolitics in the Middle East," in Esman and Rabinovich, *Ethnicity, Plu-*

ralism and the State in the Middle East (Ithaca, N.Y.: Cornell University Press, 1987), pp. 3–28.

16. Ian J. Seccombe, "The Persian Gulf," *Journal of the Royal Central Asian Society,* 25 (July 1938), p. 357.

17. Rosemarie Said Zahlan, *The Making of the Modern Gulf States: Kuwait, Bahrain, Qatar, the United Arab Emirates and Oman* (London: Unwin Hyman, 1989), pp. 54–58.

18. For further details on the HEC leaders' demands, see Muhammad Ghanim al-Rumaihi, *Bahrain: A Study on Social and Political Changes Since the First World War* (London: Bowker, 1975), pp. 289–290.

19. *Akhbar al-Khalij,* 24 December 1992.

20. Rouhollah K. Ramazani, *Revolutionary Iran: Challenge and Response in the Middle East* (Baltimore, Md.: Johns Hopkins University Press, 1986), pp. 48–49.

21. *Al-Dustur* (London), 6 May, 1 July 1985.

22. *Al-Ra'y al-'Amm,* 31 August 1979. Mudarrisi was given Bahraini nationality, of which he was stripped in September 1979 as the result of his activity to undermine the rule of the Al Khalifa family.

23. For a study dealing with the impact of the Islamic revolution, see Rouhollah K. Ramazani, "Socio-Political Change in the Gulf: A Climate for Terrorism," in S. H. Richard and J. E. Peterson (eds.), *Crosscurrents in the Gulf: Arab Regional and Global Interests* (Washington, D.C.: Middle East Institute, 1988), p. 136.

24. Ramazani, *Revolutionary Iran,* pp. 50–51.

25. *Al-Dustur,* 11 January 1988.

26. *Al-'Alam* (London), May 1995.

27. *Middle East Economic Digest,* 27 April 1992.

28. *Al-Quds al-'Arabi,* 21 December 1994.

29. *Middle East International,* 28 April 1995.

30. See, for example, *Mideast Mirror,* 14 December 1994.

31. *Al-Quds al-'Arabi,* 21 November 1992.

32. *Middle East Economic Digest,* 6 March 1992.

33. *Gulf States Newsletter,* 10 February 1992.

34. *Al-Quds al-'Arabi,* 21 November 1992.

35. *Akhbar al-Khalij,* 24 December 1992.

36. *Akhbar al-Khalij,* 28 December 1992.

37. *Middle East Economic Digest,* 8 May 1992.

38. For a full account of the petition, see *al-'Alam,* May 1995. For more on the suspended National Assembly, see *Le Monde* (Paris), 20 December 1994.

39. *Sawt al-Bahrain* (London), January 1995.

40. Speaking on behalf of the opposition, the London-based Bahrain Freedom Movement was naming the latest "martyrs," *Gulf States Newsletter,* 22 May 1995.

41. A. Rathmell, "Opposition in the Gulf," p. 309.

42. *Al-Salama al-Mamnu'a* (London), February 1995.

43. *Sawt al-Bahrain,* January 1995.

44. *Al-Majd* (Amman), 20 April 1990.

45. *Al-'Alam,* May 1995.

46. *Mideast Mirror,* 3 April 1995.

47. *Al-Majd,* 20 February 1995.

48. The IFLB secretary-general, Muhammad 'Ali Mahfuz, went as far as to blame Britain for allowing "its nationals to head the intelligence services in Bahrain and keeping quiet about the crimes" of the authorities. See AFP, 14 December—DR, 15 December 1994.

49. *Mideast Mirror,* 3 April 1995.

50. *Al-Safir,* 27 December 1995.

51. *Sawt al-Bahrain,* January 1995.

52. *Al-'Alam,* May 1995.

53. Women were also reported to have taken part in the demonstrations that occurred in February and March. See, for example, *al-Majd,* 6 February 1995.

54. On a different level, "foreign circles" were accused of "spreading untrue reports about what is happening in Bahrain." See, for example, *al-Sharq al-Awsat,* 21 December 1994.

55. See, for example, *al-Ittihad* (Abu Dhabi), 27 December 1994. See also *Mideast Mirror,* 19 April 1995.

56. *Jumhuri-ye Islami,* 8 January—DR, 12 April 1995.

57. See, for example, 'Ali Khamene'i's speech, Radio Tehran, 3 February—DR, 12 April 1995.

58. *Al-Sharq al-Awsat,* 24 January 1995.

59. A monthly newsletter published in London by the movement is called *Sawt al-Bahrain* (*Voice of Bahrain*).

60. The BFM's broad popular basis is indicated by the backgrounds of al-Jamri and al-Yusuf. Jamri is the son of a well-known Shi'i cleric, whereas Yusuf is a former International Monetary Fund official.

61. See also an interview given to *al-'Arabi,* 2 January 1995 by 'Abd al-Rahman al-Nu'aymi, a leading figure in the BFM.

62. See, for example, an interview given by Shaykh 'Ali Salman to *al-'Alam,* May 1995.

63. *Al-Hayat,* 13 January 1995.

64. *Al-Quds al-'Arabi* (London), 3 January 1995.

65. *Al-Istiqlal* (Gaza), 23 December 1994.

66. See, for example, an interview given to *al-Safir* (Beirut), 27 December 1994, by Shaykh Muhammad 'Ali Mahfuz, secretary-general of the IFLB.

67. *Al-Majd,* 8 May 1995.

68. *Gulf States Newsletter,* 22 May 1995.

69. *Al-Quds al-'Arabi,* 12 March 1996.

70. See, for example, the heir apparent's interview to *al-Sharq al-Awsat,* 7 March 1996.

71. WAKH, 14 March—DR, 14 March 1996.

72. AFP, 15 March—DR, 15 March 1996.

PART FOUR

Conclusion

10

The State and Minorities Toward the Twenty-first Century: An Overview

Gabriel Ben-Dor and Ofra Bengio

The main conclusions to be drawn from the study of minorities in the Arab world revolve around several salient and recurrent themes in the various case studies: democratization, centralization, federalism, leadership, and the search for unifying national themes and motifs.

When assessing majority-minority relations, it is important to note that the concept of a minority is intimately related to one's definition of a majority. In other words, because there are different kinds of majorities, there are different kinds of minorities. Furthermore, it is evident from the cases analyzed that a complex process of transformation turns a more or less objective social structure into a political concept of majority and minority. The conditions and circumstances of this process differ substantially from country to country, as the various chapters in this volume demonstrate.

In some cases, such as that of the Kurds in Iraq, the minorities are Muslims but not Arabs. In other cases, such as that of the 'Alawis in Syria, they are Arabs but not Muslims. In the extreme case of the Sudan they are neither Arabs nor Muslims; there, reinforcing cleavages inevitably exacerbate ethnic tensions. These different patterns lead to divergences in the fundamental quest for political orientation.

When the minority is Arab but not Muslim, the natural tendency is to seek themes of Arab nationalism in order to stress the common denominator. When this is not feasible, or when it is not fashionable, themes of one-country patriotism-nationalism come in handy instead; this can be seen in Egypt, which has a large minority of Christian Copts who are unquestionably Egyptians and are as Arab as other Egyptians. This makes for a particular patriotic and nationalistic fervor, which at times denies the uniqueness of the minority;

the minority is referred to merely as a group within the society, as a community within the family of the nation.

Things are different when the minority is Muslim but not Arab, as with the Kurds in Iraq and the Berbers in Algeria. In such cases, logic would dictate an appeal to the Islamic character of the state in order to emphasize the factor that holds the people together at the expense of that which separates them. Things are not so simple, however, because those Islamic themes are not always available. In Algeria they are not available because of the massive, violent confrontation between the incumbent regime and militant Islamic movements. They might also be unavailable because of the process of secularization, which has affected broad strata of Algerian society and makes emphasis of Islamic motifs either unappealing or self-destructive. Given this difficult set of constraints, the regime cannot appeal to Islam as the unifying factor in the country. Obviously, Arab nationalism is neither feasible nor available; therefore, an appeal must be made to local Algerian nationalism.

The situation of the Egyptian Copts is somewhat similar to that of the Algerian Berbers. In general, it seems that the Berbers are at a stage of consciousness reminiscent of an earlier stage in the political evolution of the Coptic minority in Egypt. It remains to be seen how long the low level of political assertiveness among the Berbers will remain as calm and passive as it is at present. The answer, of course, depends partly on the political fortunes of the country at large. Clearly, the violence and confrontation of the late 1990s has increased the politicization of all groups in society, while possibly stifling temporarily all cleavages in Algerian society other than the overwhelming one between the secular regime and the Islamic opposition.

The pattern in Lebanon, which pits the Maronite Christians against various Muslim factions and the Druze, is unclear. No group has a clear majority, and for that reason the definition of minorities is always somewhat hazy. All groups are minorities in the sense that they are not numerical majorities at the moment, nor can they hope to be in the foreseeable future. Furthermore, there are no natural or permanent ethnic arrangements in Lebanon that could regulate intergroup relations in a stable manner so as to create an enduring majority in the political as much as the demographic sense of the term. The concept of Muslims, for example, is not strong enough as a unifying factor, because of the complex and ever-changing differences between the Shi'is, who are the largest group; the Sunnis, who are the more powerful one; and the Druze, who are not strictly Muslims but are traditionally quite hostile to the Maronite Christians. These differences do not allow for the emergence of the secure feeling associated with a stable majority.

In Sudan, we witness the extreme case of a conflict between the clear majority, which is Arab, Muslim, and territorially concentrated in the north, and the non-Arab, non-Muslim south. Not surprisingly, the conflict there—due to these reinforcing cleavages, which are among the most severe in any

Arab country—has been particularly violent, involving a bloody civil war that has lasted for many years and is still far from being resolved. The government cannot easily appeal to a unifying set of principles, because the Arab and Islamic themes are nonexistent and others are hard to find. The national Sudanese slogans are not very credible because the ruling regime is so closely identified with Islamic fundamentalism and because the entire concept of a Sudanese nation is unclear. The differences between the groups make Sudan a mere geographic unit, more than a meaningful political center of gravity in the people's consciousness.

The intra-Islamic pattern seems less intractable but is in fact very difficult to handle in the constraints of the rough and tumble of realpolitik. The case of Bahrain, analyzed in this volume, is a purely Shi'i-Sunni affair. There is also a Shi'i-Sunni cleavage of great significance in Iraq (in addition to the formidable Kurdish issue). Such a set of cleavages also exists within the Muslim "majority" in Lebanon, and similar examples can be found elsewhere in the Arab world, where, due to the Iranian revolution and its ramifications, the increasing political consciousness of the Shi'is is gradually finding concrete political manifestation.

In Bahrain there is a clear Shi'i majority, yet power is exclusively in the hands of the Sunni elite; this is also the case in Iraq. It is not just a question of who is in power, however; it also has to do with the social bases of that power. Clearly, the intra-Islamic cleavage coincides with a social one. The Shi'is are the lower classes, the working classes, those elements in society that have less of what there is to have: wealth, education, prestige. As we know from general theory, such situations are bound to be explosive, always containing within them the revolutionary potential of violent and drastic change once the underdog's consciousness reaches a critical threshold of activism and despair.

The analysis of Bahrain in this volume indicates that the options of the ruling elite are quite limited. The lessons of the past seem to indicate that the old strategies of muddling through and buying off the opposition by making relatively inexpensive and politically insignificant gestures are not likely to work in the future. The choice seems to be reform or revolution:[1] either there will be structural changes in the system to allow for massive improvement in the Shi'is' ability to participate in the political process and thereby to improve their social and economic standing, or there will be a violent explosion that might blow the entire system apart. This is an important conclusion, one that logically derives from the intersection of socioeconomic and ethnic cleavages, even if the latter are strictly intra-Islamic.

In the future, when Iraq returns to a more normal pattern of politics as the international embargo is lifted and some of the more pressing regional animosities are resolved, there may be a similar potential for drastic action in Iraq, too. For the time being, this is not likely to happen, because the Kurdish and international issues divert attention from the main cleavage in the country, while the regime's stranglehold on political life disguises many of the main currents of potential activism. Yet that, too, may change in the not-too-distant future (such has been the general trend in the region), and when it does, some of the tensions seen in Bahrain might be echoed in the large country to the north.

The Jordanian case is even more difficult to characterize and to fit into any logical typology. The principal cleavage there pits Arab Sunni Muslims against each other, on a basis that is more national than ethnic. The Palestinians and Jordanians in the kingdom have no need to resort to the usual myths and legends of ethnicity, nor to the more complicated anthropological features of cultural differentiation. The differences between them are real enough, and their direct and immediate political implications have been observable in the country's recent history.

This looks almost like one of the most classic political divides known to the human race, that between two nations inhabiting a single piece of land, ironically not entirely unlike the picture west of the Jordan River. As the analysis in this volume clearly indicates, the solution to the problems of the Palestinians in Jordan may have to do with the fate of the Palestinians in the West Bank and Gaza. Nevertheless, it does not depend entirely on the outcome of that process, nor does an acceptable solution to the problems of the Palestinians elsewhere guarantee a solution to their problems in Jordan. In the past it was expected that the Palestinians would be gradually integrated into the Jordanian mainstream to produce a single nation in the realm. Evidently, this has not yet happened, and the process might take a very long time.

However, the case of Jordan demonstrates the importance of two political processes that are critically important to the future resolution of the problems of minorities in the Arab world: democratization and devolution (or federalism). In the past, numerous proposals were put forth for some form of federal future for Jordan. Initially, these proposals were made while the West Bank was still entirely under Israeli control, with no prospect of a negotiated Israeli-Palestinian settlement in the offing. The proposals came from Jordan as well as from Israel, with the idea of stabilizing the future solution to the problem of the West Bank and integrating it somehow with the larger political unit that is Jordan, while at the same time maintaining its unique Palestinian character.

Indeed, the theory of federalism admits that at times federalism is precisely the art of having one's cake and eating it, too.[2] A federal solution can provide a large degree of political satisfaction for the ethnic or national group in question, while tying it to another political entity in a relationship that is less than total independence. Federal arrangements exist with various degrees of symmetry between the subentities involved. There are numerous examples of such federal arrangements around the world, many of them involving complex, delicate, and creative relationships between ethnic and national majorities and minorities.

Some such device seems urgently needed in various parts of the Middle East. Observers of Sudan have pointed time and again to the need for a solution that would link the two rival regions in a federal framework, maintaining a reasonably strong and effective central government while offering a large degree of autonomy to the south, thereby satisfying as many of its demands as possible without blowing apart the national framework of the state. The same rationale has been used to suggest seemingly reasonable solutions to the problems of Iraq and Lebanon, and most frequently and prominently in the Palestinian context. However, none of these has worked so far.

Elsewhere, we have argued that the federal idea has not been popular in the Arab world, and that in fact it has never worked there at all, with the important exception of the United Arab Emirates, which has not played a central role in Arab politics.[3] In general, federal ideas have worked better in the more developed parts of the world, whereas in the so-called Third World their record has been less impressive, albeit with notable exceptions, such as India.

The reasons why federalism is not popular in Arab politics are not too difficult to comprehend, but what is important is to assess trends for the future and the potential for change. Arab political history has made it logical that Arab political thought should put a premium on unity and the oneness of the nation, which once inhabited a single, large Arab homeland and more recently on unity within the boundaries of each individual Arab country. In any case, the history of struggling against the perceived political, economic, military, and cultural encroachment of an aggressive and dynamic West made it necessary to concentrate resources on the struggle to maintain the independence and integrity of the nation, not on catering to the needs of the constituent parts. Thus, the leading trend in nationalist thought, which carried over to routine politics, was that of unity and not the delegation of authority.

Some of the ideological tension of the struggle against imperialism and Zionism has abated, but much of it still exists. Some of the tension has been carried over into the realm of inter-Arab politics and via that channel into local political systems, at times with ideological claims undermining the legitimacy of ruling regimes and states.[4] This, too, was more characteristic of earlier periods than it is today, but the fears, suspicions, and apprehensions generated in the process still persist.

An important factor militating against the tolerance and pluralism associated with federal politics has been the nature of most regimes in the Middle East. In the vast majority of cases, Arab regimes have faced serious challenges to their legitimacy because they captured power through the use or threat of force and have used coercion to keep themselves in power, at the expense of such legitimizing processes as free elections with mass participation. Such regimes find it difficult to delegate power to other elements in the country or to share it with them, and sharing power on a regional basis is the very foundation of federalism. True, many of the regimes have been in power for so long that they have managed to increase their legitimacy and to do away with serious challenges to their existence, but this has been a protracted and painful process. The memories and traumas created en route are certainly not conducive to power sharing, without which there cannot be any prospect for federal solutions to political problems.

In the course of the past two generations, a fairly large degree of political stability has finally been achieved. This stability has to do with the ability of ruling regimes to eliminate the opposition and to enhance their rule by developing and refining various governmental technologies.[5] In this they have been brilliantly successful. However, the stability created in this difficult process is of a formal nature, which means that regimes endure for longer periods of time because they are good at manipulation and coercion, not because the challenges to their legitimacy have disappeared. As long as this is the case, willingness to devolve, delegate, and share power is understandably limited.

During this period of political development, the overwhelming strength of the Arab state has been evident. Elsewhere, we have analyzed in detail the thesis that the state is the most important structure in Middle Eastern politics and that all challenges from the realms of pan-Arab nationalism, socialist ideologies, and Islamic fundamentalism have been beaten back successfully.[6] According to this thesis, the state has been the most successful import from the West with respect to political ideas and structures. It has struck deep roots in the political soil of the Middle East at a time when other political imports, such as democratic ideals and federal structures, have met with little enthusiasm.

The strength of the Arab state is also evident from the analyses of the cases studied in this volume. The ethnic challenge to the state has been extraordinarily strong, but in no case has the state succumbed. This is true even in the most extreme cases surveyed here. Sudan has been torn apart by a lengthy civil war, yet the Sudanese state has remained intact. Lebanon still exists, despite contending ethnic claims, the lack of a majority, the massive presence of the Syrians, and the Israeli "security zone" in the south.[7] The Iraqi regime has been challenged significantly not only by the Kurds but also by the emerging threat of a Shi'i majority and prolonged international sanctions. Yet the Iraqi state seems to be as potent as ever. Thus, the analysis in this volume lends credence to the thesis that there is a combination of domestic political circumstances, regional and international conditions, and considerations of improved governmental technology (such as control of intelligence and security services) that allows states in the Middle East to overcome even the harshest and most blatant challenges.

This fact of political life—the strength of the Arab state—might help control and perhaps even resolve ethnic and minority problems. Scholars have at times failed to notice that power in poorly integrated and institutionalized political systems is not something to be had but something to be created through a good deal of effort. In other words, in highly developed political systems where there are numerous political institutions and where political power is organized according to accepted traditions and structure, it makes sense to speak of devolving power, because power has been there long enough to be recognized by everyone, because it is salient enough not to be questioned, and because it is centralized enough to beg for decentralization. In such cases, federal solutions to the problems of minorities and ethnic groups make sense.

This is not necessarily the case in less developed systems, where power is not always visible, where traditions and legacies of having and exercising power are by no means universally accepted, and where the problem of power in general is that there is too little of it.[8] This is true notwithstanding all the pomp and display of power by various dictators and juntas that control governments in such countries. They frequently put on shows aimed at impressing their constituencies with their control and power, but they do so precisely because they feel insecure. The show is often but a poor substitute for the real thing, which is the ability to exercise power in an orderly institutional framework, and where the need to resort to the use or threat of force is minimal.

For such juntas and dictators to devolve power to regions and groups would approximate political suicide, because it would fragment the little power that they do have.[9] However, once such systems have enjoyed a relatively long period of stability and have demonstrated their ability to survive challenges from the opposition, thoughts of giving up some power can be more seriously entertained.[10] In such cases, possible federal solutions begin to make sense.

One major payoff of a comparative analysis should be the ability to come up with lessons to be learned from the various strategies adopted by regimes to deal with the problems of minorities. The analysis presented here may not allow for profound comparison because of the authors' different perspectives. Even so, it seems worth trying to make a tentative list of strategic choices and decisions that will reflect some of the basic convictions of these regimes regarding the problem of minorities and ethnic groups, as well as their overall posture toward national politics.

First, in the vast majority of cases, Arab regimes seem only to consider minorities and ethnic groups a problem. While one can argue that diversity of groups in a country enriches its culture and society, in practice Arab regimes tend to emphasize themes of national unity, and any tendency that has diversity and variety as its point of departure is suspect at best. This line of thinking is also manifest in the terminology used, as regimes try to speak of communities and groups rather than minorities. This is best demonstrated in the case of Egypt (which is relatively tolerant as far as Arab regimes go), where no effort is spared to prevent the discourse on the Copts from treating them as a minority, that is, as a different group opposed to the mainstream or the majority. The Egyptian regime works instead to build a picture of a society that is basically unified around its fundamental political characteristics, having only a certain diversity in terms of subgroups.

In some countries, however, it is simply not possible to pretend that society has any basic unity; in Lebanon, for instance, ethnicity is by far the most dominant variable in politics. However, Lebanon is no longer free to express this openly because of the Syrian dominance of much of its territory. Interestingly, some observers suggest that one major reason for Syria's continued involvement in Lebanese affairs is the fear that ethnic disintegration in Lebanon might spill over to neighboring Syria.

The point of departure, therefore, is Arab regimes' fear of ethnic challenge and the resulting defensive orientation, which often leads to the cultural denial of the rights of minorities and even their very existence. Development of greater self-confidence on the part of these regimes and greater willingness to integrate into some prevailing global norms of recognition of minorities— along with various strategies involving democratization and federalism, as suggested above—may make a decisive difference in the future, but it is bound to take time.

A second major theme is that of co-optation as opposed to exclusion, the two clearest alternatives at opposite ends of the spectrum. It makes sense to include some leading elements of the minorities in the regime if this would make it possible to buy off some of their most important constituents. Such a strategy would be rational in every way, at least to the point at which it starts to curtail the power of the dominant group. Yet in practice few regimes have exercised this strategic option effectively. Regimes that routinely use force to hold onto power do not, as a rule, like to share power unnecessarily. They do so only when they have no choice, at which time the strategy is obviously the product of dire necessity. The strategy of sharing is much more effective when it is done early and has a preventive capacity, namely, when it is a step taken while the group out of power considers it a real concession rather than a desperate measure in a situation beyond control. It appears, though, that the prevailing political culture of the region is not hospitable to giving up any power without a pressing need to do so;[11] this creates a vicious cycle that is difficult to break.

Even when co-optation is an option, it can be confined within limits that are simply too narrow and which, therefore, cannot satisfy the genuine political needs of the minority in question. In Egypt there have been Copts at various levels of political activity; the highly visible example of Boutros Boutros-Ghali, who went on from Egyptian political activity to serve as secretary-general of the United Nations, is a good case in point. However, Copts have never occupied positions of real power and have not been allowed to reach the highest echelons of the political structure. Even Boutros-Ghali was prevented from being foreign minister, having to settle for the position of secretary of state for foreign affairs. In that sense, the minority in Egypt is likely to feel that co-optation is meant only to reassure it without really meeting its needs, and this perspective may make it feel more alienated and offended than reassured.

A somewhat different dilemma faces a minority regime that has to co-opt the majority, as is the case in Syria. Here the situation is very complicated. Obviously, the regime wishes to rid itself of the image of being a minority or an ethnic regime, not only because it would reflect badly on its legitimacy but also because it would be suicidal in a country where the minority is so small and where the majority (Sunni Muslims) is so strong in most neighboring countries. Yet a policy of co-optation must be used carefully in this case as well. It is vital to have visible Sunni Muslim figures in key government posts, and indeed Syria has done this in recent years. The presence of Sunni Muslims is quite salient in the political structure, the formal offices of government, and the most visible positions in the military hierarchy. The problems the regime faces in this situation are the classic ones of co-optation in general, namely, making sure that the persons and forces co-opted do not gain too much power, while trying to keep them from feeling used or slighted. So far, the Syrian regime appears to have had considerable success.

Still, experience around the world shows that sooner or later the co-opted tend to become sufficiently ambitious to try to capture a share of real power. They do so when they are no longer content with figurehead positions or just the semblance of power, and when they owe their positions to the goodwill of the co-opting rulers rather than to their own standing. The rulers seem reasonably well prepared for such an eventuality, as the regimes in the region have generally been sensitive to any challenges to their power. When Middle Eastern regimes—the majority of which captured power by force—really open up their political systems to genuine competition, the entire structure of minority-majority relations is likely to change. This will be particularly true in cases in which the minority now rules and the majority is co-opted.

The logical alternative to co-optation is exclusion, namely, keeping the minorities out of power altogether. This is even more salient where the minority is regionally based and focuses on trying to capture some regional power, as in the case of the Kurds in Iraq. There have been past attempts to co-opt some Kurdish leaders into the echelons of power. At times these were leaders with a genuine power base in Kurdistan; others, as Stephen H. Longrigg put it drily, were "Kurds for ministerial purposes," that is, politicians in the center who could claim at least genealogical descent from the group in the periphery.[12]

Yet once the armed struggle intensified in the Kurdish region itself, the Kurds as such were kept out of the centers of national power. To reach a comprehensive political compromise in the future, it may be necessary to treat the Kurds as more than just a local power and to consider them one of the three main constituents of the national body politic. If this is done, they will naturally be offered some share of power in the center—some form of co-optation at the least, or in the case of substantial political evolution, a real share of the resources at the regime's disposal. If this happens, it will be an interesting attempt to transform the very nature of a minority problem: to delocalize and nationalize it in order to take away the regional sting—which would force the regime to delegate a great deal of power in the periphery in favor of a national emphasis, allowing them to delegate much less power at the center. Perhaps something along these lines could be contemplated in the Sudan, whether or not a genuine federal solution is adopted. Such attempts would obviously require imagination and a willingness to take risks, but they may appear attractive when nothing better offers itself. Rulers may well contemplate these solutions simply because minority problems are getting worse; in an age of mass communications it will be difficult to bring them under control in any less costly way.

Several other variables may have a particularly strong impact on the future of majority-minority relations in Arab countries. Two that seem particularly relevant, based on the cases analyzed in this volume, are the prospects of regime succession and future developments in Islamic politics with respect to minorities and ethnic groups. We are dealing both with republican regimes that were born, by and large, in revolutions or other means of capturing power by force, and hereditary dynasties, many of which had a similar genesis. Both monarchies and republics have struggled with questions of legitimacy, which have become more acute since the collapse of the Soviet Union and the ensuing trends of democratization around the world. Many of them have taken steps toward greater democratization, as shown in this volume and elsewhere,[13] for reasons that are all too obvious.[14] However, the vast majority of regimes depend on a single person or on a ruling junta, rather than on a mass political force institutionalized in the formal structures of parties and ideological movements. Hence, changes in the person of the ruler or the key members of the junta might make a decisive difference not only in the policies of the center but also in the image it projects and in its associated ability to create and maintain an aura of legitimacy.

In the case of Syria, for example, there is a real question regarding to what extent the vast majority of the citizenry regards the Asad regime as government by a minority. There are many reasons to think of it as such, and there are many reasons for the ruler to project a different image via strategies of co-optation, nationalist propaganda, and the like. As long as Asad remains in power, the full impact of the question is not apparent, not only because he dominates the system personally but also because of his enormous prestige and his success in making Syrian power and prosperity and the stability of his own rule one and the same in political discourse. When his own term ends, the regime might be put to a stiff test.

This test will have to be passed before the regime is successfully institutionalized as a national one and not the property of the 'Alawi minority. If the transition is to another 'Alawi personality within the security establishment, the other constituents of the Syrian body politic may reject the entire transaction as transparently keeping power within a single sect. If power is transferred to a Sunni figurehead with real domination by the 'Alawi officers and security chiefs, the situation will be different. There is also the possibility that a member of Asad's family will inherit the mantle of formal leadership, while making other, more dramatic, but less visible changes on other levels of power.

Given the nature of the Arab state system, it is easy to appreciate Arab rulers' fear of outside intervention in the domestic affairs of the countries in the region, ostensibly on behalf of the minorities.[15] One should keep in mind traumatic historical memories of the days when European powers used the Christian minorities in the Middle East as a pretext for rather massive intervention in local politics, at times going so far as to gain extraterritorial rights and build states within states, eventually leading to various forms and degrees of colonization. In light of this historical legacy, the regimes' genuine fear that minorities will be used as triggers for foreign intervention has to be appreciated. The Kurds in Iraq are a salient case in point. Even now, when the Kurds seem to enjoy a fair degree of protection from annihilation in their areas of concentration in northern Iraq, this momentary success is due not to an increase in their own abilities or resources but to the temporary constellation of interest on the part of the allies, primarily the United States. Kurdish history suggests that if the policies of these powers change, the Kurds' fate will once again take a turn for the worse.

This fear of foreign intervention makes it more difficult for local elites to appreciate the problems of the minorities for what they really are: namely, a domestic political issue—ethnic competition within the process of state building, something that can be seen all over the world. The strong ideological commitments to large entities, the obsession with protecting the regime, the pressures of legitimacy, and the fear of outside intervention all prompt the leaders to deny the existence of the problem of minorities, rather than deal with it openly and honestly, let alone with a degree of tolerance and creativity.[16]

An additional factor that makes regime manipulation easier is widespread factionalism among the minorities themselves. This is now most obvious among the Kurds of Iraq, but the Christians in southern Sudan, the Druze, the Berbers, and others have been plagued by it as well. Several anthropologists argue that it is a feature of Middle Eastern culture and society in general.[17] Be this as it may, the existence of bitter, fratricidal struggles within the minority communities and among their leaders, even at times of acute confrontation with regimes, makes it possible for their enemies to manipulate their politics in ways favorable to the existing regimes. This is something that may be overcome in the future, if social change transforms the structure within the groups concerned. So far, it has led many politicians in the region to concentrate on manipulation, rather than on a genuine effort to build political structures capable of accommodating the needs and demands of the minorities.

A twofold process may be at work here. On the one hand, as the Arab state continues to survive as the strong and overwhelming entity that it has been for the past two generations, it will gain more confidence in dealing with problems that reflect upon the structure of the state, but not necessarily on its very existence.[18] On the other hand, as minorities learn to play the political game within this state, they will adjust to the reality of the territorial state that has not allowed any change in boundaries and has not fallen apart even in the face of the most severe challenges.[19] They may also learn that in order to maximize their prospects of success, they will have to overcome factionalism, or at least keep it within manageable boundaries, which they have generally been unable to do so far.[20]

The cases surveyed in this volume underscore the argument of Saad Eddin Ibrahim (Sa'd al-Din), one of the most prominent Arab analysts of the political sociology of minorities in the region, that the problem of minorities in Arab countries should be considered within a broad, general framework of political evolution, a process that is now unfolding across the region. Ibrahim raises the possibility of a comprehensive solution that would provide for linkage between the needs of the state system and those of the minorities. This would be based on the "triangle of federalism, democracy, and civil society."[21]

The first principle, federalism, would suit certain Arab countries, such as Iraq and Sudan, which have minorities in specific areas within their territory. If adopted in these countries, federal solutions would give the minorities political autonomy, the right to use most of the natural resources located within their territories, and the right to retain and develop their own cultures. They would also have the right to make their own laws. According to Ibrahim, the federal solution, which has been found quite successful by such countries as Switzerland and the United States, could also have been successful in Arab countries where governments have paid lip service to the federal principle without really putting it into practice.[22]

Because many minorities are not concentrated in clearly designated territories, their problems must also be addressed within a framework of democracy, which is an ideal formula for multiethnic societies. Democracy allows individuals and groups to participate in deciding their fate, planning their own future, protecting their vital interests, and running their own affairs by administering their own societies. Above all, argues Ibrahim, democracy allows for "peaceful coexistence between the ethnic identity on the one hand, and the national (wataniyya) one on the other." Because ethnic identity is authentic and deeply rooted, it cannot be permanently suppressed.[23]

The third leg of the triangle is the principle of civil society,[24] a term that refers to "all the non-governmental and non-hereditary organizations which are set up to make up for the common principles and interests of their members."[25] Such organizations include parties, unions, voluntary associations, and clubs. These institutions are perceived to be the main vehicle for reconciling the principles of self-government for the group with the fears of the central regime. The fears referred to are the government's apprehensions that concessions to minorities would strengthen their identities at the expense of the national (*watani* and *qawmi*) identity. In Ibrahim's view, organizations of civil society that cut across ethnic and primordial loyalties are likely to extricate the ethnic groups from their social, political, and psychological isolation and in a more advanced phase may even give them greater opportunities for voluntary association (*indimaj*) within society at large. Ibrahim realizes that these three principles are the most creative ideas not only for solving the problems of the minorities as such but also for enabling "the Arabs as a whole to come out of the alley of history [and join] the quick road of humanity towards the twenty-first century."[26] As such, his analysis, which seems by far the most sophisticated study of the problem from within the Arab world, reinforces the view that the problems of minorities there in general cannot be understood in isolation from the problems of the societies in which they are situated; in other words, it is impossible to define a minority without also defining the majority. Indeed, it is the relationship between the two that is the linchpin of the problem, and when the majority changes, the entire relationship is, by definition, dramatically transformed.

For the time being, there is not much room for optimism. In the short run, the Arab world is not likely to adopt democracy and federalism as principles of a living reality, and the development of civil society is a lengthy and complex process at best, depending on a plethora of complicated social, economic, political, and cultural factors. But an honest discussion of the issue of minorities, such as the one advanced by Ibrahim, is an important step toward coping with some of the key problems and is itself a sign of dramatically changing times. Within the context of such a process, thoughtful writing about minorities in the Arab world by a range of authors can contribute to the developing dialogue about the direction of political evolution in Arab countries. It is hoped that this volume has made a modest contribution to this dialogue, beyond the obvious need to gain more knowledge about and insight into minorities in general. After all, the problem is not one that affects the Middle East alone; it is found throughout the world in the post–Cold War era.

Notes

1. For an extremely lucid exposition of the theory of such choices, see Samuel P. Huntington's classic *Political Order in Changing Societies* (New Haven, Conn.: Yale University Press, 1968).

2. The phrase comes from Daniel J. Elazar, a leading theoretician of federalism (oral communication).

3. Gabriel Ben-Dor, "Federalism in the Arab World," in Daniel Elazar (ed.), *Federalism and Political Integration* (Ramat Gan, Israel: Turtledove, 1979).

4. See the classic exposition of this process in Malcolm H. Kerr, *The Arab Cold War,* 3d ed. (New York: Oxford University Press, 1972).

5. This refers to the mechanics of running a governmental apparatus efficiently. The term *technology* indicates the possibility of imitation and learning, as well as that of divorcing the technique from the ideological principles of the regime in question. See Gabriel Ben-Dor, "Civilianization of Military Regimes in the Arab World," *Armed Forces and Society* 1, no. 3 (May 1975), pp. 317–327.

6. Gabriel Ben-Dor, *State and Conflict in the Middle East: Emergence of the Postcolonial State* (New York: Praeger, 1983).

7. Gabriel Ben-Dor, "Stateness and Ideology in Contemporary Middle Eastern Politics," *The Jerusalem Journal of International Relations* 9, no. 3 (September 1987), pp. 10–37.

8. This point was first articulated by Aristide R. Zolberg in *Creating Political Order: The Party-States of West Africa* (Chicago: Rand McNally, 1966).

9. This way of thinking is analyzed in detail, with reference to many cases around the world, in the works of Zolberg and Huntington cited in notes 8 and 1, respectively. For the application of these frameworks to specific Arab cases, see Ben-Dor, "Federalism in the Arab World."

10. For the time being, whatever political power there is tends to be used up for the twin challenges of meeting external (real or perceived) threats and defending the regime against (real or perceived) challenges.

11. The political practice of the region has built up a set of habits, customs, symbols, and beliefs that give meaning to the political acts and speech of the participants in the system. These condition the political minds of the actors. By its nature, a political culture is more enduring than a given institution or procedure. See Gabriel Ben-Dor, "Political Culture to Middle East Politics," *International Journal of Middle East Politics* 8, no. 1 (January 1977), pp. 43–63.

12. Longrigg uses this phrase repeatedly in his references to ethnic politics in prerevolutionary Iraq. See Stephen H. Longrigg, *Iraq, 1900–1950: A Political, Social and Economic History* (New York: Oxford University Press, 1953).

13. See Rex Brynen, Bahgat Korany, and Paul Noble (eds.), *Political Liberalization and Democratization in the Arab World, vol. 1, Theoretical Perspectives* (Boulder, Colo.: Lynne Rienner, 1995).

14. See the analysis in Gabriel Ben-Dor, "Prospects of Democratization in the Arab World: Global Diffusion, Regional Demonstration and Domestic Imperatives," in Brynen, Korany, and Noble, *Political Liberalization*, pp. 307–332.

15. All states fear foreign intervention in their internal affairs. However, the Arab states are particularly sensitive to this for two reasons. The first is the historical legacy of colonialism, when outside powers did in fact utilize the minority issue to legitimize their presence in, and domination of, Middle Eastern countries. The second reason is that the inter-Arab system has made the boundaries between Arab countries more permeable to outside influence (from other Arab countries).

16. On tolerance, see Saad Eddin Ibrahim, "Crises, Elites and Democratization in the Arab World," *Middle East Journal* 47, no. 2 (spring 1993), pp. 292–305. Regarding creativity, see Gabriel Ben-Dor, *The Modern State in the Middle East: The Need for a Human Face* (Toronto: York University Centre for Strategic and International Studies, Occasional Paper, 1993). This work is an example of the literature that tries to

reconcile a structural study of the political sociology of the state with normative concerns for human rights and for group rights for ethnic and other minorities in society.

17. See, for example, Rafael Patai, "The Middle East as a Culture Area," *Middle East Journal* 6, no. 1 (winter 1952), pp. 1–21; and Patai, *Golden River to Golden Road,* 2d ed. (Philadelphia: University of Pennsylvania Press, 1967).

18. See Elie Kedourie, *Democracy and Arab Political Culture* (Washington, D.C.: Institute for Near East Policy, 1992).

19. For a survey of the relevant theories and literature, see Gabriel Ben-Dor, *State and Conflict.* The strength and dominance of the state, which were often disputed a decade and a half ago, are now virtually beyond dispute.

20. This is a variation on the theme of learning from the follies of the past, as described in Barbara Tuchman's famous exposition, *The March of Folly: From Troy to Vietnam* (New York: Knopf, 1984).

21. Sa'd al-Din Ibrahim (Saad Eddin Ibrahim), *Ta'ammulat fi mas'alat al-aqalliyyat* (Cairo: Ibn Khaldun Center, 1992), pp. 13–21; *Al-Milal wal-nihal wal-a'raq: al-taqrir al-sanawi al-thani* (Cairo: Ibn Khaldun Center, 1995), pp. 15–23.

22. Ibrahim also argues that federal principles in general should be a good formula for achieving Arab unity. Compare this with the analysis in Ben-Dor, "Federalism in the Arab World." Ibrahim's argument was made much earlier as part of the discourse on Arab unity and inter-Arab relations in general, but by and large to no avail.

23. See also the argument in Ben-Dor, "Prospects of Democratization in the Arab World." See also the special issue of *Middle East Journal* on democratization in the region, vol. 47, no.2 (spring 1993). For a more general view, see Samuel P. Huntington, "Democracy's Third Wave," *Journal of Democracy* 1, no. 1 (spring 1991), pp. 12–34; and Gudrun Kramer, "Liberalization and Democracy in the Arab World," *Middle East Report* 22, no. 1 (January–February 1992), pp. 22–25, 35.

24. See also Timothy D. Sisk, *Islam and Democracy: Religion, Politics and Power in the Middle East* (Washington, D.C.: U.S. Institute of Peace, 1992); Elie Kedourie, *Politics in the Middle East* (New York: Oxford University Press, 1992); Sami Zubaida, "Islam, the State and Democracy: Contrasting Conceptions of Society in Egypt," *Middle East Report* 23, no. 6 (November–December 1992), pp. 2–10; Raymond A. Hinnebusch, "State and Civil Society in Syria," *Middle East Journal* 47, no. 2 (spring 1993), pp. 243–257; and Augustus Richard Norton, "The Future of Civil Society in the Middle East," *Middle East Journal* 47, no. 2 (spring 1993), pp. 205–216.

25. Compare with the earlier literature on institutionalization and political development, namely, Huntington, *Political Order in Changing Societies*, and Gabriel Ben-Dor, "Institutionalization and Political Development: A Conceptual and Theoretical Analysis," *Comparative Studies in Society and History* 18, no. 3 (July 1975), pp. 309–325.

26. Ibrahim, *Ta'ammulat*, pp. 231–246.

Selected Bibliography

Books

'Abd al-Fattah, Nabil (ed.). *Taqrir al-hala al-diniyya fi Misr, 1995*. Cairo: Al-Ahram Center for Political and Strategic Studies, 1996.

Abdallah, Umar F. *The Islamic Struggle in Syria*. Berkeley: Mizan Press, 1982.

Abu-Khalil, Joseph. *Qissat al-Mawarina fi al-harb*. Beirut: Sharikat al-Matbu'at lil-Tawzi' wal-Nashr, 1990.

Abun-Nasr, Jamil M. *A History of the Maghrib in the Islamic Period*. Cambridge: Cambridge University Press, 1987.

Ageron, Charles-Robert. *Modern Algeria: A History from 1830 to the Present*. London: Hurst, 1991.

Ajami, Fouad. *The Arab Predicament: Arab Political Thought and Practice Since 1967*. Cambridge: Cambridge University Press, 1992.

———. *The Vanished Imam: Musa al-Sadr and the Shia of Lebanon*. Ithaca, N.Y.: Cornell University Press, 1986.

Al-'Alawi, Hasan. *Al-Shi'a wal-dawla al-qawmiyya fil-'Iraq, 1914–1990*. N.P., 1990.

Albino, Oliver. *The Sudan: A Southern Viewpoint*. London: Oxford University Press, 1970.

Anderson, Charles W., Fred R. Von der Mehden, and Crawford Young (eds.). *Issues of Political Development*. Englewood Cliffs, N.J.: Prentice Hall, 1967.

Ayoubi, Nazih. *Political Islam: Religion and Politics in the Arab World*. London: Routledge, 1991.

Baduel, Pierre Robert (ed.), *L'Algérie Incertaine*. Aix-en-Province: Institute de Recherches et d'Études sur le Monde Arabe et Musulman (IREMAM), Revue du Monde Musulman et de la Mediterranée (REMMM), 1994.

Ball, George W. *Error and Betrayal in Lebanon: An Analysis of Israel's Invasion of Lebanon and the Implications for U.S.-Israeli Relations*. Washington, D.C.: USA Foundation for Middle East Peace, 1984.

Barber, Benjamin. *Jihad Versus McWorld*. New York: Random House, 1995.

Barakat, Halim (ed.). *Toward a Viable Lebanon*. London: Croom Helm, 1988.

Batatu, Hanna. *The Old Social Classes and the Revolutionary Movements of Iraq*. Princeton, N.J.: Princeton University Press, 1978.

al-Bazzaz, Sa'd. *Harb talid ukhra: Al-Ta'rikh al-sirri li-harb al-khalij.* Amman: Al-Ahliyya lil-Nashr wal-Tawzi', 1992.

Beeri, Eliezer. *Army Officers in Arab Politics and Society.* New York: Praeger, 1969.

Bendix, Reinhard. *Nation-Building and Citizenship: Studies of Our Changing Social Order.* New York: John Wiley and Sons, 1964.

Ben-Dor, Gabriel. *State and Conflict in the Middle East: Emergence of the Postcolonial State.* New York: Praeger, 1983.

———. *The Druzes in Israel: A Political Study.* Jerusalem: Magnes, 1981.

———. *The Modern State in the Middle East: The Need for a Human Face.* Toronto: York University Centre for Strategic and International Studies, Occasional Paper, 1993.

Ben-Dor, Gabriel, and David B. DeWitt (eds.). *Conflict Management in the Middle East.* Lexington, Mass.: Lexington Books, 1987.

Bengio, Ofra. *Saddam's Word: Political Discourse in Iraq.* New York: Oxford University Press, 1998.

Bill, James A., and Robert Springborg. *Politics in the Middle East.* 4th ed., New York: HarperCollins, 1994.

Brett, Michael, and Elizabeth Fentress. *The Berbers.* Oxford: Blackwell, 1996.

Brynen, Rex, Bahgat Korany, and Paul Noble (eds.). *Political Liberalization and Democratization in the Arab World, Vol. 1, Theoretical Perspectives.* Boulder, Colo.: Lynne Rienner, 1995.

Carter, B. L. *The Copts in Egyptian Politics, 1918–1952.* Cairo: American University in Cairo Press, 1986.

Chaker, Salem (ed.). "*Berbères,* une Identité en Construction." Revue de l'Occident Musulman et de la Mediterranée, no. 44. Aix-en-Province: Centre Nationale de la Recherche Scientifique (CNRS), 1987.

Cobban, Alfred. *National Self-Determination.* Chicago: University of Chicago Press, 1944.

Collings, Deirdre (ed.). *Peace for Lebanon? From War to Reconstruction.* Boulder, Colo.: Lynne Rienner, 1994.

Dann, Uriel. *Studies in the History of Transjordan, 1920–1949: The Making of a State.* Boulder, Colo.: Westview, 1984.

Day, Arthur. *East Bank/West Bank: Jordan and the Prospects for Peace.* New York: Council on Foreign Relations, 1986.

Deng, Francis Mading. *The Cry of the Owl.* New York: Lilian Barber Press, 1989.

Deutsch, Karl W. *Nationalism and Social Communication: An Inquiry into the Foundations of Nationality.* Cambridge, Mass.: Harvard University Press, 1953.

Diamond, Larry, and Marc F. Plattner (eds.). *Nationalism, Ethnic Conflict and Democracy.* Baltimore, Md.: Johns Hopkins University Press, 1994.

Eibner, John (ed.). *Church Under Siege.* Zurich: Institute for Religious Minorities in the Islamic World, 1993.

Elazar, Daniel (ed.). *Federalism and Political Integration.* Ramat Gan, Israel: Turtledove, 1979.

Esman, Milton, and Itamar Rabinovich (eds.). *Ethnicity, Pluralism and the State in the Middle East.* Ithaca, N.Y.: Cornell University Press, 1987.

Fathi, Schirin. *Jordan: An Invented Nation? State-Tribe Dynamics and the Formation of National Identity.* Hamburg: Deutsches Orient-Institut, 1994.

Fiqqi, Mustafa. *Al-Aqbat fi al-siyasa al-Misriyya.* Cairo: Dar al-Shuruq, 1985.

Fridman, Eli. "The Muslim Brothers and Their Struggle with the Regime of Hafiz al-Asad, 1976–1982" (in Hebrew). Master's thesis, Tel Aviv University, 1989.

Fuda, Faraj, et al. *Al-Ta'ifiyya ila ayna!?* Cairo: Dar al-Misri al-Jadid, 1987.

Geertz, Clifford (ed.). *Old Societies and New States: The Quest for Modernity in Asia and Africa.* New York: Free Press, 1963.

Gellner, Ernest, and Charles Micaud (eds.). *Arabs and Berbers from Tribe to Nation in North Africa.* Lexington, Mass.: Lexington Books, 1972.

Gershoni, Israel, and James P. Jankowski. *Redefining the Egyptian Nation, 1930–1945.* Cambridge: Cambridge University Press, 1995.

Glazer, Nathan, and Daniel P. Moynihan. *Ethnicity: Theory and Experience.* Cambridge, Mass.: Harvard University Press, 1975.

Greenstein, Fred I., and Nelson W. Polsby (eds.). *Handbook of Political Science, Strategies of Inquiry,* vol. 7. Reading, Mass.: Addison Wesley, 1975.

Habib, Rafiq. *Al-Ihtijaj al-dini wal-sira' al-tabaqi fi Misr.* Cairo: Sina, 1989.

———. *Al-Masihiyya al-siyasiyya fi Misr.* Cairo: Yafa, 1990.

———. *Man yabi' Misr? Al-dawla, al-nukhba, al-kanisa.* Cairo: Misr al-'Arabiyya, 1994.

Halpern, Manfred. *The Politics of Social Change in the Middle East and North Africa.* Princeton, N.J.: Princeton University Press, 1963.

Hanf, Theodor. *Coexistence in Wartime Lebanon: Decline of a State and Rise of a Nation.* London: The Centre for Lebanese Studies and I. B. Tauris, 1993.

Hansen, Henry Herald. *Investigations in a Shi'i Village in Bahrain.* Copenhagen: National Museum of Denmark, 1968.

Hasan, Y. F. (ed.). *Sudan in Africa: Studies Presented to the First International Conference Sponsored by the Sudan Research Unit,* 7–12 February 1968. Khartoum: Khartoum University Press, 1971.

Hassanpour, Amin. *Nationalism and Language in Kurdistan, 1918–1985.* San Francisco: Mellen Research University Press, 1992.

Helou, Charles. *Hayat fi dhikrayat.* Beirut: Dar al-Nahar, 1995.

Hinnebusch, Raymond. *Authoritarian Power and State Formation in Ba'thist Syria: Army, Party and Peasant.* Boulder, Colo.: Westview, 1990.

Horowitz, Donald D. *Ethnic Groups in Conflict.* Berkeley: University of California Press, 1985.

Hourani, Albert. *Minorities in the Arab World.* New York: Oxford University Press, 1947.

Hourani, Albert. *Syria and Lebanon: A Political Essay.* London: Oxford University Press, 1946.

Al-Huss, Salim. *Zaman al-amal wal-khayba.* Beirut: Dar al-Ilm lil-Malayin, 1992.

Hudson, Michael. *The Precarious Republic: Political Modernization in Lebanon.* New York: Random House, 1968.

Hunter, Shireen (ed.). *The Politics of Islamic Revivalism: Diversity and Unity.* Bloomington: Indiana University Press, 1987.

Huntington, Samuel P. *Political Order in Changing Societies.* New Haven, Conn.: Yale University Press, 1968.

———. *The Clash of Civilizations and the Remaking of World Order.* New York: Simon and Schuster, 1996.

Hutchinson, John, and Anthony Smith (eds.). *Nationalism.* New York: Oxford University Press, 1994.

Ibn Khaldun Center. *Humum al-aqalliyyat, al-taqrir al-sanawi al-awwal.* Cairo: Ibn Khaldun Center, 1993.

Ibrahim, Sa'd al-Din. *Al-Milal wal-nihal wal-a'raq; humum al-aqalliyyat fi al-watan al-'Arabi.* Cairo: Ibn Khaldun Center, 1994.

———. *Al-Milal wal-nihal wal-a'raq: Al-taqrir al-sanawi al-thani, 1995.* Cairo: Dar al-Amin, 1995.

————. *Ta'ammulat fi mas'alat al-aqalliyyat.* Cairo, 1992.

————. *Management of Ethnic Issues in the Arab World.* Cairo: Al-Ahram Center for Political and Strategic Studies, 1995.

————. *The Copts of Egypt.* London: Minority Rights Group, 1996.

al-Jabiri, Muhammad 'Abid. *Al-'Aql al-siyasi al-'Arabi.* Beirut: Al-Markaz al-Thaqafi al-'Arabi, 1991.

Joffe, George (ed.). *North Africa: Nation, State and Region.* London: Routledge, 1993.

Joumblatt, Kamal. *I Speak for Lebanon.* London: Zed Press, 1982.

Jumayyil, Amin. *Al-Rihan-al-kabir.* Beirut: Dar al-Nahar, 1988.

Jumhuriyyat Misr al-'Arabiyya, Wizarat al-difa'. *Al-Aqalliyyat fi al-mintaqa al-'Arabiyya wa-ta'thiruha 'ala al-amn al-qawmi al-'Arabi.* Cairo, 199?).

Kasfir, Nelson. *The Shrinking Political Arena: Participation and Ethnicity in African Policies with a Case Study of Uganda.* Berkeley: University of California Press, 1976.

Kedourie, Elie. *Democracy and Arab Political Culture.* Washington, D.C.: Institute for Near East Policy, 1992.

————. *Politics in the Middle East.* New York: Oxford University Press, 1992.

Kerr, Malcolm H. *The Arab Cold War.* 3d ed. New York: Oxford University Press, 1972.

Khalaf, Samir. *Lebanon's Predicament.* New York: Columbia University Press, 1987.

Khoury, Philip. *Syria and the French Mandate: The Politics of Arab Nationalism.* Princeton: Princeton University Press, 1987.

Khoury, Philip S., and Joseph Kostiner (eds.). *Tribes and State Formation in the Middle East.* Berkeley: University of California Press, 1990.

Khuri, Fuad I. *Tribe and State in Bahrain: The Transformation of Social and Political Authority in an Arab State.* Chicago: University of Chicago Press, 1980.

Kramer, Martin (ed.). *Shi'ism: Resistance and Revolution.* Boulder, Colo.: Westview, 1987.

LaPalombara, Joseph. *Politics Within Nations.* Englewood Cliffs, N.J.: Prentice Hall, 1974.

Laroui, Abdallah. *The History of the Maghrib: An Interpretive Essay.* Princeton, N.J.: Princeton University Press, 1977.

Lauren, Paul Gordon (ed.). *Diplomacy: New Approaches in History, Theory and Policy.* New York: The Free Press, 1979.

Lawson, Fred Haley. *Bahrain: The Modernization of Autocracy.* Boulder, Colo.: Westview, 1989.

Layne, Linda (ed.). *Elections in the Middle East; Implications of Recent Trends.* Boulder, Colo.: Westview, 1987.

————. *Home and Homeland: The Dialogics of Tribal and National Identities in Jordan.* Princeton, N.J.: Princeton University Press, 1994.

Legum, Colin (ed.). *African Contemporary Record,* vol. 13, 1980–81. New York: Holmes and Meier, 1981.

————. *African Contemporary Record,* vol. 14, 1981–82. New York: Holmes and Meier, 1983.

Lewis, Bernard. *The Middle East: 2000 Years of History, from the Rise of Christianity to the Present Day.* London: Weidenfeld and Nicholson, 1995.

————. *The Political Language of Islam.* Chicago: University of Chicago Press, 1988.

Longrigg, Stephen H. *Iraq, 1900–1950: A Political, Social and Economic History.* New York: Oxford University Press, 1953.

Luizard, Pierre-Jean. *La Formation de L'Irak Contemporain: Le Role Politique des Ulemas Chiites a la Fin de la Domination Ottomane et au Moment de la Con-*

struction de l'État Irakien. Paris: Centre National de la Recherche Scientifique, 1991.

Maddy-Weitzman, Bruce, and Efraim Inbar (eds.). *Religious Radicalism in the Greater Middle East.* London: Frank Cass, 1997.

Makiya, Kan'an. *Cruelty and Silence: War, Tyranny, Uprising and the Arab World.* London: Penguin Books, 1994.

Ma'oz, Moshe. *Asad—The Sphinx of Damascus* (in Hebrew). Tel Aviv: Dvir, 1988.

Mazlish, Bruce, Arthur D. Kaledin, and David B. Ralston (eds.). *Revolution.* New York: Free Press, 1971.

McDowall, David. *A Modern History of the Kurds.* London: I. B. Tauris, 1996.

McLaurin, Robert D. (ed.). *Political Role of Minority Groups in the Middle East.* New York: Praeger, 1979.

Middle East Watch. *Genocide in Iraq: The Anfal Campaign Against the Kurds.* New York: Human Rights Watch, 1993.

———. *Syria Unmasked: The Suppression of Human Rights by the Asad Regime.* New Haven, Conn.: Yale University Press, 1991.

Milson, Menahem (ed.). *Regime and Society in the Arab World* (in Hebrew). Jerusalem: Van Leer Institute, 1977.

Montville, Joseph V. (ed.). *Conflict and Peacemaking in Multiethnic Societies.* Lexington, Mass.: Lexington Books, 1987.

Moosa, Matti. *Extremist Shi'ites: The Ghulat Sects.* Syracuse, N.Y.: Syracuse University Press, 1987.

Al-Mudarrisi, Muhammad Taqi. *Al-'Iraq wal-haraka al-Islamiyya.* London: Al-Sifa lil-Nashr wa-al-Tawzi', 1988.

Mustafa, Hala. *Al-Dawla wal-harakat al-Islamiyya al-mu'arida bayna al-muhadana wal-muwajaha.* Cairo: Markaz al-Mahrusa, 1995.

Nakash, Yitzhak. *The Shi'is of Iraq.* Princeton, N.J.: Princeton University Press, 1994.

Nelson, Harold D. *Area Handbook for the Democratic Republic of Sudan.* Washington, D.C.: Government Printing Office, 1973.

Neuberger, Benyamin. *National Self-determination in Postcolonial Africa.* Boulder, Colo.: Lynne Rienner, 1986.

Norton, Augustus Richard (ed.) *Civil Society in the Middle East.* Leiden, Netherlands: E. J. Brill, 1995.

Owen, Roger (ed.). *Essays on the Crisis in Lebanon.* London: Ithaca Press, 1976.

Pakradouni, Karim. *La Paix Manquée* (Hebrew translation). Tel Aviv: Ma'arachot, Israel Ministry of Defense, 1986.

Patai, Rafael. *Golden River to Golden Road.* 2d ed. Philadelphia: University of Pennsylvania Press, 1967.

Peake, Frederick (Peake Pasha). *A History of Jordan and Its Tribes.* Coral Gables, Fla.: University of Miami Press, 1958.

Piscatori, James (ed.). *Islamic Fundamentalism and the Gulf Crisis.* Chicago: University of Chicago Press, 1991.

Polk, William R., and Richard Chambers (eds.). *Beginnings of Modernization in the Middle East.* Chicago: University of Chicago Press, 1968.

Rabinovich, Itamar. *Syria Under the Ba'th, 1963–66: The Army-Party Symbiosis in Syria.* New York: Praeger, 1971.

———. *The War for Lebanon, 1970–1985.* Jerusalem: Israeli University Press, 1985.

Ramadan, 'Abd al-'Azim. *Jama'at al-takfir fi Misr.* Cairo: al-Hay'a al-Misriyya al-'Amma lil-Kitab, 1995.

Ramazani, Rouhollah K. *Revolutionary Iran: Challenge and Response in the Middle East.* Baltimore, Md.: Johns Hopkins University Press, 1986.

Reporters Sans Frontiers. *Le Drame Algérien: Un Peuple en Otage*. Paris: Éditions La Découverte, 1994.

Richard, S. H., and J. E. Peterson (eds.). *Crosscurrents in the Gulf: Arab Regional and Global Interests*. Washington, D.C.: Middle East Institute, 1988.

Rogan, Eugene, and Tariq Tell (eds.). *Village, Steppe and State: The Social Origins of Modern Jordan*. London: British Academic Press, 1994.

Rothschild, Joseph. *Ethnopolitics: A Conceptual Framework*. New York: Columbia University Press, 1981.

Ruedy, John. *Modern Algeria: The Origins and Development of a Nation*. Bloomington: Indiana University Press, 1992.

al-Rumaihi, Muhamad Ghanim. *Bahrain: A Study on Social and Political Changes Since the First World War*. London: Bowker, 1975.

Salem, Paul. *Bitter Legacy: Ideology and Politics in the Arab World*. Syracuse, N.Y.: Syracuse University Press, 1994.

Salibi, K. S. *A House of Many Mansions: The History of Lebanon Reconsidered*. Berkeley: University of California Press, 1988.

———. *Crossroads to Civil War: Lebanon 1958–1976*. London: Ithaca Press, 1976.

———. *The Modern History of Jordan*. London: I. B. Tauris, 1993.

Salih, Khaled. *State-Making, Nation-Building, and the Military: Iraq 1941–1958*. Goteborg, Sweden: Goteborg University, 1996.

Schulze, Kirsten E., Martin Stokes, and Colm Campbell (eds.). *Nationalism, Minorities and Diaspora: Identities and Rights in the Middle East*. London: Tauris Academic Studies, 1996.

Seale, Patrick. *Asad of Syria: The Struggle for the Middle East*. London: I. B. Tauris, 1988.

———. *The Struggle for Syria: A Study of Post-War Arab Politics*. London: Oxford University Press, 1965.

Shehadi, Nadim, and Bridget Harney (eds.). *Politics and the Economy in Lebanon*. Oxford: The Centre for Lebanese Studies, 1989.

Shehadi, Nadim, and Dana Haffar Mills (eds.). *Lebanon: A History of Conflict and Consensus*. London: The Centre for Lebanese Studies, 1988.

Sisk, Timothy D. *Islam and Democracy: Religion, Politics and Power in the Middle East*. Washington, D.C.: U.S. Institute of Peace, 1992.

Smith, Anthony D. *Nations and Nationalism in a Global Era*. Cambridge, U.K.: Polity Press, 1995.

———. *The Ethnic Origins of Nations*. Oxford: Oxford University Press, 1986.

———. *The Ethnic Revival*. Cambridge: Cambridge University Press, 1981.

Sowell, Thomas. *Race and Culture: A World View*. New York: Basic Books, 1994.

Susser, Asher. *On Both Banks of the Jordan: A Political Biography of Wasfi al-Tall*. London: Frank Cass, 1994.

Susser, Asher, and Aryeh Shmuelevitz (eds.). *The Hashemites in the Modern Arab World*. London: Frank Cass, 1995.

Tapper, Richard (ed.). *Some Minorities in the Middle East*. London: Centre of Near and Middle Eastern Studies, 1992.

Tiryakian, Edward D., and Ronald Rogowski (eds.). *New Nationalisms of the Developed West: Toward an Explanation*. Boston: Allen and Unwin, 1985.

Tuchman, Barbara. *The March of Folly: From Troy to Vietnam*. New York: Knopf, 1984.

Tueni, Ghassan. *Une Guérre pour les Autres*. Paris: Jean-Claude Lattes, 1985.

Vali, Abbas. *Kurdish Nationalism: Identity, Sovereignty and the Dialectics of Violence in Kurdistan*. London: I. B. Tauris, 1996.

van Bruinessen, Martin. *Agha, Shaikh and State: On the Social and Political Organization of Kurdistan.* Rijswijk, Netherlands: Europrint, 1978.

van Dam, Nikolas. *The Struggle for Power in Syria: Sectarianism, Religion and Tribalism in Politics, 1961–1978.* London: Croom Helm, 1979.

van Den Berghe, Pierre L. *The Ethnic Phenomenon.* New York: Elsevier, 1981.

van Dusen, Michael Hillegas. *Intra- and Inter-Generational Conflict in the Syrian Army.* Ann Arbor, Mich.: University Microfilms, 1991.

Vatikiotis, P. J. *Islam and the State.* London: Croom and Helm, 1987.

Voll, Sarah Potts, and John Obert Voll. *The Sudan: Unity and Diversity in a Multicultural State.* Boulder, Colo.: Westview, 1985.

Wai, Dunstan M. *The African-Arab Conflict in the Sudan.* New York: Africana Publishing Company, 1981.

Waterbury, John. *The Commander of the Faithful: The Moroccan Political Elite, A Study in Segmented Politics.* New York: Columbia University Press, 1970.

Wheatcroft, Andrew. *The Life and Times of Shaykh Salman Bin Hamad Al-Khalifa, Ruler of Bahrain, 1942–1961.* London: Kegan Paul, 1995.

Wilson, Mary. *King Abdallah, Britain and the Making of Jordan.* Cambridge: Cambridge University Press, 1987.

Wilson, Rodney (ed.). *Politics and the Economy in Jordan.* London: Routledge, 1991.

Ya'ari, Ehud, and Zeev Schiff. *Israel's Lebanon War.* New York: Simon and Schuster, 1984.

Yaniv, Avner, Moshe Ma'oz, and Avi Kuver (eds.). *Syria and Israeli Security* (in Hebrew). Tel Aviv: Ma'arachot Press, 1991.

Young, Crawford. *The Politics of Cultural Pluralism.* Madison: University of Wisconsin Press, 1976.

Zahlan, Rosemarie Said. *The Making of the Modern Gulf States: Kuwait, Bahrain, Qatar, the United Arab Emirates and Oman.* London: Unwin Hyman, 1989.

Zolberg, Aristide R. *Creating Political Order: The Party-States of West-Africa.* Chicago: Rand McNally, 1966.

Articles

Adekson, Bayo J. "Ethnicity, the Military and Domination." *Plural Societies* 9, no. 1 (spring 1978), pp. 85–110.

Ansari, Hamied. "Sectarian Conflict in Egypt and the Political Expediency of Religion." *Middle East Journal* 38, no. 3 (summer 1984), pp. 397–418.

Axelrod, Laurence. "Tribesmen in Uniform: The Demise of the Fida'iyyun in Jordan, 1970–71." *Muslim World* 68, no. 1 (January 1978), pp. 25–45.

Bellin, Eva. "Civil Society: Effective Tool of Analysis for Middle East Politics?" *Political Science and Politics* 27, no. 3 (September 1994), pp. 509–510.

Ben-Dor, Gabriel. "Civilianization of Military Regimes in the Arab World." *Armed Forces and Society* 1, no. 3 (May 1975), pp. 317–327.

———. "Institutionalization and Political Development: A Conceptual and Theoretical Analysis." *Comparative Studies in Society and History* 17, no. 3 (July 1975), pp. 309–325.

———. "Political Culture to Middle East Politics." *International Journal of Middle East Politics* 8, no. 1 (January 1977), pp. 43–63.

———. "Stateness and Ideology in Contemporary Middle Eastern Politics." *The Jerusalem Journal of International Relations* 9, no. 3 (September 1987), pp. 10–37.

————. "The Intellectuals in the Politics of a Middle Eastern Minority." *Middle Eastern Studies* 12, no. 2 (May 1976), pp. 133–158.

————. "The Military in the Politics of Integration and Innovation: The Case of the Druze Minority in Israel." *Asian and African Studies* 9, no. 3 (1973), pp. 339–369.

————. "The Politics of Threat: Military Intervention in the Middle East." *Journal of Political and Military Sociology* 1 (spring 1974), pp. 57–69.

Chaker, Salem. "Quelques Evidences sur la Question Bérbére." *Confluences Méditerranée: Comprendre l'Algérie,* no. 11 (summer 1994), pp. 103–111.

Chouet, Alain. "Alawi Tribal Space Tested by Power: Disintegration by Politics." *Maghreb-Machrek,* no. 147 (January–March 1995), pp. 93–119.

Connor, Walker. "The Politics of Ethnonationalism." *Journal of International Affairs* 27, no. 1 (January 1973), pp. 1–21.

Donnet, Joel. "Renaissance Berbére au Maroc." *Le Monde Diplomatique,* January 1995, p. 18.

Faksh, Mahmud A. "The Alawi Community of Syria: A New Dominant Political Force." *Middle Eastern Studies* 20, no. 2 (April 1984), pp. 133–153.

Francke, Rahim. "Race to Finish Line." *Middle East Insight* 10, no. 4–5 (May–August 1994), pp. 36–43.

Fuccaro, Nelida. "Ethnicity, State Formation, and Conscription in Postcolonial Iraq: The Case of the Yazidi Kurds of Jabal Sinjar." *International Journal of Middle East Studies* 29, no. 4 (November 1997), pp. 559–580.

Galand, L. "Berbers: Language." *Encyclopedia of Islam.* New edition, vol. 1. Leiden, Netherlands: E. J. Brill, 1960, pp. 1180–1185.

George, Alexander L., and Timothy J. Mckeown. "Case Studies and Theories of Organizational Decision Making." *Advances in Information Processing in Organizations* 2 (1985), pp. 21–58.

Gershoni, Israel. "The Arab Nation, the Hashemite Dynasty and Greater Syria in the Writings of 'Abdallah." Part 2. *Hamizrah Hehadash* (in Hebrew) 25, no. 3 (1975), pp. 161–183.

Ghiles, Francis. "Algeria Again at the Crossroads." *Middle East International,* no. 417 (24 January 1992), pp. 3–4.

Gurr, Ted Robert. "Peoples Against States: Ethnopolitical Conflict and the Changing World System." *International Studies Quarterly* 38, no. 3 (September 1994), pp. 347–377.

Hinnebusch, Raymond A. "State and Civil Society in Syria." *Middle East Journal* 47, no. 2 (spring 1993), pp. 243–257.

Huntington, Samuel P. "Civil Violence and the Process of Development." *Adelphi Papers,* no. 83 (1972).

————. "The Clash of Civilizations?" *Foreign Affairs* 72, no. 3 (summer 1993), pp. 22–49.

————. "Democracy's Third Wave." *Journal of Democracy* 1, no. 1 (spring 1991), pp. 12–34.

Ibrahim, Saad Eddin. "Crises, Elites and Democratization in the Arab World." *Middle East Journal* 47, no. 2 (spring 1993), pp. 292–305.

Kelidar, Abbas. "Religion and State in Syria." *Asian Affairs* 61 (1974), pp. 16–22.

Khazin, Farid. "The Communal Pact of National Identities: The Making and Politics of the 1943 National Pact." *Papers on Lebanon,* no. 12 (1992).

Kirisci, Kemal. "Provide Comfort or Trouble: Operation Provide Comfort and Its Impact on Turkish Foreign Policy." *Turkish Review of Middle East Studies* 8 (1994–1995), pp. 43–67.

Kramer, Gudrun. "Liberalization and Democracy in the Arab World." *Middle East Report* 22, no. 1 (January–February 1992), pp. 22–25, 35.

Lak, Amara. "On Tamazight and Its Writing." *The Amazigh Voice* 4, no. 1 (March 1995), pp. 7–8.

LaPalombara, Joseph. "Macrotheories and Microapplications in Comparative Politics: A Widening Chasm." *Comparative Politics* 1, no. 1 (October 1968), pp. 52–78.

Lewis, Bernard. "Why Turkey Is the Only Muslim Democracy." *Middle East Quarterly* 1, no. 1 (March 1994), pp. 41–49.

Lijphart, Arend. "Comparative Politics and the Comparative Method." *The American Political Science Review* 65, no. 3 (September 1971), pp. 682–693.

Luizard, Pierre-Jean. "The Iraqi Question from the Inside." *Middle East Report* 25, no. 2 (March–April 1995), pp. 18–22.

Maila, Josef. "The Document of National Understanding: A Commentary." *Prospects for Lebanon,* no. 4. Oxford: The Centre for Lebanese Studies, 1992.

Mayer, Thomas. "The Islamic Opposition in Syria, 1961–1982." *Orient* 24, no. 4 (December 1983), pp. 589–609.

McCarus, Ernest N. "Berber: Linguistic 'Substratum' of North African Arabic." *The Washington Report on Middle East Affairs* (January–February 1995), p. 31.

Mutlu, Servet. "Ethnic Kurds in Turkey: A Demographic Study." *International Journal of Middle East Studies* 28, no. 4 (November 1996), pp. 517–541.

Nader, George. "Interview with General Michel Aoun, Prime Minister of Lebanon." *Middle East Insight* 6, no. 3 (fall 1988), pp. 24–27.

Newman, Saul. "Does Modernization Breed Ethnic Political Conflict?" *World Politics* 43, no. 3 (April 1991), pp. 451–478.

Norton, Augustus Richard. "The Future of Civil Society in the Middle East." *Middle East Journal* 47, no. 2 (spring 1993), pp. 205–216.

Olmert, Yosef. "Britain, Turkey and the Levant Question During the Second World War." *Middle Eastern Studies* 23, no. 4 (October 1987), pp. 437–452.

Patai, Rafael. "The Middle East as a Cultural Area." *Middle East Journal* 6, no. 1 (winter 1952), pp. 1–21.

Pennington, J. D. "The Copts in Modern Egypt." *Middle Eastern Studies* 18, no. 2 (April 1982), pp. 158–179.

Perlmutter, Amos. "The Arab Military Elite." *World Politics* 22, no. 2 (January 1970), pp. 269–300.

Pickering, Samuel J. "Pedagogia Deserta: Memoirs of a Fulbright Year in Syria." *American Scholar* 50, no. 2 (spring 1981), pp. 179–196.

Pipes, Daniel. "The Alawi Capture of Power in Syria." *Middle Eastern Studies* 25, no. 4 (October 1989), pp. 429–450.

Rabinovich, Itamar. "The Compact Minorities and the Syrian State, 1918–45." *Journal of Contemporary History* 14, no. 4 (October 1979), pp. 693–712.

Rathmell, Andrew. "Opposition in the Gulf—Further Insights." *Jane's Intelligence Review* 7, no. 7 (July 1995), pp. 309–310.

Riggs, Fred W. "Ethnonationalism, Industrialism and the Modern State." *Third World Quarterly* 15, no. 4 (December 1994), pp. 583–611.

Roberts, Hugh. "The Economics of Berberism: The Material Basis of the Kabyle Question in Contemporary Algeria." *Government and Opposition* 18, no. 2 (spring 1983), pp. 218–235.

———. "The Unforeseen Development of the Kabyle Question in Contemporary Algeria." *Government and Opposition* 17, no. 3 (summer 1982), pp. 312–334.

———. "Towards an Understanding of the Kabyle Question in Contemporary Algeria." *The Maghreb Review* 5, nos. 5–6 (September–December 1980), pp. 115–124.

Salibi, Kamal. "The Maronite Experiment." *Middle East Insight* 5, no. 1 (January–February 1987), pp. 21–30.

Satloff, Robert B. "Prelude to Conflict: Communal Independence in the Sanjak of Alexandretta, 1920–38." *Middle Eastern Studies* 22, no. 2 (April 1986), pp. 147–180.

Scott, George M., Jr. "A Resynthesis of the Primordial and Circumstantial Approaches to Ethnic Group Solidarity: Toward an Explanatory Model." *Ethnic and Racial Studies* 13, no. 2 (April 1990), pp. 147–171.

Seccombe, Ian J. "The Persian Gulf." *Journal of the Royal Central Asian Society* 25 (July 1938), pp. 19–31.

Seffal, Rabah. "Remember Me?" *The World and I* (September 1992), pp. 612–623.

Shehadi N. "The Idea of Lebanon." *Papers on Lebanon,* no. 5 (1987).

Sivan, Emmanuel. "The Arab Nation-State: In Search of a Usable Past." *Middle East Review* 19, no. 3 (spring 1987), pp. 21–30.

Skocpol, Theda, and Margaret Somers. "The Uses of Comparative History in Macrosocial Theory." *Comparative Studies in Society and History* 22 (1980), pp. 174–197.

Smith, Charles D. "Imagined Identities, Imagined Nationalisms: Print Culture and Egyptian Nationalism in Light of Recent Scholarship." *International Journal of Middle East Studies* 29, no. 4 (November 1997), pp. 607–622.

Springborg, Robert. "Egypt: Repression's Toll." *Current History* 97, no. 615 (January 1998), pp. 32–37.

van den Berghe, Pierre L. "Ethnicity: The African Experience." *International Social Sciences Journal* 23, no. 4 (April 1971), pp. 505–518.

Yaffe, Gitta. "Suleiman al-Murshid: Beginning of the Alawi Leader." *Middle Eastern Studies* 29, no. 4 (October 1993), pp. 624–640.

Yver, G- [Ch. Pellat]. "Berbers: Distribution at Present." *Encyclopedia of Islam.* New edition, vol. 1. Leiden, Netherlands: E. J. Brill, 1960, pp. 1177–1178.

Zamir, Meir. "Politics and Violence in Lebanon." *The Jerusalem Quarterly,* no. 25 (fall 1982), pp. 3–26.

———. "The Lebanese Presidential Elections of 1970 and Their Impact on the Civil War of 1975–1976." *Middle Eastern Studies* 16, no. 1 (January 1980), pp. 49–70.

Zisser Eyal. "The Renewed Struggle over the Succession." *The World Today* 50, no. 7 (1994), pp. 136–139.

———. "The Succession Struggle in Damascus." *Middle East Quarterly* 2, no. 3 (September 1995), pp. 57–64.

Zubaida, Sami. "Islam, the State and Democracy: Contrasting Conceptions of Society in Egypt." *Middle East Report* 22, no. 6 (November–December 1992), pp. 2–10.

The Contributors

Ami Ayalon is senior research fellow at the Moshe Dayan Center for Middle Eastern and African Studies and associate professor, Department of Middle Eastern and African History, Tel Aviv University. He is author of *Language and Change in the Arab Middle East* (1987), *The Press in the Arab Middle East, A History* (1995), and numerous articles on modern Arab political and cultural history; editor of *Regime and Opposition in Egypt Under Sadat* (1983, in Hebrew); and coeditor of *Demography and Politics in the Arab States* (1995, in Hebrew).

Gabriel Ben-Dor is professor of political science and director of the Graduate Program in National Security Studies at the University of Haifa. He is a former rector of the university, as well as past president of the Israel Political Science Association. Ben-Dor is a specialist in Middle East politics, and he has written and published extensively on the role of the military in the politics of the region, minorities and ethnic politics in the Middle East, inter-Arab relations, and the Arab-Israeli conflict, as well as security and strategic issues in the area. The books he has authored or edited include *The Druzes in Israel: A Political Study; State and Conflict in the Middle East; The Palestinians and the Middle East Conflict; Political Participation in Turkey; Conflict Management in the Middle East; Confidence Building in the Middle East;* and the recent special issue of the annals of the American Academy of Political and Social Sciences entitled *Israel in Transition.*

Ofra Bengio is senior research fellow at the Moshe Dayan Center for Middle Eastern and African Studies and assistant professor, Department of Middle Eastern and African History at Tel Aviv University. Her fields of specialization include contemporary Middle Eastern history, modern and contemporary politics of Iraq, and the Arabic language. She is author of *The Kurdish Revolt in Iraq* (1989, in Hebrew), *Saddam Speaks on the Gulf Crisis: A Collection of Documents* (1991); *Political Discourse and the Language of Power* (1996, Hebrew); *Saddam's Word* (1998); and articles.

Joseph Kostiner is senior research fellow at the Moshe Dayan Center for Middle Eastern and African Studies and associate professor, Department of Middle Eastern and African History at Tel Aviv University. He has published several papers on the subject of the history and current affairs of the Arabian Peninsula states. He is author of *The Struggle for South Yemen* (1984), *South Yemen's Revolutionary Strategy* (1990), and *From Chieftaincy to Monarchical State: The Making of Saudi Arabia 1916–1936* (1993) and coeditor (with P. S. Khoury) of *Tribes and State Formation in the Middle East* (1991).

Bruce Maddy-Weitzman is senior research fellow at the Moshe Dayan Center for Middle Eastern and African Studies. His fields of specialization include contemporary Middle Eastern history, inter-Arab relations, and the modern Maghreb. He is author of *The Crystallization of the Arab State System: Inter Arab Politics, 1945–1954* (1993) and articles on regional Arab politics and Maghreb affairs. He is coeditor of *Religious Radicalism in the Greater Middle East* (1997) and editor of the center's annual year-book, *Middle East Contemporary Survey.*

Uzi Rabi is instructor at the Department of Middle Eastern and African History at Tel Aviv University. He specializes on modern history of the Gulf states.

Yehudit Ronen is research fellow at the Moshe Dayan Center for Middle Eastern and African Studies and lecturer at the Department of Middle East and African History. She is author of *Sudan in a Civil War: Between Africanism, Arabism and Islam* (1995, in Hebrew) and editor of *The Maghrib: Politics, Society, Economy* (1998, in Hebrew). She specializes in Sudan, Libya, and the Maghreb.

Asher Susser is senior research fellow at the Moshe Dayan Center for Middle Eastern and African Studies, a former head of the center, and associate professor in the Department of Middle Eastern and African History at Tel Aviv University. He specializes in the history and politics of Jordan and the Palestinians and religion and state in the Middle East. He is author of *Between Jordan and Palestine: A Political Biography of Wasfi al-Tall* (1983, in Hebrew), *The PLO After the War in Lebanon* (1985, in Hebrew), and *On Both Banks of the Jordan* (1994) and coeditor of *At the Core of the Conflict: The Intifada* (1992, in Hebrew) and *The Hashemites in the Modern Arab World* (1995).

Meir Zamir, professor of political science, teaches at the Department of Middle East Studies and the School of Management at Ben-Gurion University in the Negev. He is author of *The Formation of Modern Lebanon and Lebanon's Quest: The Road to Statehood, 1926–1939.*

Eyal Zisser is research fellow at the Moshe Dayan Center for Middle Eastern and African Studies and lecturer in the Department of Middle Eastern and African History, Tel Aviv University. He is author of several studies on modern Syrian and Lebanese politics.

Index

About the Book

Questions of identity and ethnicity have always been part of the intricate web of politics in the Arab world, but the recent expansion of political participation has made these issues more political, more visible, and more acute. This book offers a comprehensive discussion of minorities and ethnic politics in eight Arab countries. Focusing on the strategic political choices made by minorities, majorities, and regimes in power, the authors also point to probable future developments in majority-minority relations in the region.

Ofra Bengio is senior research fellow at the Moshe Dayan Center and assistant professor of Middle Eastern and African history at Tel Aviv University. **Gabriel Ben-Dor** is professor of political science and director of the graduate program in national security studies at the University of Haifa.